DATE DUE

Advance Praise for *Song for My Fathers*

"Finally, a book about New Orleans music from a totally fresh perspective. Tom Sancton was fortunate to have had a very colorful upbringing in the cradle of jazz and we're fortunate that he wrote about it so rivetingly."
—Woody Allen

"This is an important inside look into an underinvestigated period of New Orleans music. It tells a story with an insider's heart, a reporter's eye, and the pure feeling of a New Orleans musician. Enjoyable, informative, and engaging."
—Wynton Marsalis

"For me, Tom Sancton has long been the face of New Orleans. And now with this exquisite memoir, he is also that lost city's voice."
—Graydon Carter, editor in chief, *Vanity Fair*

"This is a book writers dream of writing and readers dream of reading. It's about everything—family secrets, first loves, the deepest roots of American jazz, the world (New Orleans) before the flood—but mostly it's about fathers, all the ways they find to disappoint us, and how they make us all that we become."
—James R. Gaines, author of *Evening in the Palace of Reason* and former managing editor of *Time*, *Life*, and *People*

"*Song for My Fathers* brings vividly to life the vanished world of New Orleans in the 1950s and 1960s. Lovingly described, the colorful musical life of the founding fathers of traditional jazz interweaves with that of a middle-class white boy, growing up in the last vestiges of the Old South. Tom Sancton is a rare and privileged individual, who absorbed his jazz from such revered musicians as George Lewis, Creole George Guesnon, and Harold 'Duke' Dejan, but who also learned how to write with skill and passion from his own father, who never found the success his talent deserved. Sancton's narrative deftly brings together the two sides of his life, and in doing so captures the sights, sounds, smells, and society of a magical city living on borrowed time."
—Alyn Shipton, jazz critic, *The Times* (London), and author of *A New History of Jazz*

"Tom Sancton has written a lush, gorgeous elegy to the place where he grew up—a place now gone not only from him but from the world. His portrait of his hometown and of his Southern gothic family is like the New Orleans jazz he learned to play: at once sad and spirited, enduring and ephemeral. *Song for My Fathers* is a beautiful book."
—James Atlas, author of *My Life in the Middle Ages: A Survivor's Tale*

"Tom Sancton's memoir is a passionate hymn to the souls of great men and a great city. It is lyrical, loving and haunting, like a melody that stays with you even when the musicians have left the stage."
—Christopher Dickey, *Newsweek* Paris bureau chief
and author of *Summer of Deliverance:*
A Memoir of Father and Son

Song for
MY FATHERS

Song for
MY FATHERS

A NEW ORLEANS STORY *in* BLACK AND WHITE

TOM SANCTON

Other Press • New York

Some parts of the Introduction have previously appeared, in slightly different form, on the Web site of *Vanity Fair*. Used with permission.

Production Editor: Robert D. Hack

Text design by Kaoru Tamura
This book was set in Janson Text by Alpha Graphics of Pittsfield, NH.
ISBN-13: 978-1-59051-243-2

10 9 8 7 6 5 4 3 2 1

Library of Congress Cataloging-in-Publication Data

Sancton, Tom.
    Song for my fathers : a New Orleans story in black and white / Tom Sancton.
        p. cm.
    ISBN 1-59051-243-X
    1. Sancton, Tom.   2. Clarinetists–United States–Biography.   3. Jazz musicians–United States–Biography.   4. Jazz–Louisiana–New Orleans–History and criticism.   I. Title.
    ML419.S197A3 2006
    781.6509763'35–dc22
                                                        2005033079

For my parents

INTRODUCTION

My heart leapt when we reached the top of the Causeway Boulevard overpass and saw the skyline of downtown New Orleans. "It's still there, Clay," I said. "It's still there!" My Mississippi cousin, riding shotgun in our borrowed Ford pickup, pointed to the distant Superdome. Three quarters of its roof had been peeled away like an onion skin. And sunlight danced on the watery arteries that once were streets and avenues.

But we were not there on that September day to gawk at the stricken city. We were on a mission: first, to see what was left of my family home; second, to retrieve some vital objects for my parents. Both ninety years old and living alone, they had reluctantly joined the New Orleans diaspora on August 28, when my sister forced them into her car and headed for Florida. My father's cracking voice had announced their imminent departure in a brief voicemail message that I received in my suburban Paris home on a beautiful summer day: "Tommy, the worst storm in U.S. history is about to hit New Orleans. We are leaving town with Beth." That was the last I heard from them for nearly a week.

In the meantime, like TV viewers around the world, I saw the horrific scenes from New Orleans and the Gulf Coast: whole neighborhoods under water, bodies drifting through the flooded streets, thousands of refugees herded into the reeking bedlam of the Superdome and the Convention Center, miles and miles of beachfront property reduced to piles of shattered timber. And as much as I worried about the fate of my family, I worried about the future of that strange, magical city that had been my home until I left for college.

As the days went by, I frantically dialed Beth's cell phone number. I finally got through to my other sister, Wendy, who told me my parents were staying with family friends near Pascagoula, Mississippi, in a house with no electricity or running water. Wendy's bungalow in nearby Moss Point had survived, but Beth's antebellum home on the coast at Pass Christian had been totally destroyed.

That news hit me almost as hard as a death in the family. Starting out with nothing but her irrepressible energy and determination, Beth had worked all her life to get that dream house. Built in 1830, the colonnaded wood and brick structure had been through many a ferocious storm. It was badly battered by Hurricane Camille in 1969, and was little more than an empty shell when Beth bought it several years later. She spent a quarter century restoring it into an elegant showplace with twin rows of oak trees in front and stables in back. She filled it with antique furniture and family photos and cherished it like Scarlett O'Hara cherished Tara. Four generations of our family had gathered there the previous Christmas, little knowing it would be for the last time. But when all the pelicans disappeared from the coast a week before the storm, Beth took it as an omen. While on her way to Florida, with my parents in tow, she had stopped in Pass Christian and literally kissed the old place good-bye. She went back a week later to sift through the ruins. All she found was a few pieces of silver, some broken china, and parts of her antique bed. "I'll just have to start all over," she vowed, like Scarlett at the end of the Civil War.

My parents eventually made it to Jackson, Mississippi, where my mother was born in 1915 and still had some family. I met them there after flying in from Paris. They were okay, but feeble and shaken. My mother, almost totally deaf and suffering from a heart condition, needed her medicine and her amplifying telephone. My father, a writer struck nearly blind by macular degeneration, needed his reading machine in order to finish what he had long assured us would be his masterpiece. And he was frantic over the state of his house.

It must once have been a majestic place—two stories high, white fluted columns, large breezy verandas with elegant banisters upstairs and down. The house had enjoyed a brief moment of glory after Hurricane Betsy battered it in 1965. My father, who never seemed to have any money or a stable job, had used the insurance settlement to fix the place up. Seven years later, though, a fire started in the downstairs rental unit and gutted much of the old wooden structure. The upstairs, where my parents lived, received cursory repairs that made it marginally inhabitable. But it was all jerry-rigged—extension cords dangling every which way, dysfunctional plumbing, open gas heaters with no ventilation system. The downstairs apartment, a vital source of rental income, was simply boarded up, charred timbers and all, and remains so to this day.

As my parents got older, the place disintegrated into moldy decadence, with broken furniture, threadbare carpets, rusted-out screens, dust and clutter everywhere. Cardboard boxes filled with my father's files multiplied and devoured one room after another. In the kitchen, decades of grease and grime covered the walls; the door of the refrigerator was coated with rust and, more often than not, food was left on the countertop overnight for the roaches to feast on.

The outside of the house was no less chaotic. Climbing vines ran wild. The phalanx of trees that Daddy had long ago planted to block out the outside world pushed the side fence down and cracked the foundations of the house with their root systems. A thick carpet of rotting leaves and fallen palm branches covered what was once the front lawn. The backyard was invaded by a ten-foot-high thicket of bamboo. More than once, I was stopped on the sidewalk by passersby who wanted to buy what they thought was an abandoned ruin.

My sisters and I hoped that Katrina's wrath would do what no rational discussion could ever accomplish: force my father to accept the fact that, at ninety years old, confronted with multiple infirmities, he and my mother could no longer live alone in their disheveled New Orleans nest. I rented them a clean, functional house in the leafy neighborhood that my mother had grown up in. Her Mississippi family—we have a lot of "kissing cousins" in the South—provided the perfect support network. From storerooms and attics and basements, they retrieved the wherewithal to furnish the new place and make it cozy. But my father soon dispelled any idea that he would accept Jackson as a long-term proposition.

"Listen to me," he croaked, riveting me with what I had known since childhood as *the look*. It was a hard, cold, gaze of his blue eyes, now narrowed by age into little slits, but still hurtful and fearsome in their brutal penetration. "I know you children have some idea that we are going to stay here. Understand this well: we are going back to New Orleans. What would I do here? There's nothing for me in Jackson. I'd die here."

"What about Mother? Don't you think she'd be happier in a clean, decent place, surrounded by her family?"

"She's happy with me. I'm the only person who can make her happy. I'm her caregiver. She needs me."

"But she doesn't need to go back to that shambles of a house. Do you have any idea how far removed your living conditions are from the way most people live in civilized countries? The place is a mess, it's a firetrap, the plumbing doesn't work, the neighborhood is not safe, you live up two flights of stairs over a burnt-out shell, and neither one of you can hear the telephone."

"That's your reality. You go back to Paris and live in your reality, and let me and Seta go back to New Orleans and live in our reality. You think you can live over in Europe and play your music and then come here for a few days and tell us what to do? I'm still the head of this family."

"We don't have to fight this battle now," I said.

"There's not going to be any battle. The battle is over. Look at me—look me in the eyes." His face was six inches from my own. His deep-set eyes looked like sockets under the bushy white eyebrows that he had always stubbornly refused to trim. When he was at peace, it was simply the face of an old man. But when he was angry, it was a grotesque and frightening mask. And he was angry now.

"Look me in the eyes. I'm your boss."

"No, Daddy, you are not my boss."

"Yes I am, and I am tougher than you are. We are going back to New Orleans."

There was no point trying to find out what my mother wanted. Her hearing was so bad, I could no longer carry on a real conversation with her. Besides, she always went along with whatever my father decided. In their sixty-four years together, I don't think she ever contradicted him. And now, her memory was starting to slip. She asked Daddy to explain to me how to get to their house—the place I had grown up in.

My father once told me that if I ever wrote about him, I should do it "warts and all." But there weren't always so many warts. In earlier years, Tom Sancton was a tall, dashing young writer who charmed the ladies with his good looks and impressed his peers with his quirky brilliance. He won a Nieman Fellowship at Harvard, became managing editor of the *New Republic* at age twenty-eight, was recruited by Henry Luce to write for *Life*, and established himself as one of the country's most outspoken and radical voices in favor of racial equality. Inspired by his early idol, Thomas Wolfe, he wrote two novels set in New Orleans and hoped to carve out a name for himself as a great Southern author. That didn't happen. His career went off the rails then, and he never really got back on track. Instead of the next Thomas Wolfe, he wound up more like one of those tragic, broken figures in a Tennessee Williams play.

Most of that went on over my head when I was a child. Whatever storms were raging in Tom Sancton's heart and soul, he was my hero. He told me magical bedtime stories that made me squeal with laughter, took me fishing and crabbing, and made the world's greatest gumbo. He taught me about writing, books, and ideas, and pushed me to get ahead. Maybe he pushed too hard, but I guess he did what he thought he had to do. He called it "coaching." Some of it did me a lot of good. And, as he never failed to remind me, he saved my butt on more than one occasion.

I thought about all that as my cousin Clay Alexander and I headed to New Orleans in his Uncle Hebron's shiny new pickup truck. Clay had offered to share the driving with me and—armed with his .45 automatic—act as a bodyguard in case we ran into looters. He assured me he was a "damn good shot." I prayed he wouldn't be put to the test.

Arriving by the Old River Road, we easily talked our way past a police checkpoint though the city was officially closed. We turned onto St. Charles Avenue, a graceful thoroughfare lined with moss-draped oaks and stately homes. There were a lot of fallen trees and branches, but most of the buildings looked unscathed and the ground was dry. Same story in the Garden District, where the city's wealthiest "old-line" families live. The rich, at least, had been spared.

I was starting to think all the apocalyptic TV images were wrong. Then we headed up Napoleon Avenue. Within a couple of blocks, there was water up to our hubcaps—black, viscous, foul-smelling water full of floating branches and garbage, and so teeming with malevolent microorganisms that the whole surface seemed to vibrate in the steamy, late-summer heat. Clay and I put on surgical masks to counter the stench and sprayed each other with insect repellent.

We turned onto a side street and approached Gen. Pershing. My parents' corner house looked no worse than usual—but certainly no better. Some of the man-eating vines that climbed up the side of the house had been ripped loose by the wind—good riddance. Here and there, a rusted-out gutter was sagging. More worrisome, though, the house was surrounded by a polluted moat, and the high watermark showed that the old brick foundation had been soaked to a level of about three feet—not a good sign for a structure that has been settling for years.

We put on our knee-boots and jumped into the sludge. My father had bolted the front door from inside, so we had to go up the back way—a perilous path, since the rear steps had nearly rotted off the house. For days, I had had nightmares about what we would find inside—rats, snakes, squatters, looters—but my fears proved unfounded. The smell of death filled the house when Clay unwisely opened the refrigerator. But he quickly slammed it shut and we went about our business. Clay wandered through the cluttered rooms and shook his head. "I just can't understand Seta living like this."

There was no time for me to explain my mother's long descent from Jackson aristocracy to the current decadence. We scooped up various items and struggled to bring my father's heavy reading machine down the rickety back stairs. At that moment, we looked like nothing so much as a pair of looters. I was afraid a cop, soldier, or vigilante might take a potshot at us. But there was no one to be seen—no people, no cars, no movement at all. Apart from the occasional military or emergency vehicle, the streets were empty. A city of half a million people had turned into a virtual ghost town.

As we drove away from the relatively high ground near the riverfront, we began to encounter the kind of catastrophic flooding that we had seen on TV. The truck could not make it very far into those areas, but we could see the partially submerged cars and houses all around us. The dark waters filled many of the old cemeteries, with their above-ground crypts. "They had just buried my niece," one old black woman told me. "Her casket done rose up and float away."

The most dramatic views were to be had from the overpasses. We parked on the nearly deserted I-10 highway to gaze down at a broad avenue that looked like a black river. Door frames, tires, branches, and green scum floated on the surface of the sluggish stream. Another man stood at the railing and shook his head in amazement. I asked him if he knew the name of the street down there. "Carrollton Avenue," he said. I was stunned: I had once lived just a couple of blocks from there, but I couldn't even recognize it.

We headed down to the French Quarter. To my amazement and relief, that whole historic area—St. Louis Cathedral, Jackson Square, the old French Market—was dry and relatively undamaged. I walked the abandoned streets and approached the spot that, in my youth, had seemed like the very heart of New Orleans and the passionate center of my existence: Preservation Hall. I had heard wild rumors that this world-renowned Mecca of traditional jazz was under ten feet of water. But as I walked up St. Peter Street from Bourbon, I saw it was intact.

I placed my hands on the wrought-iron gates and peered into the carriageway. It looked just as it had on that hot summer night when my father first took me there, more than fourty years earlier, and opened the door to the most profound experience of my life. At that time it was just a one-room hole-in-the-wall frequented by a cult-like handful of traditional jazz fans. I immediately fell in love with the music, the people, and the funky atmosphere—and decided to become a jazz musician myself.

Thus began my apprenticeship alongside some of the city's legendary old black jazzmen. They became my idols and mentors. They taught me about their music, of course, but more than that. They taught me about their world, their neighborhoods, their humor and anger, their fears and disappointments, their courage in the face of poverty and prejudice, sickness and death. Most of all, they taught me their humanity. They called themselves "the mens."

This book is a song for my fathers—the white one who sired, raised, and coached me, and the black ones who inspired and encouraged me, and enriched my life beyond measure. It also recounts the life and times of a middle-class white boy growing up in New Orleans in the 1950s and '60s. New Orleans is more than a backdrop to this drama; it is perhaps the central player, for this story could not have taken place in any other city in the world.

The book was written over a period of several years, before Katrina smashed into my beloved town and changed its face forever. In the wake of that cataclysm, these memories of New Orleans may seem particularly poignant and nostalgic. In fact, the New Orleans of which I speak had mostly faded into history long before Katrina struck—a victim of time, progress, and the eternal passing of generations.

But this is the way it was.

Paris, September 28, 2005

CHAPTER ONE

They buried Papa Celestin on a raw winter day. It was early in the morning when the mourners started arriving at the funeral home on Louisiana Avenue. By noon, five thousand people and two brass bands jammed the broad two-lane thoroughfare outside, waiting to take the great trumpeter on his last ride. Two dozen motorcycle cops revved their engines, preparing to escort the cortege—and ready to deal with any violence if things got out of hand.

Inside the crowded funeral parlor, black friends and relatives of the fallen jazzman mingled with his many white admirers—among them, the mayor, a congressman, prominent businessmen, lawyers, university professors, socialites, writers, and journalists. There were few places in New Orleans where the races could gather under one roof in those Jim Crow days; segregation was the law of the land in Louisiana. But they made an exception for Papa Celestin. Apart from Louis Armstrong, perhaps, he was the closest thing to a local hero that the city could claim. President Eisenhower had even honored him at the White House and told him he was "a credit" to his race.

I was five years old and knew nothing about Papa Celestin. But there I was in the middle of the pressing crowd, bundled up against the December wind and clutching my mother's hand. Nearby, my father hovered protectively over my sisters, Wendy, nine, and Beth, eight. Mother had questioned the wisdom of bringing us here, but my father had insisted. "In New Orleans," he said, "a jazz funeral is a cultural event. These kids will be telling their grandchildren about the day they buried the great Papa Celestin."

"Who was Papa Celestin?" Wendy asked.

My father knelt down on the grassy median and pulled the three of us close to him. "His real name was Oscar," he said. "Oscar played the music we all loved when we were young. He had a band called the Tuxedo that played the music for our dances. I used to hear him at the Yacht Club, out by the lake. When we would walk out on the pier at the end of the Yacht Club, we could look back and see the people dancing past the windows. We could hear the waves splashing in through the pilings. The lights of autos would be passing on the lakefront road. Out on the water, the sailboats came by—and we could hear people talking and laughing on the boats, and see the sails in the darkness. Oscar would be playing his trumpet. It was beautiful, the way the horn notes came over the lake, and mixed up with the waves booming through the pilings and hitting against the seawall. When you are that young, you think these things will last forever. But you grow older, and life goes in other directions. Then you begin to remember how things felt when you were very young."

"You're not old, Daddy," Wendy said, and held his hand.

Beth snuggled up against him and grabbed his other hand.

"Oscar got very famous. He made records. He played for Carnival balls and parades. He played funeral music when Negroes were buried in the old days. Then, for about ten years—longer than you have been alive—things changed, and nobody would pay Oscar to play music. So he had to get other jobs. Then, when he was an old man, people began to remember him. They asked him to get his band together and play again. And he did."

My sisters and I liked the ending.

Then my father told us he was going into the funeral home to pay his respects to Oscar. Mother stayed on the sidewalk with us kids. When Daddy came out, he told Mother that Oscar looked like "a dead king, with his head on a satin pillow." We wanted to see the dead king, too, but Daddy said we were too young.

A bitter wind sliced down the avenue and the crowd was getting restless. "Come on, brothers," someone shouted, "let's hear some music." Another voice chimed in, "Yeah, you right, man, we ain't gonna wait here all day. It's gettin' *cold* out here."

The cops gunned their engines. Reflections of the low winter sun danced on the polished brass of the tubas and trumpets. The drummers adjusted the straps of their harnesses. The crowd filled the street from sidewalk to sidewalk, separating the two bands and surrounding the hearse and limousines that waited in front of the funeral parlor with their motors idling, blowing clouds of gray exhaust into the frigid air.

Suddenly someone cried, "Here come the body! They bringin' out the body!" The door of the funeral home opened and six black pallbearers slowly descended the steps bearing the silvery casket to the sound of muffled snares. The bass drummer pounded a somber cadence: Boom . . . Boom . . . Ba-DOOM! Then two dozen horns cut in with a chilling burst of notes.

The hearse and limousines advanced slowly to the head of the cortege, flanked by the throaty motorcycles. With trumpets blaring and clarinets soaring like women's voices, the Eureka Brass Band, followed by the Tuxedo, fell in behind the vehicles. The musicians swayed like elephants as they marched, leaning first to one side, then to the other.

Trailing behind the bands, five thousand men, women, and children formed the second line of this unwieldy procession. They flowed around the trees and parked cars like a river rushing over submerged rocks. The dirge music had calmed them, but it was clear from the painted umbrellas that poked up here and there that the second-liners were waiting to cut loose and dance to the hot music that would erupt once Papa was in the ground. That was the New Orleans way.

I doubt that I had ever heard the word *funeral* before, nor, probably, did I even know what death was. But I knew something solemn and majestic was happening that day. I could feel it in the slow pounding of the bass drum, hear it in the power of the trumpets, the thunder of the tubas, and especially in the mournful, high-pitched song of the clarinet—strange and wondrous instruments whose names I did not know, but whose magic I felt that day deep in my five-year-old guts.

The moment exists for me now in that vague cloud of childhood memory—part recollection, part imagination, part reconstruction from later tellings of the tale. But there is one thing I recall quite clearly. As I walked along holding my mother's hand, she said something to one of the musicians—a slender, dark-skinned clarinet player with a black parade cap on his head.

"Aren't you George Lewis?" she asked.

"Yes, ma'am, that's me," he replied with a smile like a sunburst, then put his horn in his mouth and continued playing. The sound he made was like nothing I had ever heard before. It was like a woman singing, or crying, or both.

Who could have known that this little man would one day become my idol, my friend, my teacher? And that many of the men playing alongside him would fill my world with joy, wonder, and a sense of purpose.

CHAPTER TWO

Some say my mother deserved better. Daughter of a Mississippi supreme court justice; debutante and Carnival Queen in her native Jackson; member of the Junior League, the Daughters of the American Revolution, and the Society of Colonial Dames—in short, a pure product of the white, uppercrust southern establishment. She was about to give her hand to a promising young hometown medical student, when, as a favor to a friend, she accepted a blind date with a handsome, hard-drinking New Orleans newspaperman named Tom Sancton.

The tall stranger from that sinful, cosmopolitan river port was a dreamer, a talker, a charmer. Before the night was over, Seta Alexander had slipped off her cotton glove so she could hold hands with him in the backseat of the car. When she returned home that night, she woke her mother and said, "Oh, Mama, have you ever seen such blue eyes?" My grandmother mumbled, "Poor Fred"—the medical student—and went back to sleep.

That was the beginning. Now we lived on the second story of a run-down two-family house on Carondalet Street in New Orleans. The Garden District, where the wealthy old-line families lived in grand white-columned homes shaded by live oaks and palmettos, was just two blocks from us. That's where Seta Alexander Sancton rightfully belonged, but we were definitely on the wrong side of St. Charles Avenue. The house needed paint, and not a blade of grass grew in the dusty yard. A sprawling black neighborhood was just a few streets away, and colored people, as we called them then, were always walking past our house on their way to the St. Charles streetcar line. We could hear them talking and laughing, and sometimes they would ask if they could come into our yard and pick up the nuts that fell from our pecan tree. My father always said yes.

Our upstairs apartment seemed comfortable enough to me. I had a back room to myself. A mouse, or rat, had made a nest in the attic just over my head and I went to sleep each night to the sound of his teeth gnawing on the rafters. I called him "Jiggits"—that was the sound he made. He was my secret friend. My older sisters, Wendy and Beth, shared a bedroom toward the front of the house. My mother slept in a small room next to theirs. My sisters said they could sometimes hear her crying at night.

The big front bedroom with its balcony and private bath was my father's domain. He said he had to have that room to himself because that's where he did his writing, and the sound of his late-night typing would keep my mother awake if she shared it with him. There wouldn't have been much room for her, because he had jammed an immense leather-topped desk and a metal typewriter stand into the space between the four-poster bed and the glass doors that led out onto the balcony.

When my Mississippi grandparents came to visit, my grandfather, Judge Alexander, played ragtime banjo and told us magic stories about the pixies that lived in his big garden in Jackson. My grandmother—we called her "Marnee"—told no fairy stories. She was bright eyed and quick-tongued, and wasn't afraid to say what she thought. She sat in the living room over coffee one afternoon, gazing at the torn wallpaper and the yellowed paint peeling off the ceiling. Suddenly she said to my mother, "Seta, how can you live like this?" My mother shrugged. "I'm used to it." Marnee snapped back, "Well don't get *too* used to it."

But she did. My parents lived like gypsies. Meals were catch-as-catch-can—a peanut-butter-and-jelly sandwich, a bowl of vegetable soup, or tuna fish salad eaten standing up in the kitchen. I don't remember any sit-down meals like the ones at my grandmother's home in Jackson, with starched napkins and iced tea and black servants. That would have been impossible in our house. There was no dining room, and the tiny kitchen table wouldn't have held us all at once. My father was rarely with us at mealtimes in any case. He was either working at his newspaper job for the New Orleans *Item* or hunkered down in his room writing his novel.

The book was his ace in the hole. He was convinced, and had persuaded my mother, that he would hit the jackpot with it. He had abandoned a promising career as a magazine writer and editor in New York to move back south and write the Great American Novel. The *Item* job was just to pay the rent until the book was published and the royalties started to pour in. Then things would change. They would move into the Garden District, or buy an antebellum mansion on the Gulf Coast, or a stately home in Jackson with servants and gardeners like my grandparents. At least that was my mother's dream. My father, a political radical who secretly scorned the fancy trappings of bourgeois society, was more interested in the fame of authorship. "Fame is the spur," was one of his favorite sayings.

The book filled their conversation. They lived with the characters—Brad, Hester, Phazma the Phlame Girl, Count Casimir Poliatoffsky. My parents talked about them so much I thought they were family members.

I loved to fall asleep in my father's four-poster bed while he wrote. It was the only room with an air conditioner. Everybody else in the family could swelter in the stifling, wet-blanket heat of the New

Orleans summer, slapping at the mosquitoes that entered through the torn window screens, but my father had to be in what he called the "blessed cool" in order to do his work.

He typed in rapid-fire bursts on his gray Underwood Number 4, pausing now and then to chuckle at something he had written. He wrote on rolls of teletype paper pilfered from the *Item* so he wouldn't have to stop and crank a new piece of paper into his typewriter every ten minutes. On a good night, the roll of manuscript snaked all the way to the far wall and back. His desktop was littered with coffee cups and half-empty Coke bottles—he had long since given up alcohol.

He rarely talked to me while he was writing, but I know he felt my presence as I lay curled up on his bed, sucking my thumb, clutching my teddy bear and my favorite blue blanket. The bear had a music box in its belly that played a tune I called "Tommy's Bear." (It was actually Brahms's "Lullaby.") I would keep rewinding it until I drifted off, lulled by the tinkle of the music, the hum of the air conditioner, and the clackety-clackety-clack of my father's typewriter.

My father seemed to have a good time writing. One night he burst out laughing, and I asked him what was funny. "Oh, something Casimir just said," he replied. "He's a little crazy sometimes." I said it must be fun to type all night and have your characters talk to you and make you laugh. He took a sip from his Coke bottle and said softly, "Son, don't ever be a writer."

Whenever I went to sleep in my father's room, I always woke up in my own bed. I guess he would take me back there and tuck me in once I had drifted off. I don't know why he bothered, because he hardly ever used his own bed—a beautiful four-poster antique made by a slave carpenter on an antebellum plantation. In fact he never seemed to sleep much in those days. He wrote through the night and left for work at 5 a.m. I asked why he left so early, when it was still dark. He said the *Item* was an afternoon paper, so he had to finish all his stories before noon. When he came home, he always had mother make him a pot of coffee and sat down at his typewriter again. It was only on the weekends that my father would lie down, always with a pillow over his head, and then he could be out cold for twelve hours at a time.

Many years later, I learned the secret of his strange sleeping pattern: he was hooked on Dexedrine diet pills that some society doctor had prescribed for my mother. My father had tried one and found it pepped him up and helped him write. He was soon an out-and-out addict, popping ten to fifteen pills a day.

Maybe that had something to do with the laughing spells that would grip him while he wrote. Or with his shifting moods. Sometimes he was all smiles and good humor; at other moments, his thick brows were knitted by bouts of deep depression. That's when he would make my sisters and me sit down in front of him and lecture us until Mother pleaded for him to stop. "Tom, please don't fuss at the children." There never seemed to be any reason for the tirades. They just welled up inside him like a Gulf squall, then raged and thundered and finally blew over. Until the next time.

In between the storms, there were wonderful moments. Like the Freddy Elf stories he told me when he was feeling good. Freddy Elf lived in Africa, and the only way to get there was on my dad's flying bed. At story time, he took a framed map of New Orleans down from his wall and put it on the floor. Then he opened the doors onto the balcony and got on the bed with me. We had to say the magic words to make the bed fly: "A saucer and a dish, and a big red fish, I wish, I wish, I wish, I wish, I wish this bed would fly away to the jungles of Africa . . ."

The bed would jiggle and shake. He leaned over and showed me the map of New Orleans, and pointed out all the landmarks we were flying over: St. Charles Avenue, Robert E. Lee Circle, Canal Street, the Mississippi River, Lake Pontchartrain. He clutched me tight as we flew over the ocean. The bed always landed with a jolt in a jungle clearing. Daddy described the trees and birds and strange animals surrounding us—monkeys, parrots, zebras. Then we heard an eerie, high-pitched voice singing this song: "Oh, my name is Freddy Elf and I'm all by myself, and I wish I had a little boy to come and play with me." "Freddy, it's me!" I cried and Freddie said, "Oh, there's my boy! There's Tommy!" Freddy was dressed all in green, with a floppy little hat and pointy shoes with bells on the toes. He had a gray beard and long gray hair. I saw him hundreds of times.

For some reason, my sisters were never there when we flew to Africa to see Freddy. They were older than me, Beth by three years, Wendy by four. Maybe they were too big for elf stories?

Sometimes my father took a break from his writing to give us kids a treat. On warm evenings, he took us for "dream walks." They would start with snowballs from a local stand, doused with cherry, grape, or bubble gum syrup, followed by a stroll through the semi-darkened streets as he and my mother held hands and talked. The night air smelled of jasmine, honeysuckle, and magnolia, and the locusts droned their deep-summer song.

We would walk down St. Charles Avenue all the way to Lee Circle. My parents sat on a bench there, while my sisters and I climbed the steps at the base of the monument—a larger-than-life statue of General Robert E. Lee, who "never turned his back on the North." Bathed in floodlights, the cement steps formed a stage on which we danced and sang like Shirley Temple. "Hello everybody, hello! We hope you enjoy our little show. We'll dance for a nickel, we'll dance for a pickle, hello everybody, hello!"

On really special nights, my father piled us into his beat-up Ford station wagon and drove us out to Pontchartrain Beach, the big amusement park on the shores of Lake Pontchartrain. The owner gave my father free tickets because he worked for the newspaper and once wrote a big feature piece about the park. I always thought we got the tickets just because we were special. We ate ice cream and cotton candy and rode the roller coaster—the Big Zephyr— until our stomachs churned.

My father would also take us to West End Park, not far from Pontchartrain Beach, where we watched the fountain shoot jets of colored water high into the night sky and sat on the seawall while the sun set over the lake. West End is where I took my very first steps, and where my visiting grandfather Alexander—we called him Dede—taught me to fish in the little lagoon using a bent pin and a piece of bread.

Gerry Gerdes, who lived across the street from us, was the king of the neighborhood. He was older and bigger than us, and a bit of a bully at times. He once threw a rock at me and narrowly missed putting my eye out; I still have the scar. Gerry was always thinking up interesting things for us to do. One time he decided to promote a boxing match between me and another neighborhood boy named Phillip. I said I didn't want to fight anyone, but Phillip's father was in the navy and the boy had apparently been bred for combat. He pushed me in the chest, but I didn't push back. Then he punched me on the shoulder and I started crying and ran home.

My father, who had watched the whole scene from the kitchen window, was waiting for me at the top of the stairs.

"Don't you ever let me catch you running away from a fight," he said, glaring at me with his deep-set blue eyes. "Only a coward runs away from fights. You want to be a coward?"

I shook my head. My cheeks were still wet with tears and my lip was quivering.

He slapped me in the face. I cried.

He slapped me again. I cried louder.

"You like that?"

I shook my head.

"Then what are you going to do about it?"

I made a little fist and hit him in the stomach.

"Harder," he said and slapped me again.

I punched him in the knees and stomach with both hands.

"Harder!"

I punched harder. He slapped me again.

I flailed wildly at him, raining little mini-blows wherever they would fall.

"That's better," he said finally. "Now go back out there and finish your fight."

I ran back out in the street, where the neighborhood group was still buzzing about the fight. Before Phillip knew what was happening, I was punching him over and over like a jackhammer tearing up a sidewalk. He backed away, but I advanced and kept swinging. Phillip let out a whelp and ran home. All the kids cheered and Gerry held up my hand like a prizefighter. "The winner!"

But I didn't hang around to bask in my glory. I ran back upstairs and found my father sitting at the kitchen table, where he had watched the rematch through the window.

"Daddy, Daddy, did you see that?"

"Yes, I saw it. Don't you like that better?"

I nodded and wiped a lingering tear from the corner of my eye. He sat me on his knee and gave me a hug. "Don't ever run away from a fight, son," he said softly. "Always make the other guy run away."

Whenever Daddy watched us from his balcony, there was a chance I'd get in trouble. One time I was playing ball in the street with some neighborhood children when I heard my father's voice calling down to me. "Tommy," he shouted, "get out of the middle of the street before a car runs you over." I moved to the sidewalk, then edged my way back into the street, taking care to stay near the curb. Five minutes later I heard my dad's voice again. "Tommy! Didn't you hear me tell you to get out of the street? Come up here."

I knew I was about to get punished and started sniffling as I climbed the stairs. My father stood at the top of the stairway glaring at me. "Son," he said, "you've never had a spanking from me, but you're going to get one now." He grabbed me by the shoulders, yanked my pants down and bent me over his knee. He had his arm raised over his head and was about to slap my bare butt when I blurted out a desperate argument for the defense.

"But I did what you told me, Daddy!" I cried. "You said get out of the middle of the street, so I stayed on the side."

He hesitated, then slowly dropped his arm. "You really thought I was just talking about the middle of the street?"

"Yes, Daddy, that's what you said."

"Well, I can't spank you if you thought you were doing right. But don't play in the street, son. It's dangerous."

Then he told me a story. "There was a caveman one time who told his son, 'There are two roads through the forest. I know this one is safe. But I saw a bear on the other road. He may still be there, he may not. But if you take that road, the bear might get you.' The boy thought he knew better than the papa caveman and took the second road. He never came back to the cave, because the bear ate him up." I would hear about that damn bear for the rest of my life.

The streets might be dangerous, but they were also full of excitement and adventure. During Mardi Gras season, all the parades passed down St. Charles Avenue just a block from our house. Crowds gathered along the broad, oak-lined avenue and the grassy median—the "neutral ground," as we call it in New Orleans. Vendors sold cotton candy, caramel-covered apples, and a kind of taffee called Roman candy from mule-drawn carts. The sweet smell of their wares mingled with cigar smoke and beer.

The first sign that the parade was coming was the passage of the motorcycle cops with their red lights flashing and sirens blaring. Soon you would hear drums and trumpets approaching, along with the roar of ten thousand voices shouting, "Throw me something, mister!"

A dozen elaborately decorated floats followed. Perched atop them, maskers in sequined costumes threw glass beads and trinkets by the handful. My Uncle Buck rode in the Rex parade every year and he would shower us with "throws" when he got to our street corner. On Mardi Gras Day, most of the crowd was also in costume—there were devils, witches, cowboys, Indians, spacemen, and a lot of transvestites. For some reason, I always dressed as a pirate.

Even when there were no parades, the streets around our house were full of strange and wondrous things. I was fascinated by the black vendors who passed along Carondalet Street. There was the iceman who came by on a wooden wagon pulled by a mule. He would chip ice off big blocks in the back of his wagon or deliver whole blocks with a big pair of metal tongs. Another man sold avocadoes—known locally as "alligator pears"—from a big burlap bag slung over his shoulder. He would cry out "Alligator, p'alligator, alligator, p'alligator . . ." It was a repetitive drone that reminded me of the locusts' song.

Then there was Dora Bliggen, the blackberry woman. She wore a long dress and apron that reached all the way to the sidewalk and had a big white bandanna wrapped around her head. On top of the bandanna, she balanced an enormous basket of blackberries that she picked out in the country. She sang a haunting chant: "Blackberries, blackberry! Sweet and fine . . . Blackberries, blackberry, fresh from the vine . . . Blackberries, blackberry!" You could hear her coming from blocks away.

One day a man named Fred Ramsey came to visit my father, who had known him in New York. He had cowritten a famous book called *Jazzmen* years earlier and was now traveling through the South recording Negro folk music. My dad told him about Dora Bliggen and Fred decided to record her street call.

He set up a tape recorder in my father's front bedroom and ran a microphone out onto the porch. Pretty soon, we could hear Dora's call coming toward us from blocks away. "Blackberries, blackberry . . ."

As the sound got louder, Fred's eyes lit up. "This is marvelous," he whispered to my father while the tape turned and captured her song. When Dora arrived in front of our house, my father rushed down, bought her entire stock of blackberries, and asked if she would come up and sing so Mr. Ramsey could record her voice. She seemed hesitant about coming into our house, but finally, agreed after some more money was pressed into her hand.

Dora stood in our living room, still wearing the bandanna, with large beads of sweat coming down her brow, cooling herself off with a palmetto fan. She did her blackberry cry, then sang a musical version of the Lord's Prayer in a wavering, contralto voice with bluesy quarter-tone inflections. It was strange, haunting, beautiful.

Even apart from the music, Dora's visit was a special event. Louisiana was segregated in those days, and it was against the law for blacks and whites to be under the same roof—except if the blacks were working for the whites. I guess Dora, like cooks, maids, nannies, and handymen, qualified as hired help. In fact, the only regular contact I had with black people was when they came into my world as servants.

We had a cleaning woman, Justina, who came two days a week. My Aunt Pat's more affluent family had servants every day. Mary Jiles was my favorite. Not only did she make the world's best fried chicken and garlic spinach; she was a great talker, with an encyclopedic knowledge of baseball and opinions on just about any subject under the sun.

Mary was short, dark, and skinny as a stick, with bushy hair and twinkling black eyes. She had fine features and must have been a very pretty young woman. She was only in her forties at this time, but to me that seemed ancient. I would sit on a high stool in Aunt Pat's kitchen while Mary, neat as a pin in her white-starched uniform, prepared dinner, cutting up the chicken pieces, dipping them in egg batter, rolling them in flour and bread crumbs, and throwing them into a deep cast-iron skillet full of sputtering oil.

Mary had lived in St. Louis as a young woman and got hooked on baseball when Jackie Robinson was signed by the Brooklyn Dodgers in 1947 and became the first black man to wear a major league uniform.

"Tommy," she told me, "whenever the Dodgers came to town, I be there screamin' 'Jackie Robason! Jackie Robason!' I didn't care nothin' about them Cardinals." Robinson had made her an unconditional Dodger fan, and she passed that allegiance on to me.

Aunt Pat was my father's sister and guardian angel. In fact, she was everybody's guardian angel. Endowed by nature with the genes of kindness and self-denial, she was slavishly devoted to her mother,

her aged aunts, her brother, and, of course, her husband, Uncle Buck, whose success in the rubber goods business gave her the means and leisure to spend her life doing good for others.

Aunt Pat's only child, my cousin Claudia, was two years older than me. Claudia and I were very close. We shared the Sancton blue eyes and we both had very curly hair, which Beth liked to describe as "kinky." As very young children, we even took baths together. She often had me over to spend the night in the special child-sized bedroom that had been built for her in the attic. We would read *Winnie the Pooh* and plot to raid the icebox once her parents went to sleep. But we always drifted off long before they did.

Uncle Buck was a dapper, good-looking man, despite his premature baldness and the prominent ears that made him look "like a loving cup from behind," as Aunt Pat had told him on their first date. I found him a bit intimidating with his deep voice and droopy-lidded eyes that would look disapprovingly at me whenever I neglected my table manners or forgot to flush the toilet in his bathroom. But he never scolded me. In fact, I rarely heard him raise his voice—except to curse President Kennedy or Martin Luther King Jr. every time he saw them on the TV news.

Like most New Orleans socialites, he was fond of his drink. When he was feeling good after a couple of highballs, he would point proudly to the framed pictures that showed him dressed up in his carnival costumes as a member of the Rex krewe and, one year, as King Proteus in a jeweled crown, false beard and white tights that showed off his athletic legs to good advantage. This was all quite serious to him. In New Orleans, membership in the Mardi Gras organizations was the key to social success, a sign that one had made it in this class-conscious city.

Aldwyn "Buck" Harold didn't start at the top of the New Orleans social ladder. The son of an impoverished English emigrant, he grew up in a large working-class family and never got past high school. But he had the good fortune to be brought into a rubber goods company started by his older brother Claude. The Harolds prospered in a rising economy and eventually wound up millionaires. My uncle's wealth was the source of the little envelopes Aunt Pat slipped regularly to my father, who was always short of cash. Daddy secretly resented his success even as he took his money. Uncle Buck must have sensed this, because he loved to tell his intellectual brother-in-law things like, "Tom, I never got much schooling, but I can sure as hell sell rubber!"

CHAPTER THREE

My father was different from all the other dads in the neighborhood. He didn't drink. He worked all night. He slept all weekend. But most of all, he was a writer. That made him a local celebrity, since his byline was in the paper every day and the *Item* billed him as their "ace reporter." From my very first day at school, McDonogh Number 10, two blocks from our house, teachers would perk up when they learned my name. "Tommy Sancton? Are you related to Tom Sancton of the *Item*?" I would proudly tell them he was my dad. And that made me special.

My father was tall and good looking, with penetrating blue eyes, thick eyebrows, and, in those days, black hair combed straight back. He cut an imposing figure when he went to work in his natty business suits with a white handkerchief stuffed in the breast pocket.

Sometimes he took me to the office with him. Everybody made a big deal over him when he strode into the city room. The copy boys revered him and called him "chief." The other reporters would gravitate to his desk to tell him how much they "dug" his last piece and ask what he was working on today. The photographers, a crude and tough-talking lot, would come over and swap jokes and bawdy stories with him.

Tom Sancton was the star of the *Item* city room, and I was delighted to bask in his reflected glory. "Who's this?" they'd say. "Little Tommy? You gonna be a writer like your dad?"

I'd say I didn't know. But I always felt a thrill when my father rolled up one of his finished stories and let me put it in the vacuum tube that sent it flying down to the Linotype operators on the ground floor. It made me feel like I was working on the paper too. And when the presses started up around 11 a.m., the whole building shook like a spaceship about to take off. It was exciting.

My father was also the center of attention at the evening journalism classes that he taught at Tulane University for a couple of years. Sometimes he would take me there, too. I sat in the back of the classroom while he told two dozen admiring undergrads to throw away their textbooks and write "gutsy" stories that people wanted to read. "Forget about the professors," he'd say. "You gotta write for the lip readers."

That didn't ingratiate him with the other faculty members, but the kids loved him. Some of them were varsity athletes who took his course because they thought it would be easy. It wasn't. He made his students rewrite their stories over and over until he got something he considered readable out of them. And they loved him all the more for it. Especially the young women, who seemed to get giddy and girlish in his presence.

One of his students was an intense young man who was interested in writing fiction. My father lent him some books and talked to him for hours about the art of the novel. The boy went on to write a novel himself, a colorful fantasy about New Orleans, but no one wanted to publish it. He later killed himself. His name was John Kennedy Toole, and his book, *Confederacy of Dunces*, won a Pulitzer Prize after its posthumous publication in 1980.

My mother was also different from the others in our neighborhood. She had a Mississippi accent, spoke some French, and painted watercolors. She didn't work in those days, but she stayed plenty busy.

She served as a volunteer saleswoman at the Junior League thrift shop. She was on the altar guild at Trinity Episcopal Church, which meant she arranged flowers on the altar and also worked at the church rummage sale. And when she wasn't doing those things, she was taking watercolor lessons or painting landscapes in Audubon Park or on the levee. Sometimes she would take me with her and let me paint, too. She even tried her hand at golf, but quit after she got "exposed at" by a strange man while she was trying to retrieve her ball in the rough.

Mother came from a different world—the affluent, genteel society of Jackson, Mississippi. My sisters and I loved to visit Jackson with her. We would stay at my grandparents' big white house on Poplar Boulevard, with its huge oak tree in the front yard, and its half-acre of lawn and gardens in the back. Jackson seemed like paradise to us. We could play with our cousins, roam through the woods, wade in the creeks, ride our bikes on the quiet, hilly streets, sit on Marnee's porch swing in the cool of the evening while the old folks drank iced tea and talked into the magnolia-scented night.

On Sundays, Marnee would have my two uncles and their families over for lunch, which the Jackson folks called "dinner." The food was typical southern fare: baked chicken, rice, okra, butterbeans, turnip greens, crowder peas, cornbread, and iced tea with fresh mint from the garden. There was never any fish on my grandmother's table: Jackson was too far inland. The only seasonings they ever seemed to use were salt and bacon grease. My mother told me she had never even smelled garlic until she moved to New Orleans.

Unlike my father, who was kept out of World War II by a heart murmur, my uncles, Julian and Clay, were war heroes who had flown many missions over Europe at the controls of their B-25 and B-28 bombers. They had seven kids between them, so there was quite a crowd around the dinner table.

Uncle Julian was a lawyer who had used his war-hero status and his father's illustrious name to get elected Hinds County district attorney. I learned many years later that he was also an alcoholic and a compulsive gambler who beat his children and finally squandered most of my grandmother's fortune, over which he had power of attorney. But in those days, he was living high off the hog, with a big, white-columned home, two cars, and a vacation house and deep-sea fishing boat on the Gulf Coast at Pass Christian. Sometimes he and his family would invite us to go swimming with them at the Jackson Country Club. One of my cousins later told Beth how ashamed they had all been whenever we would show up there in my father's rusty Ford.

My grandfather Alexander was a prominent man in Jackson—a Princeton graduate, associate justice on the Mississippi supreme court and a Sunday school teacher at First Presbyterian Church, where his father had been a famous preacher. The Judge was an influential jurist and scholar, author of a two-volume text on jury instructions, and of some eloquent opinions that went on to become permanent fixtures of American law. My grandmother came from well-to-do families, the Roberts and Whartons, who traced their lineage all the way back to the Mayflower.

I remember my grandfather mainly for his fairy tales and his banjo playing. But I also got some sense of his importance when I would ride in the car with my mother to pick him up at the state capitol after work. It was a thrill to see that big domed building with the gilded eagle at the top. As soon as I spied Dede coming with his bulky briefcase in his hand, I would hide on the floor in the back of the car. He would get in the front seat, kiss my mother on the cheek, and say, "Oh, Seta. You didn't bring my boy. If only you had brought my boy." Then I would poke my head up and squeal, "I was fooling you!"

Judge Alexander probably didn't like the idea of his precious daughter marrying a New Orleans newspaperman—and a Catholic at that. When he first heard they were dating, he asked my mother, "Is he a sot man?" He even used his judicial connections to get background information on Tom Sancton from colleagues in New Orleans. The report came back that Sancton was a "fine man," so the judge finally blessed the marriage that his daughter had her heart set on.

But he was never really comfortable with his son-in-law. He probably never knew the extent of my father's political radicalism, or his involvement in the first stirrings of the civil rights movement. But he could tell that Tom Sancton's views about race did not exactly square with those of the Southern establishment. And at a time and place when class was almost as important as race, he could not have been overly eager to hand his daughter over to this half-orphaned son of a modest working-class family. Aunt Pat later told me how nervous she and her mother had been as they headed up to the wedding on the Illinois Central train. "The Alexanders were such big society people, we were afraid they would look down on us. But the Judge was a real gentleman, he never made us feel that."

In my last memory of him, Dede was standing next to his bed in an undershirt and boxer shorts, packing clothes into a tan leather suitcase. We had spent Christmas with my grandparents, and this was New Year's Eve. "Are you taking a trip, Dede?" I asked.

"Yes, I am," he said. "Marnee and I are driving to New Orleans. We're going to the Sugar Bowl."

"What's that?"

"It's a big football game between Ole Miss and Georgia Tech. We'll be right back once it's over."

When he had packed the bags into the trunk of his shiny blue Plymouth—he called it "My Blue Heaven"—he came back into the house and dragged the Christmas tree out the back door. "It's bad luck to leave your tree up after New Year's," he said.

We waved good-bye as my grandparents drove down the back driveway and turned into St. Ann Street. Then my sisters and I went back to our games.

The next day, we had a special treat. *Peter Pan* had just come out and Mother took us to see it in the local movie theater on Capitol Street. As we headed back up the driveway to my grandparents' house, I saw my great-uncle Ramsey Roberts—we called him "Rannie"—waiting by the side porch. He was usually smiling and twinkle-eyed, but now his face looked grim. When mother got out, he pulled her aside and whispered something in her ear.

"No!" she said. "No!" Then she started crying.

My sisters and I stood there clutching her legs, uncomprehending until Rannie told us what had happened. "Dede's gone to heaven," he said. He'd had a heart attack during the game and died right there in his fifty-yard-line seat in Tulane Stadium with my grandmother sitting helpless and horrified at his side. When I finally realized I would never see Dede again, I grabbed Rannie's hand and told him, "Rannie, you have to be my grandfather now." He said he would.

None of my mother's people could ever get used to the fact that she had married a poor writer. But Tom Sancton couldn't care less what the Alexanders thought of him. He was convinced that he would have the last laugh when his books made him rich.

His first novel, *Count Roller Skates*, came out in December 1956. It tells the story of "Count" Casimir Poliatoffsky, a romantic, semi-mad Polish seaman, champion roller skater, and self-proclaimed nobleman who marries a working-class New Orleans girl and dreams of creating a utopia on earth by putting mankind "on wheels." Peopled with corrupt cops, dissolute seamen, buxom showgirls, and a barrelhouse piano player named Fewclothes Stagney, it was a colorful, vigorous first novel and a promise of things to come.

The publication of *Count Roller Skates* was a big event in our lives. We were living in Jackson at the time—my father had taken a leave of absence from his *Item* job. I remember newspaper reporters coming over to interview him in Marnee's living room. He told one of them that the Count was a symbol of "the egotism in all human nature." There was a big book signing party on Capitol Street. Everyone was flocking around my father as he autographed stacks of books.

Eudora Welty, a lifelong friend of my mother's, was there, flipping through her signed copy and saying how "very fascinating" it looked. She was a nice lady, but I thought she looked like a toad and I was afraid to let her kiss me. A review or jacket blurb by Eudora would have boosted the sales, but she provided neither. My father never forgave her.

Back in New York, the only place that really counts in the publishing world, the book hardly made a blip on the radar screen. Daddy complained to Mother that his old New York friends—like the critics Max Geismar, Edmund Wilson, Malcolm Cowley, and Lionel Trilling—had declined to review it. According to a clipping that I later found in my father's files, *Time* magazine gave it a condescending and flippant mention, calling it an "uneven, offbeat first novel" that "whizzes its screwball hero right through the mentally sound barrier."

"My friends didn't want to acknowledge that I had written a serious novel," Daddy told me many years later. "I was a pretty boy from the South. It was alright for me to write about race relations and politics, but in their eyes I wasn't supposed to be a novelist. They froze me dead."

A week after *Count Roller Skates* went on sale, my father drove to New Orleans and stuck his head into the big Doubleday Bookstore on Canal Street to see how the book was selling. A clerk told him they had sold their two copies and didn't plan to restock. "What?" said my father. "A book by a New Orleans author, set in New Orleans, published by Doubleday, and you're not going to restock it?" The man just shrugged. My father was furious and called his editor at Doubleday, the legendary Lee Barker (known in the book trade as "the Baron Barker"). "I'm sorry to hear that, Tom," Barker said, "but, you know, we really don't have any control over the individual bookstores." My father put down the phone and told Mother, "Seta, my book is dead."

He was devastated. His manic high over the book's publication gave way to the deepest of depressions—made worse by his cold-turkey kicking of his diet pill addiction. The failure of *Count Roller Skates* also marked the end of our idyllic Jackson life. My dad's leave of absence was up, and his book advances long since spent, so he had no choice but to move back to New Orleans and return to work at the *Item*. So we bade good-bye to our schoolmates, our cousins, and our grandmother, and climbed into Daddy's banged-up old station wagon for the long drive back.

CHAPTER FOUR

We arrived in New Orleans at the beginning of the summer and moved into my other grandmother's house at the far end of Canal Street. This was where my father grew up, a two-story Victorian house that my grandmother had remodeled in the Spanish mission style and divided up into low-rent apartments during World War I. It had changed little since that time. The facade was covered with a beige stucco, and the original wooden columns had been transformed into arches that made the place look a little like the Alamo. The front porch had half a dozen rocking chairs where the roomers would sit and try to cool off on steamy New Orleans evenings. The Canal Street trolley line ran right in front of the house, its bell clanging far into the night. One block further down the broad avenue was Metairie Cemetery, the city's biggest and best-known burial ground.

Our apartment was on the ground floor, just off the porch. It had a living room, bedroom, kitchen, and bath. My parents slept in the bedroom—the first time, in my memory, that they used the same bed. My sisters shared a convertible sofa in the front room, and I slept on a folding cot. There was just a small patch of grass in the back—a mere postage stamp compared to my grandmother Alexander's lush lawns and gardens. At the rear of the backyard was a wooden tool shed with a corrugated tin roof. Thanks to the New Orleans humidity, the wood was half-rotten, and the whole backyard had a musty smell. There were lots of centipedes and lizards to chase after, but no room to run around or play ball as we had done in Jackson.

During my first days on Canal Street, I spent a lot of time riding my bike around the neighborhood looking for interesting things to do. I thought the cemetery was spooky, so I never rode in that direction. I also found the back streets a bit frightening, with their rusty garbage cans and run-down houses and men in sleeveless undershirts drinking beer on their front steps. It was all so different from the stately homes and gardens of Poplar Boulevard.

My grandmother, Amelia Palanque Sancton, was a strong-willed widow with braided black hair rolled up in a bun, heavy red lipstick, thick glasses, and penetrating blue eyes like my father. She and my father had lots of arguments—my dad said they were like "two diamonds scratching against each other"—but she doted on her grandchildren. Wendy was her favorite.

Meme loved to have the kids visit her upstairs apartment, with its big screened windows framed by the thick branches of live oak trees. It just had one bedroom, jammed with dressers and wardrobes, and a tiny front room that was originally the upstairs porch. It was here that my father had spent most of his first twenty years, sleeping on a day bed while his older sister Ursula shared the big bed with my grandmother.

Meme's father had emigrated to New Orleans from Bordeaux just after the Civil War, arriving as a child in a city still occupied by Yankee troops. Eagerly embracing the lost cause of his new neighbors, Simon Palanque had the distinction of getting himself arrested at the age of ten for firing a popgun at some federal troops down by the river. They gave him a scolding and turned him over to his mother.

I don't know what Simon did for a living, but he apparently spent a lot of time in the bedroom. He fathered thirteen children, all of whom lived together in half of a "shotgun" house—those long, narrow wooden dwellings typical of New Orleans's working-class neighborhoods. The boys were mostly bums and ne'er-do-wells—one of them was clinically insane—and the girls went to work early to support the family. Meme, the middle daughter, managed to escape from the crowded, carping household by marrying a bright and ambitious neighborhood boy named George Sancton.

George worked as a machinist and dreamed of becoming an engineer. A couple of years into their marriage, he jumped at the chance to earn good money working on the Panama Canal. So they moved to Panama City with their first-born child in tow and another baby on the way. That's how my father came to be born in Panama on January 11, 1915. He was a strapping nine-and-a-half pounds at birth. George wrote to his family back home what a "beautiful baby" Tom was. Meme looked at him with a slightly more critical eye, writing that "baby is very determined, but very affectionate."

My dad recalled nothing about Panama, except for the smell of his father's Bay Rum after-shave. But Ursula, better known as Pat, was three years older and had vivid memories of that brief, determining interlude in their lives. She remembered the lush tropical vegetation and the lizards and the mosquitoes and the quinine they had to take to ward off malaria. She remembered swimming with her father when he came home from his job at the canal. And she remembered seeing him off at the garden gate one morning, just hours before he stepped onto a scaffolding to free a trapped cable at the Miraflores locks. A bolt sheared and he fell forty feet to the ground.

"When Mother broke the news to me," Aunt Pat told me many years later, "she said, 'Daddy has gone to Heaven.' And I said, 'Well, when is he coming back?' She said he wasn't coming back.

So I said, 'When are we going to see him again?' And Mother said, 'When we go to Heaven.'"

My grandfather had not died immediately. With a ruptured spleen, a crushed chest, and numerous broken bones, he lingered for six days in a military hospital. With his dying breath, he told his young wife to take good care of five-year-old Ursula and two-year-old Tom, and to see that the boy made something of himself. "And don't ever let anybody make a fool of you, Meme," he said. At age twenty-nine, George Sancton became one of the 22,000 men who lost their lives digging that famous waterway.

Meme never forgot George's final injunction. With her meager settlement from the government, $3,820, she made a down payment on the Canal Street house and shrewdly turned it into a source of rental income. A brief second marriage did little to relieve her burden: her husband, a Scottish-born veterinarian whom the children adored and called "Daddy Doc," turned out to be a deadbeat and a philanderer. Their divorce left my father with a new sense of loss and deprived him of the male role model that he badly needed.

Tough-minded and demanding, Meme raised her children with an iron hand and was forever prodding her son to be diligent and get ahead. But he was dreamy and distracted.

"He was the sweetest little fellow, and smart as a whip, but he was always a free spirit, a little dreamer," Aunt Pat later told me. "Meme would send him to the store for groceries, and he'd forget half the things on the list and drop the change on the way home. Mother would lose her temper and beat him, really beat him. It just broke my heart to see that. I always wanted to protect him. I still do."

Meme's thrashings left my father with a deep hurt that mingled with his grief over his own lost, unknown father. He was sensitive, brooding, melancholy. His happiest moments were the six summers he spent at a Boy Scout camp in Slidell, across the lake from New Orleans. That was where he got away from his mother's temper, and the cramped apartment, and experienced the exhilarating freedom of sleeping under the open skies.

Camp Salmen was a magical place of awakening and discovery and communion with nature; a place whose piney-woods smells and star-drenched nights he could feel in his bones; a place where he could swim and fish, build bonfires, and earn merit badges; a place where he and his fellow campers experienced "first love" in heady nighttime rendezvous with vacationing society girls across the bayou.

Years later, in a 1944 essay titled "The Silver Horn," he wrote of his love "for the rhythms of nature, for tropical rains that came sweeping through the pines and oaks, for the fiery midday sun, for long evenings, and the deep black nights. . . . We felt the beauty of this wilderness like a hunger." That poignant, fleeting beauty was symbolized for him by the silver trumpet on which a fellow scout would blow taps each evening. "It was at bedtime that Paolo gathered up into his clear, thin music all the ineffable hungering of our awakening lives," he wrote. "Somehow the music spoke for us, uttered the thing we knew but had no words for, set up a wailing in the pine trees of the brevity and splendor of human life."

My father always knew he would be a writer. Even at Warren Easton High School, he had shown a flair for writing and thereafter looked on that as his ticket to wealth and fame. So did his mother and sister. "He had such talent," my aunt told me, "that we always thought he would make his fortune writing books. We all counted on that." They were so sure of it that Aunt Pat, in the first of her countless sacrifices, dropped out of college after two years, went to normal school, and began teaching to help put my father through Tulane.

Daddy's writing skills, and his college connections, landed him a job with the New Orleans *Times-Picayune* as soon as he graduated from Tulane in 1935. He blossomed in the bustling old city room on Lafayette Square, writing crime reports, obituaries, city hall stories, human interest features, pieces on prison escapes and oil-refinery fires, and the endlessly colorful political scandals in Huey Long's Louisiana. He was never much of a stickler for factual detail—he was really more of a storyteller than a reporter. What counted to him was the human juice and readability, the stuff that made the lip-readers keep turning the pages.

Years later a reporter for a rival paper, Iris Kelso, described the frustration of going up against him on a story. "I worked against a man, Tom Sancton, who was a novelist, and very imaginative," she said. "He would not only write what happened, he'd write what should have happened or might have happened. And when I would get back to the office, my editor would be furious that I didn't have all these interesting details."

Few things interested my father more than race relations. Growing up poor and half-orphaned in a working-class neighborhood, he had a deep and instinctive sense of kinship with what W. E. B. Du Bois called "the souls of black folk." But he did not dare write about the subject in the New Orleans press, for it was taboo to question the sacrosanct Jim Crow system or wring one's hands over the plight of the blacks. "Separate but equal" was the law of the land in the ex-Confederacy. And no sane white man, at least in the South, would openly question it. Anyone who did so in those days would have been looked on as a social pariah, becoming virtually unemployable and even exposing himself to physical danger. But my father could not suppress his sense of outrage. He started contributing articles to the so-called Negro press, passionately exposing the travesty of segregation, denouncing the Southern caste system, and cheering on the early civil rights movement.

No white people in New Orleans ever read the Negro press, of course, so his writings remained underground. Until the day when a black postman proudly showed my grandmother a piece her son had written. "Darling," she told me in hushed tones years later, "I almost died. You see, he was *for* the colored people!" Little by little, word started to get around town that Tom Sancton was a radical, a Communist, and—worst of all—a "nigger lover."

By that time, though, my father had already found his ticket North. In 1940 the Associated Press sent him to New York, where he renewed his courtship with Seta Alexander, who was taking summer school courses at Columbia. In 1942, the year my parents were married, my father won a Nieman Fellowship and headed off to Harvard. He was there only a few months when he was offered a job as managing editor of the *New Republic* at the precocious age of twenty-eight.

In the North, my father had more freedom to write and speak out about race. He hung out with white progressives and black writers like Langston Hughes, Ralph Ellison, Roi Ottley, and Henry Lee Moon. He conversed and corresponded with the great W. E. B. Du Bois, a founder of the N.A.A.C.P. and longtime editor of its magazine, *The Crisis*. In one published 1942 letter, he asked Du Bois, "What white men now alive or in recent years, either writers or doers, do you think have really understood, have really felt, have really helped the progress of Negroes to the decent things of life?" There is no record of the old man's answer, but this was clearly the role Tom Sancton hoped to play.

"The black intellectuals trusted me," my father once told me, "because they knew I respected them, that I loved them for who they were, and that I could not accept the permanent injustice of one race subjugating another just because they were different. Roi Ottley said, 'Sancton passes the test. He fully understands the humanity of the Negro.' He told me, 'Tom, you don't have any problem in Harlem.'"

My father's fiery race articles in the *New Republic* got a lot of attention. They were even denounced on the floor of Congress by some fire-breathing southern senator, a fact that he thereafter wore as a badge of honor. One typical sally, after the Detroit race riots that left thirty-one blacks dead in July 1943, bitterly took President Roosevelt to task for letting the racial climate fester: "Why, in these months when the peril of open race war hung upon the air, hasn't Mr. Roosevelt come to us with one of his greatest speeches. . . . Why hasn't he come to us and talked to us in the simple and genuine language that Lincoln might have used . . . of a land where all men are endowed with inalienable rights, of a country where all are created equal?"

His writings finally caught the attention of Henry Luce, who invited him to lunch one day and hired him to write about race relations for *Life* magazine. But something went wrong at *Life*. He didn't hit it off with his editor, John Shaw Billings, and couldn't get his pieces into the magazine. After just a few weeks, he knew he had no future there. That's when he decided to move back South and write the Great American Novel.

CHAPTER FIVE

We stayed only a couple of months at Meme's. Toward the end of the summer, my parents rented a downstairs apartment in a two-family house on Short Street. It was a pleasant, tree-lined uptown neighborhood, just a block off tony Fontainebleau Drive, and—to my delight—four blocks from Aunt Pat's. I would often bike over to her house to play with Claudia and, especially, eat Mary Jiles's fried chicken.

Lafayette School, just across the street from us, was a wrenching change from the coddled gentility of Jackson. Some of the sixth-grade boys had failed so many times they had mustaches and sideburns. One of them even chewed tobacco and spewed streams of brown spittle onto the schoolyard. He carried a knife and used curse words I had never heard before, like "shitass," "bastit," and "morfadike." Another kid had his name, Tony, crudely tattooed on his right hand and smoked during recess. Then there were kids in khaki uniforms from the Waldo Burton boys' home. Some of them were orphans, others were from broken homes, and still others were delinquents sent there by juvenile court. All of them were tough as nails. Finally, there were the special classes filled with spastics, cripples, retards, and mongolians.

It was the kind of place where you had to learn to stand your ground or get run over. Fortunately, I had been prepared for this kind of challenge by my father's stern injunction never to run away from fights. As soon as any kid gave me a shove, slap, or punch, I flailed out at him with both fists. I didn't pick fights, and I didn't always win them, but if anybody hassled me, I pasted him. Partly as a result of that, and partly because I liked to talk in class and play the smart aleck, I was identified as a "behavior problem."

A teacher named Mrs. Wiederman—better known to us as "Old Lady Wiederman"—called my father in one day to inform him that little Tommy was always getting into fights. She asked him to make me stop. "I'm sorry, I can't do that," he replied. "I'm rearing a boy to be a man."

The thing that worried me most in those days was not schoolyard fights or teachers' reprimands. It was the Russians. On October 4, 1957, they launched their Sputnik satellite and all the kids said they would use it to drop atom bombs on Lafayette School. We were scared to death, and the teachers didn't help when they started making us do regular air-raid drills in class. The drills consisted of crouching on the floor under our desks when the midday siren went off. Apparently, the desks could shield us from atomic radiation. But what if the bombs hit when we were at home?

While I was busy worrying about the Russians, my sisters were getting interested in boys—and vice versa. Beth, then in fifth grade, was very good looking, with green eyes, blond hair, and high, Slavic cheekbones. Wendy, a year older, was plainer, with reddish brown hair and big brown eyes. Both were starting to develop, especially Beth, whose precocious and well-shaped breasts were beginning to attract lots of attention.

Wendy was quiet, sensitive and easily hurt—as much as she tried not to show it. She made up for her vulnerability with a kind of bossy, I-know-better attitude. But she was also the most thoughtful of the children. She never forgot a birthday card and, in later years, would phone our parents every day to make sure they were okay.

Beth was different. She was hard-headed, hot-tempered, and absolutely fearless. She and Daddy had a stormy relationship. Beth was the one who got the most scoldings from him, especially when she started wearing makeup and hanging around with boys. And she was the only one of us who would talk back to him—a trait that would stay with her well into middle age.

Beth was hell-bent-for-leather. When she was in sixth grade, she saved up her money and bought a quarter horse. She got it real cheap because it was never properly broken in. The first time she mounted the beast, it threw her into a barbed wire fence and cut her arms and face so badly she needed to go to the hospital for stitches. The next day, she was begging Daddy to take her back to the stables. He returned to the stables himself, but only to sell the horse back to the former owner. Beth never forgave him for keeping the money.

People often remarked that I didn't look anything like my sisters. There was a reason for that. My parents had despaired of having children after my mother had suffered a miscarriage and then had a stillborn baby. So they adopted a baby girl from a Catholic orphanage. That was Wendy. Shortly after that, the nuns contacted my parents again and begged them to take in another girl, an infant who had been breast-fed by her mother for a few weeks then put up for adoption. Ripped from her mother's arms, the baby had lost the will to live. The nuns feared she would die if she did not soon have a mother to cuddle and comfort her. My parents did not hesitate to take the second little girl into their home. That was Beth. My arrival in March 1949 came as a big surprise to everybody.

The fact that they were adopted was something I knew but paid no attention to. It was like saying Beth had blond hair or Wendy had brown eyes. Our parents treated us no differently. And it made absolutely no difference in the way I felt about them, or in my sense of kinship with them as my sisters. But to them, it was the source of a secret hurt and shame. They felt they had been rejected by their "real" parents, whereas I was the "real" child of the Sancton family. Not a word of this was ever uttered between us at the time. It was only years later that I would learn the extent of their pain, and bitterness, over our different origins.

CHAPTER SIX

My father's dreams of literary stardom had been shaken by the failure of *Count Roller Skates*. He had already received—and spent—the advance on a three-book contract with Doubleday, so he had little choice but to continue the projected trilogy. He finally dusted off the half-finished manuscript of a second book, cranked a telex roll into the old Underwood, and started typing again. This book had to be the Hail Mary pass.

By Starlight, published in 1960, tells the story of young Brad Poliatoffsky, the son of the mad Count from the earlier book. It is a highly autobiographical work: Brad, like Tom Sancton, is raised in a rooming house by a single mother and a doting sister, and awakens to the mysteries of life, love and death during one long summer at a Boy Scout camp. It is in fact, a novelized version of his 1944 essay, "The Silver Horn," with a central plot that revolves around an intriguing love tale: Brad falls for a vacationing society girl from across the bayou, but is ultimately seduced by her mother—a sexy, frustrated alcoholic on the threshold of middle age.

The plot, if not the setting, is similar to that of *The Graduate*, published three years later and made into one of the most successful movies of its era. My dad would later tell me that the plots of no fewer than five major bestsellers had been "stolen" from his books—as if the young man–older woman story were not as ancient as *Oedipus Rex*. He never got over the reply I gave him as a cynical college boy: "All that has a perfect reality for you, doesn't it?"

My father had big movie plans for *By Starlight*. He and my mother even used to discuss the casting. They finally settled on an actor for the role of Brad: the young Anthony Perkins. He would have been perfect for the part. But there was no movie. And though the book sold respectably, and went through a couple of paperback editions, it fell far short of best-sellerdom and failed to earn back its advance.

To make matters worse, the *Item* was sold that year to its competitor, the New Orleans *States*, thereby depriving my father of his day job. Proud as he was, he went hat in hand to beg the *States* editor, Frank Allen, to take him on staff. Allen refused: not only did he cost too much—the *States* would have had to match his *Item* salary of $175 a week—but he had the reputation, for all his acknowledged brilliance, of being a prima donna. So there was Tom Sancton, at forty-five, with two failed novels behind him, three kids to feed, and no job.

In desperation, he rented a tiny office in the American Bank Building on Canal Street and had his name painted on the door: Thomas Sancton, Public Relations. No one could have been more ill-suited to a career in the P.R. business—or any business, for that matter—than this former leftist radical, this sworn enemy of segregation and the Southern caste system, this dreamy, romantic free-spirit, this ungovernable, headstrong individualist. Not surprisingly, the society types who ran the New Orleans business world were not exactly lining up at his door.

The handful of clients he did manage to attract were mostly a collection of eccentrics and crackpots—a fly-by-night entrepreneur with a scheme for selling lumber "by the pound"; a Mississippi real-estate promoter who dug an artificial inland lake because "people are getting tired of all those hurricanes on the Gulf"; a megalomaniac politician. Eventually, even this trickle of clients dried up. My father finally gave up his Canal Street office and answered an ad for a $5,000-a-year job as a publicist for the Louisiana Heart Association.

It was at this bleak moment that Tom Sancton wandered through the French Quarter one evening and passed by the open wrought-iron gate of 726 St. Peter Street. He heard a familiar sound coming from within—the old jazz strains of his youth, the nostalgic soundtrack of those glorious Yacht Club evenings and Tulane fraternity parties. A pretty young woman sat on a stool at the entrance, cradling a wicker basket full of coins. She smiled at him and said, "Come listen to the music, it's only fifty cents."

He paid his money, advanced into the carriageway and, to his astonishment, recognized three familiar faces on the makeshift bandstand: George Lewis, Jim Robinson, and "Slow Drag" Pavageau. He had heard these men, and befriended them, when they were playing in New York in the 1940s. He and my mother had danced to their music almost every night at the Stuyvesant Casino on Second Avenue. Now here they were back in their hometown, playing for coins in a French Quarter art gallery.

My father spoke to them during the break, feasted on their warmth, their humor, and the instinctive folk-genius of their music. In the midst of the most devastating spiritual storm of his life, he had found a haven of humanity.

Daddy was in a euphoric mood when he got home that night. He told my mother he had heard some great music at a place called Preservation Hall, and he wanted to take us all back there the next night to hear the "old men" play jazz.

Mother seemed delighted. It would be a welcome change from seeing my dad stretch out on the sofa—his favorite posture—and spend the evening working his way through the stack of books and magazines that permanently cluttered the coffee table.

I was more into baseball and rock 'n' roll than old-time jazz. But I agreed to go; at thirteen years old, I didn't get many chances to visit the Quarter. As for my sisters, I thought the last thing they wanted, in their teenage sophistication, was to go out on the town with their parents and little brother.

It was just a single room with a splintery wooden floor, some rough benches and kitchen chairs, and smoky-looking paintings on the walls. At the entrance, over the wrought-iron gate, hung a pair of musical instrument cases with the words "Preservation Hall" written on them in brass letters. The place smelled of dust and cigar smoke and sweat. On that early summer night in 1962, the humid heat of New Orleans pervaded the room and embraced its occupants like a warm, wet blanket.

We sat on a bare bench right in front of the band. On the far wall, just behind the drummer, a hand-painted black-and-white sign read *Traditional request $1*; *Others $2*; *The Saints $5*. A rickety electric fan behind the piano was blowing on the band, recycling the cigar smoke and warm, sticky air, but not doing much to cool off the musicians. Their white, short-sleeved shirts were soaked in sweat, and beads of moisture trickled down their cheeks.

But they didn't seem to care. They were happy and exuberant—especially the tall, dark trombone player, who was always jumping to his feet, clapping his enormous bear-paw hands, and encouraging the sparse audience to clap along. He smiled a lot and his teeth were capped with gold. Sometimes he pulled a white handkerchief out of his rear pocket, waved it playfully, then wiped his broad, high-cheekboned face. When he played his horn, he shifted his weight from one foot to the other like a boxer. His brassy phrases flew out clean and snappy like combination punches. "That's Big Jim Robinson," my father whispered to me. "I knew him in New York."

The piano player was Emma Barrett. She looked about a hundred years old to me, but in fact was only in her sixties at that time. Emma wore a red beanie with her name embroidered on it in gold. On her legs, just below the knees, she wore a pair of garters festooned with bells that jingled when she tapped her feet to the rhythm of the music. They called her Sweet Emma the Bell Gal. But to me, she didn't look sweet at all. She was positively scary, with her protruding teeth, sagging lower lip, and grayish skin. When she sang, her voice had an eerie echo to it, as if it were resonating in a tomb. She made me think of Marie Laveau, the legendary voodoo queen of New Orleans, who, as Papa Celestin used to sing, "made a fortune, strange as it seems, sellin' gris-gris and interpretin' dreams."

The left-handed banjo player, Narvin Kimball, looked wise and professorial with his dark-rimmed glasses, a close-cropped mustache and halo of white hair. He accompanied the band with a rock-steady chink-chink beat. But when he stood up for his solos, his left foot on his chair and the banjo propped up on his knee, he would play the actual melodies of the tunes using whole chords and a fluttering, mandolin-like tremolo. He also sang some spirituals in a rich tenor voice, bending and shading notes like nobody I ever heard in my uptown Episcopal church.

I was starting to think that there was nothing ordinary about these people. Whether rambunctious like Jim Robinson, or spooky like Sweet Emma, they radiated a kind of spirit that I never encountered before. There was a siren-song magic about their music that was luring me into uncharted territory. I hadn't a clue where it was taking me, but I knew I would not wind up exactly where I started from.

Nothing made me feel that more strongly than the sound of George Lewis's clarinet. The band had been playing up-tempo ensemble numbers since we arrived, but at one point George stood up and announced that he was going to play a solo. "This here's the 'Burgundy Street Blues,'" he said in a deep, soft voice. "This my *own* tune."

It was a slow number, mournful and exalting, punctuated by soaring, shimmering high notes. He played chorus after chorus, building on the same simple theme. His long, tapered fingers moved easily over the silver keys. Unlike some of the other horn men who puffed out their cheeks when they played, George seemed to breathe from somewhere deep within his small, frail-looking body. The only sign of effort was the bulging, sinuous vein on his left temple.

George was so small that the clarinet looked enormous in his hands. When he played his horn, his hips moved in a gentle circular pattern. His slim body had the energy of a coiled snake. More than mere music, his clarinet seemed to fill the room with soul and spirit, something deep, dark, and eternal.

I don't know if I had ever felt passion before—that pulse-churning excitement that makes you want to possess a thing, to fuse with it and have it fuse with you, that makes that thing seem greater and more wonderful than any other thing in the world. That's what I felt for the sound of George Lewis's clarinet.

I was quite moved when my father took me up to chat with George during the break.

"George," he said, "this is my boy Tommy."

George shook hands and looked me straight in the eyes. I couldn't believe I was touching the fingers that had just made that angelic music.

"What instrument you play, Tommy?"

"I don't play anything."

"Better learn one," said George. "You got music inside you."

"How can you tell?"

"The way you move when you listen. I was watchin' you. You got the beat."

"Slow Drag" Pavageau, the bass player, was standing at George's side, sucking on a briar pipe. He studied me with twinkly black eyes.

"Get you a clarinet, play like George Lewis," he said in his Creole French accent. "Bass make you work too hard." He made a bass-playing gesture, pumping his right arm like a chicken wing and moving his left hand up and down an imaginary instrument. He chuckled, out of breath. "Old man—fatigué," he said, and went out to sit in the carriageway.

Drag had a right to be fatigué—he was born in 1888. In fact most of the musicians I met at the Hall had been born before or shortly after the turn of the century. Many of them had quit playing years earlier, and spent their time hanging out in neighborhood barrooms, on their sagging front steps or out at the racetrack. But once Preservation Hall opened for business, they began to play regularly for French Quarter audiences that, in those early days, were sparse but enthusiastic. Some of the patrons were tourists who had stumbled in on their way to Pat O'Brien's bar next door. But many of them were local regulars who returned night after night. The musicians got to know them and counted on seeing them down at the Hall. It became a kind of family.

In those days, though, blacks and whites were not supposed to enjoy each other's company in New Orleans. These were the twilight years of segregation. Whites and "colored" people attended separate schools, drank from separate water fountains, stayed at separate hotels, and went to separate restaurants, bars, and movie theaters. It was okay for blacks to play music for whites, or wait on them, or walk their children through Audubon Park as nannies. But it was technically illegal for the races to "consort" together. For a white kid growing up at the tail end of the Jim Crow era, the world of these old musicians was an unlikely fraternity. But nothing seemed more natural to me, the son of an old civil rights activist, than to admire the "mens" and embrace their culture.

CHAPTER SEVEN

Preservation Hall was like the Arabian Nights. Everything else in my life—school, friends, teenage parties, baseball—suddenly seemed ordinary and boring compared to that. It wasn't just the music that attracted me to the Hall. It was also the weird and wondrous people who hung around there. Where else would a kid my age have encountered such a colorful swath of humanity: writers, artists, pimps, hustlers, defrocked preachers, ruined heiresses, ex-cons, beautiful women, and exotic foreign travelers?

Allan Jaffe, who ran the place with his wife Sandra, was a descendant of Russian Jews who had settled in Philadelphia. Allan took great pride in the fact that his grandfather had been an influential rabbi in Vilna. A graduate of the Wharton School of Finance, he seemed destined for a career in the retail business—until he took a job as a comptroller at a big New Orleans department store in 1961 and fell in love with the jazz and the food. He knew this was the place for him the night he and Sandy puttered into town on his Vespa motorscooter and went to Mandina's restaurant for his first local meal. "As soon as I tasted their gumbo," he said, "I was hooked."

Jaffe put in his days at D. H. Holmes department store and his evenings exploring the French Quarter with his bride. They naturally stumbled into Larry Borenstein's art gallery-turned-jazz hall and soon struck up a friendship with him. The place was then being managed by a California jazz buff named Ken Mills. In a switch that left Mills and his partner Barbara Reid forever embittered, Borenstein handed over the keys to his fledgling establishment to the Jaffes.

Allan, a shrewder businessman than the dreamy Mills, transformed the Hall from a nickel-and-dime operation into a serious commercial venture. Early on, he decided to pay the musicians full union scale—$13.50 a night and double for the leader—instead of just dividing up the tips. He supplemented the kitty income with record sales. And, in a brilliant move that helped change a local jazz joint into a national institution, he started sending bands out on tour under the Preservation Hall banner.

Jaffe was not content to attract customers through the gates. He felt he was involved in a crusade to save the music and get all the old players active again—even those who had lost heart and hung up their instruments years earlier when their old-style jazz fell out of fashion. He would ride around town on his Vespa, looking up old jazz musicians he'd heard about and offering them gigs at the Hall. For many of them, it was a new lease on life.

Some cynical observers, reflecting the familiar stereotypes, said it had taken a couple of Jews like Jaffe and Borenstein to turn a kitty hall into a lucrative business. But it was far more than a business proposition to them. Like the northern Jews who had played such a prominent part in the civil rights movement, I think they were also driven by an instinctive sympathy for another oppressed group and a genuine desire to help them. The old men seemed to appreciate this. I never once heard one of these musicians make an anti-Semitic remark about their employers—or even take note of the fact that they were Jewish.

Allan was in his late twenties when I met him. He was a bit pudgy, with a round, boyish face, and always wore khaki pants and white shirts with the sleeves rolled up just below the elbow. People rarely called him by his first name. It was always "Jaffe."

He was a quiet guy, soft-spoken when he did talk, and given to long pauses in the middle of a conversation. I could never figure out whether he was being shy or thoughtful. I think now that he was probably listening to the music. He was a musician himself, a former prep school tuba player who often sat in at the Hall and played regularly with the touring band. But he never sought the spotlight. I once asked him what he had learned by playing with the old men. He thought about it a while and replied: "That the best thing you can do is stay out of their way."

Allan spent most of his time in the carriageway, the breezy corridor that led from the wrought-iron front gate to the rear patio. The carriageway was the most convivial part of the Hall, because the music was not so loud there and people could talk as they sat on the massive cypress pew that Allan had bought from the Church of the Good Shepherd before they tore it down. There was a coke machine in the corner and a pay phone on the wall, along with about a dozen framed posters advertising jazz concerts at venues from Tokyo to Toronto.

Two tall doors led from the carriageway to the main hall where the bands played. Behind the carriageway, there was a courtyard lined with banana trees. It was flanked on one side by a moss-covered brick wall and, on the other, by the former stables, now converted into apartments. In the very rear were the former slave quarters, which had been turned into a high-ceilinged studio apartment with a sleeping loft. That's where Allan and Sandy lived.

Sandy was a beauty with her black hair, big blue eyes, and enigmatic smile. She sat on a high stool at the entrance to the Hall with a wicker basket on her lap. The basket was for the donations that paid the musicians and the rent. But the crowds were sparse in the early days, and sometimes the pickings were slim.

One night, I overheard an argument between the Jaffes and the proud, irascible banjo player George Guesnon. Seems there was a disagreement about the exact amount of money in the kitty and how it should be divided.

"Y'all gave us a bad count," said Guesnon, his thick eyebrows dancing with indignation. "I'm a dice player! I'm a gambler! I can count money with anybody in the United States. I can count better than both of you together—and doubled!"

Sandy could be a tough cookie. If anybody tried to come in without paying, she locked an icy gaze on them and said, "It's fifty cents." If they still didn't pay up, she would physically block the entrance and push them out.

She was also hard on the drunks who were always stumbling in from nearby bars, especially Pat O'Brien's, whose rum-based Hurricane is a particularly potent cocktail. Whenever someone stumbled in with a Hurricane glass in hand, she would sternly announce, "No alcohol inside." This sometimes led to a boisterous protest, often accompanied by abusive language. Sandy's typical response was to stand up, still cradling the kitty, and kick the offender in the shins. By this time, Allan or Larry Borenstein or my father would move in and hustle the rowdies out.

After one of these confrontations, Sandy got hungry and went down to the corner of St. Peter and Bourbon to buy a Lucky Dog. Lucky Dogs were extra-long hot dogs served with a ladling of chili and a squirt of yellow mustard. They were sold from rolling metal carts shaped like giant Lucky Dogs and usually manned by unshaven, down-and-out type guys. The whole operation—like a lot of other businesses in the French Quarter—was run by the local Mafia.

No sooner had Sandy paid for her Lucky Dog than she was confronted by a drunk who had just been run out of the Hall. "You know what you can do with that hot dog, lady?" he growled. "You can . . ."

Before he finished, Sandy stabbed him right in the eye with her Lucky Dog. Chili and mustard splattered all over the man's face and burned his eyes, causing him to reel backward and fall, cursing and screaming, into the street.

Larry Borenstein was the evil genius behind the Hall. He was fat and grubby, with greasy black hair, sandals, thick black-rimmed glasses, and T-shirts that he wore for a week at a time. He smoked crooked, foul-smelling cigarillos that he bought in Mexico during his frequent trips to pick up the pre-Columbian sculpture and pottery (some of dubious origin) that he sold in his Royal Street gallery. He also dealt in Civil War memorabilia, paintings, coins, stamps, and all manner of collectibles, including, for reasons I shudder to guess at, black leather whips.

Larry was allegedly a nephew of Leon Trotsky, and in fact bore a striking resemblance to him. Unlike the infamous Bolshevik, though, he was a capitalist to the very marrow of his bones. Jaffe put it succinctly: "If Larry has $100 in the bank that isn't working for him, he gets nervous."

Larry was widely feared and hated—and he cherished it. But he had an engaging wit and charm under his slovenly exterior. A native of Milwaukee, he was a classic buyer and seller. Years earlier, he had tried his hand at currency speculation but "guessed wrong on the British pound," as he told my father, and got wiped out. He rebuilt his fortune through shrewd trading, then opened his art gallery and began acquiring property all over the French Quarter.

As intent as he was on making a buck, Larry did a great service to the music. At a time when almost no one was paying attention to the old jazzmen, he recognized their artistic greatness—and the commercial potential of the authentic style. It was just a matter of putting it in front of an audience. That's what he did when he started his art gallery jam sessions in the late 1950s, and the miraculous alchemy of Preservation Hall did the rest.

Sally Fellon was eighteen and long-legged as a filly, with bright blue eyes and luxuriant blond hair that she wound into a French twist. I immediately fell in love with her. Puppy love was more like it, given the age difference between us.

Sally had been introduced to the Hall by a visiting English jazz enthusiast with whom she'd had a summer fling. The guy was long gone, but she kept coming down there night after night. Like me, I guess, she found something in the mens and their music that spoke to her. She was from a simple working-class family and yearned for something more than life had given her so far.

Sally would take the St. Charles streetcar down to the quarter as soon as her high school classes ended and do her homework in the Bourbon House café until the Hall opened at 8:30. She was so beautiful that guys were always trying to pick her up, but the avuncular black waiter, Robert, would shoo them away.

Sally and I were kindred souls, the only young people among the regulars. We would spend hours sitting side by side, listening to the music and talking together in the carriageway. Sometimes my father would drive Sally home at night and I would sit with her in the backseat pretending to fall asleep so I could lean over and put my head on her shoulder. One night, she sang me a lullaby.

My crush on Sally was part of the magnetism that drew me to the Hall.

Florence Hayes was a real French Quarter character. She looked like she was ninety years old and always dressed in black. She must have been nearly bald; she wore a black straw hat from which just a few strands of gray hair protruded. There wasn't a tooth in her head, but she made up for her receding lips by drawing an enormous Clara Bow mouth with red lipstick. Florence was a dedicated fan: she would sit on those hard benches all night, clapping her hands to the beat of the music, and wouldn't leave until the last note was played.

Florence was always good-humored, but her story was tragic. Seems she was the daughter of a wealthy Baltimore businessman who sent her on a world tour after she graduated from finishing school. She had made it as far as New Orleans when the stock market crash of 1901 wiped out the family fortune, drove her father to suicide, and left her stranded. She had lived alone in the French Quarter ever since.

Mike Stark first showed up shepherding a group of deaf Sunday school students on a tour of the French Quarter. He translated all the song lyrics into sign language. He must have liked the place, because he kept coming back. Jovial and cherub-faced, Mike was a young Baptist minister who found the ambiance and the mores of the Quarter more congenial than his seminary lodgings. He took an apartment nearby and eventually abandoned his coat and tie for a full-length robe and sandals and grew a long red beard. He also walked around with a large parrot on his shoulder. I don't know what became of his ministry, but he eventually started a French

Quarter shelter for wayward teenage boys. He must have gotten into some kind of trouble there, because I heard the cops ran him out of town. He later returned and opened a shop selling Mardi Gras masks.

Frank Amacker always wore a straw hat and dressed to the nines: starched white shirt, gold cufflinks, a bright-colored silk tie with a diamond-studded horseshoe stickpin. The suits were chocolate brown or mustard yellow, sometimes pale lavender, always immaculate. He had a gold watch chain and two-toned shoes shined to a mirror finish. The musicians called him "the Dude." He was one of the few black people who came to the Hall to listen, not to play.

Frank told me he was born in 1890 and worked as a "professor" in Storyville. I asked if he taught music. "No, son, I didn't teach no music," he chuckled. "I played the piano in the red light district. Entertain the customers while they drinkin' champagne with the girls before they—you know—go upstairs." I must have looked confused, so he went on. "See, fellas paid money to be with the girls, know what I'm sayin'? I had some girls workin' for me. And sometimes I did specialty work—there was this white guy liked to get hit with a board."

Though Frank had played piano and guitar in the old days, I never heard him make any music. Not on an instrument, at least. He always arrived by taxi and paid the driver from a fat roll of bills. He walked slowly through the iron gate, nodding and smiling pleasantly, and took his regular seat in the carriageway. Once he was settled in, he would take a deep breath and emit a high-pitched falsetto warble to accompany the music coming from inside the Hall. Never any words or melody, just a sort of formless wail.

"Voice like a nightingale," he would say when the number ended. "Yes *sir*, that's a God-given voice."

But the thing Frank was proudest of was his hands. They were immaculately manicured, with long fingers and smooth brown skin. Like his round face, they had almost no wrinkles. "I keep my hands soft," he explained. "A lady want to feel silky hands on her body, she don't want no workman's hands." My mother, who was always made uncomfortable by any allusion to sex, found Amacker offensive. But to me, he was colorful and exotic.

Bill Russell was anything but exotic, but he was a legendary figure in jazz history. A conservatory-trained violinist from Missouri who once studied composition with Arnold Schönberg, he had abandoned his musical career to become a writer, historian, and record producer. Without Bill Russell, there would have been no revival of traditional jazz. He was instrumental in the rediscovery of Bunk Johnson—purportedly an ex-bandmate of the legendary Buddy Bolden and a teacher of Louis Armstrong—in the 1940s. Bill's recordings of Bunk had rekindled interest in traditional New Orleans music and, ultimately, paved the way for the Preservation Hall revival. Bill settled in New Orleans in the late '50s, ran a funky little record and violin repair shop, and became the first curator of the Jazz Archives at Tulane University.

To me, Bill Russell was just a kindly old man, very tall and pale, with a large bald dome of a head surrounded by a wispy fringe of white hair. For all his accomplishments, he was one of the most unassuming, self-effacing people I had ever met—perhaps because of his lifelong socialist convictions. We once saw him lugging a heavy tape recorder down the street under the rain and offered him a ride. "Oh, no thanks," he replied. "I wouldn't dream of bothering you."

He hovered around the carriageway every night, helping with the record sales, sometimes minding the basket for Sandy. When the last set ended, he would grab a broom and sweep out the dust and cigar butts. It was Bill who fed the stray cat that hung around the Hall. But his real allegiance was to Pretty Baby, his talking parakeet, who did a perfect imitation of Bill's Midwestern accent.

Bill lived in a St. Ann Street apartment, surrounded by floor-to-ceiling shelves full of manuscripts, photos, and jazz memorabilia, which he kept in shirt boxes acquired from the local laundry. He also kept boxes of odds and ends, bearing labels like "string" and "good string." In the middle of this dense trove, there was just a little clearing with a folding chair, a cot, and a record player. In keeping with his love of animals, he would leave food out in front of a mouse hole along a baseboard. This was both for the benefit of the mouse that lived there and for the preservation of his archives. "If Mousie is fed," he explained, "she won't eat my sheet music."

Bill's place reminded me of the famous pack-rat Colyer brothers of Harlem, who were eventually crushed to death under a fallen stack of hoarded newspapers. He had material on every musician I'd ever heard of—and a lot of others. His greatest treasure was a collection of letters, manuscripts, and sheet music written by the great Jelly Roll Morton. For all the years I knew Bill, he was working on a definitive biography of Morton, which no one thought he would ever finish.

From its shaky beginnings, Preservation Hall soon became an internationally known landmark. It was featured in major magazine articles, network TV shows, and even in the movies after Norman Jewison shot a scene there for his 1965 film, *The Cincinnati Kid*, starring Steve McQueen.

Once it became an obligatory tourist stop, large crowds lined up outside the gates, filled all the seats, milled around the carriageway buying records, and fed the kitty basket until it overflowed. All of which made the Jaffes rich, and left most of the musicians a lot better off than they ever were before.

That kind of success is sure to breed jealousies—and copycats. Still sulking over his unceremonious ouster by Larry Borenstein, Ken Mills set up the short-lived Icon Hall, which specialized in obscure, nonunion musicians and appealed only to a handful of purists. In the mid-1960s, a white Chicago-style trumpeter named George Finola helped set up Southland Hall, directly across St. Peter Street from Preservation Hall, with the express purpose of running the Jaffes out of business. They even had external loudspeakers that beamed their music directly into the carriageway of Jaffe's place. But Southland Hall folded within a few months.

The most successful of the rivals was Al Clark's Dixieland Hall on Bourbon Street, which stayed in business for a decade. The setup was very commercial, with an air-conditioned bar and a corny trio of tap dancers—Skeet, Pete, and Repeat—who finished off each set with an embarrassing minstrel routine. They wore ridiculous coke-bottle glasses and baggy pants and projected the worst stereotype of the happy-go-lucky, watermelon-eating darkie. For that reason, I never much liked going there, although Dixieland Hall's roster included some great musicians, such as clarinetist Louis Cottrell, trumpeter Alvin Alcorn, drummer Paul Barbarin, and trombonist "Frog" Joseph (so named because he hopped like a frog due to a childhood bout with polio).

Dixieland Hall, by the way, did not actually present "Dixieland" style jazz. That was the specialty of the touristy Bourbon street clubs like the Famous Door, Al Hirt's, or Pete Fountain's. Dixieland is a slick, anesthetized, "white" version of traditional jazz. It tends to be fast, loud, and soulless. Though Dixieland bands and traditional bands might play the same tunes, they are as different as muzak and Mozart, or Pat Boone and Chuck Berry. Anyone with ears can hear the difference.

None of these establishments could claim any historic ties to the birth of jazz—including Preservation Hall, which was built as a Spanish tavern in the late eighteenth century. And most of the places in New Orleans that were authentic jazz landmarks were flattened by bulldozers and wrecker's balls in the name of progress.

Some say jazz was born in Storyville, the redlight district on the downtown side of Canal and Basin Street. Legendary players like Jelly Roll Morton, Bunk Johnson, and King Oliver got their start playing in the bordellos of Storyville. Some of the older musicians I knew had worked there as young men—Frank Amacker, Papa John Joseph, Peter Bocage—and many of the others had snuck into the district as kids to listen and learn. Louis Armstrong used to hide behind the piano in Tom Anderson's to listen to Bunk. That was a big part of their apprenticeship.

This seething cauldron of jazz, booze, and sin was closed down in 1917 on orders of the secretary of the navy, who feared that venereal disease would sap fighting capacities of U.S. servicemen and cause us to lose World War I—as if the Germans didn't have their own brothels. The abrupt shutdown sent a lot of bawdy-house musicians up the river to Chicago in search of work. The historic buildings—including veritable palaces like Lulu White's and Josie Arlington's—remained behind.

They should have been preserved and even revered for their cultural significance. But the city fathers were ashamed of the district's colorful past, so they tore down these magnificent structures one by one. In their place, they built a housing project that eventually became a notorious den of drugs, guns, and violence. Some progress!

Fortunately, the French Quarter was spared that kind of large-scale destruction, mainly because the politicians realized that its unique architecture, with its shady courtyards and iron grillwork balconies, was the city's main tourist draw. One of the oldest neighborhoods in America—its seventy square blocks were laid out by Bienville in 1718—the French Quarter was a magical place, full of life and color and bustle. Its atmosphere was like no other part of the city, and it was one of the reasons I loved going to the Hall so much.

My experience of the French Quarter, in fact, went back much further than my exposure to the jazz scene. My parents used to take me and my sisters down there when we were kids to have coffee and beignets at the Café du Monde, romp on the grass in Jackson Square, and watch the big freighters go by on the Mississippi River. Sometimes we would go to Brocatto's Italian pastry shop for spumone and lemon ice. Once in a while, my dad would drive us down Bourbon Street, where we would catch a titillating glimpse of the girls dancing in the strip clubs as the touts opened the doors to lure tourists in.

Even the smell of the Quarter, pervaded by the pungent aroma of chicory coffee and the yeasty vapors from the Jax Brewery on Decatur Street, was special and exciting—if not always appetizing. One of my earliest memories was going down to the French Market with my mother when I was still in a stroller and gagging on the smell of rotting fish.

Once I started going to the Hall with my parents, I began to observe the weird and exotic people who made the Quarter such a bohemian paradise. There were poets and writers—Faulkner had lived there in the 1920s—and sidewalk artists around Jackson

Square. There was also a nutty old lady, Rosie "the duck girl," who walked her pet ducks around the Quarter on a leash. One of my friends asked her what she fed the ducks. "Duck food, asshole!" she snapped, and hit him with her purse. And of course there were the musicians—not just the jazzmen at Preservation Hall, but street musicians, blues pickers, tap dancers, and Gospel singers.

Yet even the Quarter changed over the years. The buildings remained generally intact—they were protected as historic landmarks—but the atmosphere changed. In the early years, the tourists and the gaudy commercialism were generally confined to Bourbon Street, with its nonstop row of bars and strip clubs. But the crowds of rowdy visitors gradually spilled over into the rest of the Quarter, bringing with them the inevitable fast-food stands, T-shirt shops, and clip-joint restaurants trying to capitalize on the city's culinary tradition by selling bad jambalaya and inedible gumbo.

The worst thing was the crime. The influx of well-heeled tourists attracted con men, pickpockets, and muggers, turning the Quarter into one of the city's most dangerous neighborhoods. And sometimes the violence would come too close to home. One night Sandy Jaffe's nephew, on a visit from Philadelphia, was robbed and murdered a block away from the Hall. His name was Tracy. He was nineteen years old.

CHAPTER EIGHT

I was mesmerized by George Lewis. I got a book about his life, *Call Him George* by Jay Allison Stuart, and read it over and over. I bought his records at the Hall and listened to them until I knew every note by heart. I would even stand in front of a mirror and play along with his records on a plastic flute.

When I told George I was trying to learn his music on a toy flute, I thought he'd make fun of me. He didn't. In fact, he told me, his first instrument was a tin fife. "I wanted me a clarinet real bad," he said, "but my mama wouldn't buy me one. I was a sickly child, and she thought it would take too much out of me to blow a horn." So George bought himself a fife for a quarter and practiced it until the neighbors complained about "chirping birds." That's how he started playing music. He didn't get a clarinet until he was seventeen.

As much as I loved George's sound, I never thought of playing the clarinet myself. I was afraid I would just wind up sounding like the kids in the school band—shrill and squeaky and, well, white. They learned to read the notes all right. But the magic of George's playing was not just in the notes. It was tone and feeling, soul and rhythm. And I never thought a white boy could do it. Until Sammy Rimington showed up.

He appeared at the gates of Preservation Hall one night in June 1962. He was nineteen years old, with stringy black hair, a thick Cockney accent and a clarinet case in his hand. My father, who liked to hang out in the carriageway and watch all the comings and goings, was intrigued by this skinny young man and struck up a conversation with him. It turned out that he played with a band in England. He said he and his "mates" had all learned by copying the old records, and now he had come to New Orleans to learn at the source. Most of all, he had come to meet his idol, George Lewis.

"George is here tonight," my dad said. "I'll introduce you to him."

The set had just ended and George was busy putting a new reed on his horn.

"George," said my father, "this is Sammy Rimington from England. He plays with the Ken Colyer band over there."

George flashed a broad smile. "I know Ken Colyer. He was here a few years back and sat in with my band. You got a clarinet in that case?"

"Yeah, that's right. I play clarinet."

"You want to play a few tunes with us?"

"Oh God," said Sammy. His narrow eyes gleamed with excitement, and he scratched his head nervously with long, tapered fingers. "Fabulous, fabulous."

Sammy took a seat next to George and put his horn together, giggling and bubbling over with enthusiasm.

As I watched this gangly young man from across the sea, I didn't know what to expect. But when George stomped off the first tune, Sammy's notes flew out pure and true. He sounded exactly like George—including the liquid tone. It was uncanny. George would play a solo, then Sammy would duplicate it note for note. He even played "Burgundy Street Blues" in unison with George. It sounded like one clarinet.

George was grinning from ear to ear. He'd heard other Englishmen trying to copy his sound when he was on tour over there.

But nobody had come as close to the master as young Sammy Rimington.

The small audience applauded enthusiastically, and the other musicians grinned and shouted encouragement at the young Brit. Banjoist George Guesnon, a harsh judge of musicianship, shook his head in wonder and called Sammy "a clarinet wizard." George Lewis nodded his agreement. "Yes, sir," he said, "this here boy gonna give me some trouble on that horn."

Sammy's performance was a revelation to me. Not only could a white boy capture the sound of the mens, but he could be accepted by them as a fellow musician. From that night on, I wanted to get my hands on a clarinet and play like Sammy Rimington. No, not like Sammy. Better than Sammy.

My father was fascinated by the young visitor and took him under his wing. He invited him out to our house, where Sammy had to "sing for my supper," as he put it, by playing along with George Lewis records.

Sammy also dazzled us with what he called his "conjurer's tricks," for he was a wizard with coins and cards as well as clarinets. Some fellow Brits even said Sammy was a sorcerer, adept in the black arts. I was almost willing to believe that; only someone with super-natural powers could have absorbed as much of George Lewis's spirit.

Over the next few days, my father drove Sammy across the river to George's house, photographed the two of them playing together at the Hall (the picture later appeared on a British album cover, attributed to an "unknown U.S. photographer"), and even arranged for Sammy to make a demo recording in the studios of WWL–TV, where one of his former *Item* buddies worked.

Sammy was grateful for all my father's help and attention. And he must have sensed the enormous admiration I had for him, because when he left town he thanked my dad and told him he would be "sending something to Tommy" when he got home.

Several weeks later, we found a parcel post notice in the mailbox addressed to me. My father drove me down to the post office on Girod Street and I presented the notice at the window. A few minutes later, the clerk shoved a shoe-box sized package across the counter. It was wrapped in brown paper and covered with strange-looking British stamps.

"What do you think it is?" I asked my father.

He said he didn't know, but I think he had an idea. "Open it and see," he said.

I climbed into the back of the car and started ripping off the paper and twine. When I took the cover off, my heart stopped.

"It's a clarinet!"

Before my father had driven two blocks, I hooked the joints together and put the mouthpiece on the end of the horn. It had an old, slightly chipped reed on it. I put the tip in my mouth the way I had seen George do it, took a deep breath, and blew.

Nothing.

I blew harder. There was no sound but the hissing of my own breath.

I kept trying when we got home, kept at it for hours, but could not get a note out of the horn.

"Don't fight it, son," said my father. "We'll take it down to the Hall. George will tell you what's wrong."

The next night, I showed my new clarinet to George.

"Got you a real horn? Now you gonna give me trouble, too, just like Sammy."

"I don't think so," I said glumly. "I can't get a note out of it."

"Let me try it." George wrapped his long, slender fingers around the keys and blew a short phrase. It sounded gorgeous.

"Ain't nothin' wrong with this horn, but that reed's too hard for a beginner. You need to go down to Werlein's and get you a number one-and-a-half reed. Then you got to wet it, see? Can't play on a dry reed. Got to suck on it a while and make it soft."

He played it some more and made it sing like his own Selmer.

"Yeah, Tommy, that's a nice horn," he said, handing it back to me. "Now you do like I tell you, and when you get to where you can play it a little, I'll teach you a few things."

I wasted no time. My father bought me a box of reeds and a clarinet fingering chart at Werlein's music store on Canal Street, and I was soon playing simple tunes by ear. I played so much—sometimes four or five hours at a time—that the downstairs neighbors started complaining. So I lined the walls of a walk-in closet with blankets and put a folding chair inside. I even brought our Silvertone victrola in there so I could play along with my records. It was there, in that womb of a closet, that I gestated as a jazzman. I was doing what the old musicians called "woodshedding"—spending all day in the woodshed and working out on your horn.

There was a lot of talk about bomb shelters in those Cold War days, but I considered the closet my personal shelter and practiced right through the Cuban Missile Crisis. To tell the truth, I did watch the TV reports and, like most Americans, I was scared to death at the prospect of a nuclear confrontation with the Russians. But I put my confidence in our young president, John Kennedy, one of my early heroes. Once I was assured that he was on top of the situation, I returned to my horn and my closet. None of us knew at the time what a near run thing it was.

My first lesson with George Lewis took place at our home on Gen. Pershing Street, in the uptown section of town not far from St. Charles Avenue. My father and I drove across the river to pick him up at his four-room wood-frame house in a black neighbor-hood of Algiers. George was sitting on the porch with his clarinet case in his lap. His front lawn needed mowing and a couple of dogs were barking in the junk-strewn yard next door. He waved good-bye to his daughter Shirley and her two kids and sat next to me in the backseat of my dad's VW beetle for the twenty-minute drive back to our house.

It was a sunny day and George was in a good mood. He talked about different bands he played with in the old days, when all the musicians drank homemade liquor and dances often ended with fights and gunfire. I remember him looking down from the Mississippi River Bridge at a cemetery whose above-ground tombs looked like whitewashed dollhouses from that height.

"People always talkin' about the cost of livin'," he mused, "But it cost a lot to die. I know, cause I just buried my mother a couple of years ago."

"How old was she, George?" my father asked.

"Ninety-six. All her people lived old. Her grandmother lived over a hundred."

"Did you know her?" I asked.

"Oh, yes indeed," said George. "I was ten when she died. She used to tell us all her old stories. She was born back in the slavery times, you know? And *her* mama was born in Africa, a place they call Senegal. Some fellas kidnapped her when she was a little girl and brought her to New Orleans on a ship to sell her for a slave. When she passed, she spoke African on her deathbed."

I was amazed by the connection between George and Africa. I asked him if his mother knew any African words. "No, Mama didn't speak no African," he said. "But she spoke a bunch of other languages—French, Spanish, even a little German."

"She learned all that in school?"

George shook his head. "Colored folks didn't get much schoolin' in them days. See, my grandmother went to work for a French family—rich folks—when Mama was still a little girl. They kind of raised my mama and saw to it she got an education, right along with their own kids."

George's own education had been rudimentary—he could just about read and write—and in many ways his generation of black New Orleanians was worse off than their parents and grandparents. Emancipation, in fact, had left millions of former slaves to fend for themselves—no longer valuable property to be maintained by their masters but marginal "citizens" who had neither the means nor the skills to take advantage of their nominal freedom. George's generation, born just three decades or so after the Civil War, probably represented a low point in terms of education and opportunity. Which is why music was so important to them; along with sports, it was one of the few available avenues of advancement and respect.

I could have talked to George all day, but we were soon pulling up in front of our house on Gen. Pershing Street, a big white-columned colonial with screened-in porches and two towering palm trees framing the front steps. We had moved there two years earlier because my father needed "more room to write." We rented at first, but when the house came up for sale, my dad bought it with a down payment loaned by Aunt Pat.

Having George in our own home was a big event, and my parents stayed with us the whole time. My mother kept him plied with his favorite drink—hot coffee. I remember him being very polite that day—"Yes, ma'am, thank you, ma'am"—to my mother. He always had a quiet, gentlemanly manner at the Hall, but seated there in our living room he seemed almost deferential. The primordial survival instincts of southern blacks were too deeply rooted for a man of George's generation to be entirely at ease in the home of a white man—even a dyed-in-the-wool liberal like my father.

George had the most beautiful instrument, a Selmer Albert system with polished, silver-plated keys. It had been custom-made for the great Jimmie Noone, but Noone had died before it was delivered and somehow George wound up with it. The mix-and-match horn that Sammy had given me was quite shabby by comparison. It was also virtually impossible to tune.

On George's instructions, I had to pull the barrel way out to lower the pitch. It was only later, when I took my instrument to Werlein's to get the pads replaced, that I learned what the problem was: it was a high-pitched clarinet, made before the international pitch was established in 1921. George, who had owned dozens of clarinets in his life, probably realized this.

The great thing about my horn, George said, was that it was an Albert system. The Albert system had long ago been replaced by the Boehm system, which had more keys, easier fingering, and better pitch. But Alberts just sounded better—deeper, rounder, funkier—and all the old jazz musicians used them.

George's teaching method was hands on, master to apprentice. No scales, no theory, no fingering exercises, no sheet music. George, in fact, didn't know anything about all that. He barely knew the names of the notes. As for reading music, he said, "There's readers, and there's spellers." Spellers could muddle their way through a piece of sheet music, note by note, but could not just play it straightaway. And that's pretty much how I learned to read, teaching myself the notes from a method book, but never developing any great facility with written music. "Folks don't pay nobody to read," George told me. "They pay 'em to *play*."

He played the first five notes of an old blues called "Corinne, Corinna," then stopped and told me to "make that." I copied the phrase as best I could. Then he went on to the next phrase. Sometimes I would get a note wrong, and he would show me how he placed his fingers on his own horn. "Make this-here note."

"Now, I'm gonna teach you how to variate," said George. "You got to go in and out, low register to high, and high to low. You play the melody and I'll show you what I mean."

Behind my simple statement of the tune, George started playing those beautiful phrases and embellishments that I had heard him do in the Hall or on his records. He would go up and down the horn, weaving in and out, sometimes harmonizing with the melody, sometimes leaving space and playing a counterpoint, sometimes laying down a rhythmic arpeggio. His tone was gorgeous, especially when he let his horn sing out on the long notes with his plaintive vibrato.

The lesson finally ended and my dad drove George back across the river. When we pulled up in front of his house, he told me to come inside with him. Shirley was sitting on the couch in the front room, drinking beer and watching TV with a dark, heavyset man that I took to be the father of her two boys. He glared silently at me. I gathered the intrusion of a white boy was not to his liking.

George led me into his back bedroom. It was a perfect reflection of the man: small, spare, neat as a pin. There was a large crucifix on the wall, next to a photo of George and his mother. There were lots of other pictures of him playing in clubs and concert halls around the world. Near the door was a rack that held at least twenty pairs of shoes, all shined and ready to go onstage.

He opened the closet door and pulled a clarinet case off the shelf. It was tan colored and had a little brass plaque on the top with an inscription that read "To George Lewis, from the Chris Barber band, London 1959."

"Look inside," he told me.

The case contained a beautiful Selmer Albert system clarinet, polished ebony with shining silver keys. "I can't give you this horn, Tommy, 'cause it was a gift to me. But you can use it as long as you want."

I was thrilled, but felt unworthy. "George, you shouldn't do this. I mean, you need this horn yourself."

"I ain't usin' it these days. It's just sittin' on the shelf gatherin' dust. You need a horn that's in tune. Try it out. It'll make you play better."

"It's beautiful, George."

There were other lessons—at our house, at George's house, at the Hall. Then one day George said I was ready to play in front of an audience. "Get your daddy to bring you down to the Hall on Tuesday," he said. "I'm playing there with my quartet and you can sit in with us."

We got to the Hall early that night and settled into our regular corner seats. George waved me over to him. "Come on, Tommy, and warm up with the mens." Papa John Joseph, who was tuning his bass, smiled and nodded but said nothing.

"Hello there, pardner," said Joe Watkins, bending down to adjust his bass drum pedal. "You gonna play some jazz with us tonight?"

"I'm gonna try."

Dolly Adams, the piano player, turned and looked at me through her tinted eyeglasses. "How do you do, young man."

George was blowing his usual warm-up phrase, *da de da DEE da-da*. I had heard him do it a hundred times, so I tried to play the same riff. Then George called out "Corinne, Corinna," tapped his foot three times, and we were off.

I played the melody and George "variated" around it, just like in our lessons. Then we switched and George played the melody. We had done this together many times, but this was the first time in my life I had ever played with a live rhythm section.

It was fantastic to hear that rampart of support behind the horns: Papa John with those rock-steady bass lines; Joe with his bass drum thumping like an elephant's heartbeat and those tight press rolls on the snare; Dolly with her no-frills, four-to-the-bar chords. I could feel the beat in my gut. From that moment, I was a jazzman.

After a couple of ensemble choruses, George nudged me with his elbow. "Stand up and take one, Tommy," he said. I rose to my feet and played something simple, close to the melody. It was no great shakes, but I played it from the heart. It was the tone that counted, George always told me, so I went for the tone.

Sandy Jaffe beamed at me from the carriageway door. Sally was not there that night—a huge disappointment. But the sparse audience applauded the solo with far more enthusiasm than it deserved. And that, too, was a drug. I was hooked.

I played a few more numbers with the band—"Basin Street Blues," "You Tell Me Your Dream and I Will Tell you Mine"—tunes I had rehearsed with George. When the set ended, all too soon, we had to say our good-byes—it was a school night, after all. George said I had played "real fine" and told me to come back.

During the drive home, Mother raved about the "standing ovation" I had received (from all of a dozen people) and my dad told me I sounded "like a real jazzman." I knew they were proud of me, and that made me happy.

Somebody took a picture of the band that night. I am wearing a hand-made Mexican sweater—a present from Larry Borenstein, who imported them—and slouching slightly in the high-backed chair with my long spindly legs cocked to the right and my horn pointing to the left. George wears a plaid flannel shirt, suspenders, and his usual baggy pants. He has a much more professional posture, back straight up and horn pointed directly in front of him. My cheeks are puffy. My eyes are closed. I am lost in the music and blowing my little heart out. Did I realize then that my life would never be the same?

CHAPTER NINE

George Lewis was more than my clarinet teacher and role model. As the weeks and months went by, he became a real friend to me and my parents. He took pride in my development as a musician. He laughed at my mother's jokes. But he had a special bond with my father. It came partly from his realization that my dad respected him as an exceptional man and a great artist.

But I think their special rapport also had a lot to do with the fact that both men had been raised by strong-willed mothers. My father's mother was a widow who ran a boarding house on Canal Street; George's mother was a domestic servant whose husband moved out when George was five. Both women worked hard to put food on the table, and both were determined to make something of their sons. "The secret of so many of the musicians," my father told me, "is that they're mama's boys—most of them were raised by their mothers. That's where they get their sensitivity and their strength."

But George, at least, had known his father. Henry Louis Zeno was born during the last year of the Civil War to a slave father and a Choctaw Indian mother—making George himself one-quarter Choctaw. Henry never took to life in the city, and one day moved back to the pine woods on the north shore of Lake Pontchartrain, a region where the Choctaws had lived for centuries. (George, who was christened Joseph François Zenon, took the name George Lewis when he stared playing music.)

"My daddy lived across the lake in Mandeville," George told us one night as my dad was driving him home over the Mississippi River Bridge. "He was a trapper and fisherman. Sometimes he worked as a carpenter. Built his own house. I used to spend summers with my daddy—man, I loved it over there. Fact, I played my first payin' job in Mandeville. But I haven't been back there since my daddy died in 1922."

"Did your father play any music?" I asked.

"No, he didn't play. But he was crazy about my music. He bought me a clarinet and a C-melody saxophone—but I never fooled much with the sax. One time he even tried to make me a reed out of a goat's horn."

"A goat's horn? What for?"

"He seen me fightin' with my reeds, shavin' 'em down, burnin' the tips off and all, and one day he say, 'Son, I'm gonna make you a reed that last forever.' He took one of my reeds to see how it was made, then he took his pocket knife and whittled one out of a goat's horn."

"What did that sound like?" I asked.

"Didn't sound like nothin'," George laughed. "I never could get a note out of it."

My dad had always supposed that George was an orphan, like him. The fact that George had actually known his father and spent time with him came as a revelation. "George," he said, as we pulled up in front of his house on De Armas Street, "would you like me to drive you over to Mandeville and see if the old house is still standing?"

George pursed his lips. "Yes, Tom," he said in his deep, soft voice, "I believe I would."

We were back at his house the next morning. George was sitting on the porch with Shirley and her two kids. George had four other grown children by a first marriage; I know one son still ran a grocery store in New Orleans, another one, George, Jr., was a professional boxer. But ever since George's second wife died, Shirley and her boys were his only close family.

The quickest way to Mandeville is via the twenty-five-mile causeway that cuts across Lake Pontchartrain. But my father decided to take the long way around, circling the eastern shore on Highway 11, probably because that's the way he used to go to Camp Salmen when he was a boy. The lakefront road out of New Orleans went right past the old Milneburg resort area, where both black and white bands used to play for dances and fish fries in wooden camps built out over the water. In the old days, from the late nineteenth century until the 1930s, there were more than a hundred such camps. People would come out on the Smoky Mary train and the bands would buck against each other to see who could draw the biggest crowds.

Legend had it that when Buddy Bolden played on the Lakefront, he would point his horn toward New Orleans, six miles away, so people would hear him in town and know there was a dance out at the lake that night. When he played those mighty blasts, people said Bolden was "callin' his children home." We asked George if that was true, but he said he had never heard Bolden—"and a lot of folks that claim to never did hear him either."

George sat in the front right seat, looking out the window at the passing trees, fields, and railroad tracks.

"You know, Tom," George said, "we never used to drive to Mandeville. We always took the steamer that left from Milneburg— white folks in the front of the boat, colored in back. I'm tellin' you, it took a long time to cross that lake."

"Did your mother go over there with you?" My father asked.

"Onliest time I ever saw her in Mandeville was the day they buried my daddy. She was the last one standin' there looking down into that grave. She really grieved for him. But they never could live together. It was just one of those things."

"Did your mother go hear you play in New Orleans?" I asked.

"No, my mama never come around where I was playin'. Not even when I made good and had my own band. She didn't listen to my records much, neither. I know she was real proud of me, but jazz just wasn't her kind of music. I guess it was too modern for her ears."

"She didn't like music?" I asked.

"Oh, she loved music. She worked for a white family that was always having musicians come over and play. But it wasn't no jazz bands. They had string quartets, quadrilles, classical music. She liked the French opera, high-class music. She used to sing me songs from the opera when I was a little boy."

You could tell how much George missed his mother. He talked about her a lot. And she had doted on him—her only child, the pride of her life.

"Mama passed about three years ago," George said. "Never had been sick a day in her life, but she fell down when she was gettin' out of bed one morning, then she had a stroke a couple of days later. She never did get better after that, just sort of broke down. Couldn't walk no more. I had to carry her to bed. She lost all her weight—got so thin she was like a doll in my arms. A little black doll."

George looked out the window and didn't say anything for a few minutes. The sun was high in the sky now and the waves out on the lake were dappled in light.

"A funny thing happened, though," he said. "She was lyin' on her bed 'sleep one morning, and she just stop breathin'. Didn't have no breath, no heartbeat. Her feet and legs started gettin' cold. I mean, she was *dead*. I grabbed the cord to shut the blinds, and they just come crashin' down—bang! My mama open her eyes and bolt right up in bed. It's like the noise started her heart beatin' again."

"She came back to life?" my father asked.

George nodded. "But you know something? Colored people are funny. Shirley went running out the room screamin' and shoutin' like it was some kind of voodoo or something. But it wasn't nothin' like that. She died for good a few hours later. And just before she went, she look at me and said, 'Come on, son, get on the train with me.' I told her, 'No, Mama. I ain't takin' no train. You got to take it by yourself. I'll take a later train.' Those were the last words she said: 'Come get on the train.'"

Halfway to Mandeville, we stopped by an old wooden church and had a picnic lunch under a live oak tree. My mother had packed some tuna fish sandwiches and a thermos of hot coffee for George; she would have loved to have joined us, but she had to work at the library.

Before we got back in the car, I took some pictures of George sitting cross-legged under the oak tree, hands folded over his knees, a big grin on his face. My father also wanted to get some pictures of George playing the clarinet, so we had brought my horn along. He hooked it together, put the mouthpiece on, and played some blues phrases while I snapped away.

"You ever blow out in the open like this, Tommy?" he asked me. "It's good for your tone. I used to practice in a field by my daddy's house. Drove his pigs crazy."

George always told me that getting a good tone was the most important thing—"that's the beauty part of the clarinet." George's tone was both sensual and spiritual—an exalted song of humanity delivered through a pulsating vibrato. It was male in the lower register and female in the upper register. It was sex and sin at one moment, hymn and supplication at another.

He told me I could develop a good tone by practicing softly with a hard reed. But I knew there was a lot more to it than reeds and muscle control. A player's sound starts inside him; it's what he hears in his heart before the note emerges from his instrument. George's tone came from somewhere deep within his soul.

They say that great art comes from great suffering—"You can't play the blues if you ain't paid your dues"—and George Lewis was a man who had seen hard times. Like most black people in the South, he had lived most of his life against the constant backdrop of poverty and discrimination. As he wrote to one jazz fan in 1945, when he was about to be evicted for not paying his rent, "Us color people are worse off than dogs." But George also had to deal with more than his share of sickness and injury. A derrick almost crushed him to death in 1945, while he was working on the docks. Days later, with his chest still bandaged up, he sat on the edge of his bed and recorded his famous "Burgundy Street Blues" for the first time.

"Burgundy Street" contained the secret of George Lewis's tone—it was spiritual, mystical, even religious. For religion was never far from George's thinking about his music. "I guess one reason I made it," he said, "is because every time I went on the stage in one of them big halls I prayed—like I always do everywhere—that God would stick with me and help me play my very best for these folks who'd been so good to me."

We packed up and headed on to Mandeville. It was just a sleepy little southern town strung along the lakeshore, all of ten blocks square, with wooden houses nestled under shady trees, a couple of stores and gas stations. George directed my father onto a back street on the outskirts of town. We crossed a railroad track and turned down a dirt road. Near the end of the road, on the right side, stood a small wooden shack. It needed painting and was missing a bunch of roof shingles.

"That's it," George said quietly. "That's my daddy's house. Still here."

We got out of the car and approached the sagging structure. There was an old oak tree in front of the house. Tufts of Spanish moss hung like gray shrouds from the thick branches and swayed gently in the lake breeze. The house was unoccupied, locked up tight. George had no idea who owned it now. Through the windows we could see two empty rooms—one front bedroom and a little kitchen in back. The floors were covered in dust. One of the window panes was broken. The walls were bare wood—no plaster or wallpaper had ever covered them. "Ain't been lived in for a long time," George muttered.

George stood silently on the front porch. I imagine he was remembering how his dark, taciturn father spent his days on that porch fixing crab traps and fishing nets, whittling sticks into the sharp-tipped spears that he would use to catch flounder by lantern-light on hot summer nights, stabbing them as they slept on the sandy lake bed. He remembered his aunt Pauline, his father's sister, who lived nearby and adored George. And he remembered some idyllic years he spent with his first wife, Emma, in a little rented house down the road. Emma had raised chickens and hogs and kept a vegetable garden in the backyard while George practiced his clarinet.

Mandeville had been big in George's life. It was there that he played his first paying job at seventeen with a band called the Black Eagles. And it was there that he hooked up with the trumpeter Buddy Petit, who recruited George for his band and took him back to New Orleans.

George must have felt a lot of ghosts on that creaking porch. He spent a long time sitting quietly on the front step while my dad and I stood on the grass, a little distance away. Then he turned to me.

"Tommy," he said. "Where your horn? I want to play a song for my father."

I went back to the car and got my clarinet. I put it together and handed it to George. He took a breath and started to play some velvety notes deep in the low register. It was "The Old Rugged Cross," one of George's favorite hymns. As he played the melody, simple and unadorned, I could hear the words in my mind: *"I will cling to the old rugged cross, till my burden some day I lay down . . . I will cling to the old rugged cross, and exchange it some day for a crown."*

We took the faster causeway route back to New Orleans. The two-lane bridge was dangerous. People were always trying to pass and running head-on into cars coming the other way. Sometimes speeding cars would careen through the railings and plunge into the lake. My father never sped, though. He'd trundle along at 40 m.p.h. so he would have time to look at the lake and the seagulls and think his thoughts. With him at the wheel, our biggest danger on the road was getting rear-ended.

George got to talking about all the jobs he had played out in the country when he was younger—dance halls, weddings, church picnics, funerals. "I mean, we used to play all over the place," he said. "Lafayette, New Iberia, Baton Rouge, Biloxi, Mobile." Sometimes they would drive all night in an old beat-up car, jam-packed with musicians and instruments and cardboard suitcases. "Then times got so bad we couldn't even pay for gas," George said with a little chuckle. "That's when we started ridin' the freight trains."

"Wasn't it dangerous jumping on and off trains?" I asked.

"Not as dangerous as some of the things that happened once we got to those country towns. One day, must have been nineteen and thirty-two, me and Chinee Foster and Evan Thomas was just hanging around the railroad tracks in Crowley, killin' time. Train pass by and all of a sudden, I hear somebody call my name. I look up and see it's Bunk Johnson ridin' a flatcar. He was on his way home from Kansas City. He jump off and say, 'Hi, George, y'all need a trumpet player?' We took Bunk on as a second trumpet. He and Evan started soundin' real nice together—I mean, we had us a band then. But it didn't last long. About two nights before Thanksgivin', we was up on the bandstand in Rayne, and this fella, name of John Guillory, come runnin' into the dance hall with a deer-handled dirk. Say Evan been messin' around with his wife. Evan didn't have no time to run, so he grabbed me by the shoulders and ducked down behind me."

George took a deep breath and let it out slowly. "Man, I thought I was finished. Guillory reach over me with that knife and started hackin' at Evan. His wrist kept hittin' my shoulder like this"—he patted his right shoulder three or four times—"and blood was pourin' out all over me. Evan run out the hall and fell dead in the street. Then Guillory run out after him, screamin' and cussin'."

"What did you do?" I asked.

"Packed up my horn and put it behind the bandstand. I was shakin' like a leaf. Pretty soon, Guillory run back in the hall with a shotgun, and I jump head first out the window. Everybody scattered. Then he start breakin' the instruments and throwin' 'em on the ground. Slashed Chinee's drum heads with his knife. Man, he went good and crazy. Stomped Bunk's cornet—wrecked it for good. Fact, everybody's instrument but mine was busted up. I have that clarinet case yet."

"Did they catch the killer?"

"Yes indeed they caught him," George said. "Sent him to the baddest place in Louisiana: Angola Penitentiary. Funny thing, though. I heard he broke out about a year later, and you know the first thing he did? Went into a white bar in Mandeville and ask for a beer. When they told him they didn't serve colored, he pulled out his knife and the bartender shot him dead. Some folks is just hard-headed."

Abby "Chinee" Foster, the drummer on that bloody night, disappeared for three decades. He was living as a wino in Congo Square when a young English musician, Richard Knowles, ran into him in 1961 and convinced him to play again. Chinee made a remarkable comeback and became a regular at the Hall—until he collapsed and died on a street corner in September 1962.

"Why did Chinee quit playing all those years?" I asked George.

"His drums was smashed up. I'd a quit playin' myself if that man had a' broke my horn. See, that was Depression times. Nobody could afford new instruments. Chinee went back to New Orleans and just hung around in the barrooms. Bunk, he went back to New Iberia and worked on a rice farm. And he'd have stayed there if Louis hadn't run into him."

"Louis Armstrong?"

George nodded. "Louis used to listen to Bunk when he was first trying to learn the cornet. Now, Bunk, he like to tell everybody he taught Louis to play. I don't know about that. But I know Louis used to sneak into Storyville to hear him and follow him around in the parades. Everybody was crazy about Bunk's playin' in them days. He was about the best in town. But Bunk had his ways. He could be mighty contrary when he got to drinkin' that bad whiskey—used to call me 'rat-face.'"

"Louis found him on a rice farm?"

"That's right. Must have been around six or eight years after Bunk's trumpet got stomped. Louis was touring the South with his big band and he ran into the old man down in New Iberia. Bunk told Louis he wanted to play again, but he didn't have no horn and no teeth. Louis promised to send him a brand new trumpet—said he got 'em free from the Selmer people."

"So Louis got Bunk playing again," my father said.

"Well, not exactly. See, Louis never did get around to sending Bunk no horn—too busy or something. But when Louis got back to Chicago, he told Bill Russell he'd seen the old man. Bill had heard folks talking about Bunk Johnson from the old days, but everybody thought he was dead. Now when he found out Bunk was still alive, Bill got crazy to come down and make a record with him. It was Bill and his friends that sent Bunk the money to buy a new trumpet and get his teeth fixed. Leonard Bechet—Sidney's brother—made him a new set of teeth for twenty-five dollars. That was big money in them days.

"Once Bunk got his chops fixed up, Bill Russell and a couple of other guys drove down here and made the record. I was on it, too. So was Jim Robinson. First record I ever made. We had to do it in an old piano storeroom down on Baronne Street 'cause the recording studios didn't want to fool with no colored bands. Man, it was so hot that day we had to keep the windows open and let in all the noise from the street—cars, streetcar bells, barking dogs."

I knew the album by heart—Bunk Johnson's Superior Jazz Band, 1942. It was required listening for anyone trying to learn that music. In fact, when the original 78's came out on the Jazzman label, they caused a sensation among jazz fans who looked on Bunk as a sort of unfrozen caveman playing the "pure" New Orleans style he had learned in the early days of the century.

The old style had fallen out of fashion with the rise of the big band era in the 1930s. But at the very moment when Dizzy Gillespie and Charlie Parker were inventing bebop, Bunk's rediscovery launched a nationwide revival of interest in traditional jazz. He was suddenly flooded with offers to play in San Francisco, Chicago, Boston, and New York. But Bunk did not have long to enjoy his fame: an unpredictable, self-destructive soul, he literally drank himself to death in July 1949 at the age of sixty-nine.

The whole revival could have ended there, but George took over Bunk's band and went on to become a star in his own right. For the next decade or so, the George Lewis Ragtime Band crisscrossed the U.S. and Europe virtually nonstop and made dozens of recordings. Their arrival in London's Euston station in 1959 had even touched off a pre-Beatlemania riot by young fans jostling to get a look at their heroes. In fact, one future Beatle, Ringo Starr, caught the band that year at Liverpool's Cavern Club; he later told an interviewer that Lewis's drummer, Joe Watkins, was "the most incredible one I ever saw."

By the time I met George, his career had peaked. He still did the occasional out-of-town concert or tour, but he was getting up in years and seemed content to stay at home and work two or three times a week. For many of the old musicians, Preservation Hall was a ticket out of obscurity and unemployment. For George, it was a welcome haven after his successful years on the road.

That was my good fortune, because it allowed me to spend a lot of time learning at George's feet. For the first couple of years, I would hardly listen to another clarinet player, even though men like Louis Cottrell, Albert Burbank, and Willie Humphrey were all playing great in those days. I could have learned a lot from them;

they were all schooled musicians who could read music and play in almost any key.

But George didn't need all that to teach me what he knew. With George, it was all playing from the heart. I got that almost by osmosis, by listening to him, watching him, being around him as much as I could. It was the apprenticeship method: you learn by doing, in the presence of a master.

CHAPTER TEN

Everybody who ever heard Punch Miller at the Hall knew that he was—or had been—a great trumpet player. He also turned out to be a gifted teacher. Larry Borenstein paid him a few bucks each week to lead informal Saturday jam sessions with aspiring young musicians. It was partly a way of slipping Punch some extra pocket money, but Larry also thought it would help keep the old style going if the younger generation could learn from an old master.

Punch's students were a mixed bag. There would usually be a couple of visiting Brits, Swedes, or Japanese. Larry's wife, Pat, tooted on the trumpet a couple of times. Sandy Jaffe briefly tried her hand at the drums, but she infuriated Punch with her attempts to play the melody on the tom-toms. "Aw no, Miss Sandy," he would plead, "that's the horn part. You can't play that on no drum!" To my surprise, I was the only local kid, white or black, who showed up regularly for those sessions. On many Saturdays, I was the only pupil who showed up at all.

Even though Punch was a trumpet player, he taught me a lot about the role of the clarinet in a New Orleans band. He would write out simple parts for tunes like "Tin Roof Blues" and "A Closer Walk with Thee," just about at the limit of my reading ability, then he would show me how to "get off"—the only term he ever used for improvisation. "When you get off, see, you don't just stick on the melody. You gotta use other ideas, put in some accidentals. You can play anything you want, as long as you follow the chord changes."

Punch had a sweet, melodious voice that made even his conversation sound like music. On the trumpet, though, his tone had something dark and melancholy running under the nimble phrases. In his life, as in his music, there was more than a touch of the blues.

Punch was also a great singer, full of humor and theatrical gestures when he did his favorite numbers, like "South of the Border" and "Somebody Stole my Gal." And he wrote some funny songs, like "Rita's Blues," about the time Sandy Jaffe's sister, Resa, got her foot broken by a police horse one Mardi Gras Day. ("Rita" was as close as he could get to her real name.)

When Punch demonstrated a solo, he made the same demands on himself that he had always done, even though age had slowed him down and a big callus on his upper lip made it hard for him to hit the high notes. It enraged him whenever he muffed a lick that he had hit with ease all his life. He would jerk the trumpet from his lip with a furious "goddam!" Then he would try again and again and fight the horn until at last he got what he wanted from it. Unlike some of the other players, he never simplified his style or learned to pace himself. In his mind, he was still "Kid" Punch, and when he was feeling good, you could hear the echoes of his youthful power and exuberance.

A country boy from Raceland, Louisiana, Punch—his real name was Ernest P. Burden—had gone north, played his trumpet in the Chicago clubs and speakeasies in the 1920s, then spent decades touring with a motley collection of itinerant bands, carnivals, and circuses. It was in Chicago that Punch renewed a rivalry with Louis Armstrong that had begun back in New Orleans. Louis, three years younger than Punch, dazzled listeners with his fat tone, powerful high notes, and improvisational genius. But Punch was the king of fast fingering and, in those pre-bebop days, had no equal.

Punch was convinced that it was his lightning technique that had finally run Louis out of Chicago. "Louis come in the club I was working at and he said, 'Punch, you too fast for me, man. I'm going to New York.' Oh, I was rough in them days, Tommy, yes indeed. I was a bad man."

That was not idle bragging. Punch had once been a star, and he knew it. He had made a lot of records up north, led his own band, accompanied Bessie Smith, even toured with the great Jelly Roll Morton. Punch remembered playing at a drunken party with Jelly in a Chicago brothel. Morton, a light-skinned Creole, told the girls he was white. The party got wilder and wilder, then Jelly went off with one of the women. "All of a sudden," said Punch, "a door open up and that girl is draggin' Jelly through the living room by his gland, shoutin', 'You ain't no white man! You ain't no white man!'"

Punch had doubtless lived through many such drunken scenes. But one morning, he recalled, he looked at himself in the mirror and couldn't believe his eyes. "I was so skinny and wore out, I didn't even recognize myself," he told me. "I had to turn around to see if there was somebody else standin' behind me. Boy, I dropped my whiskey bottle in the garbage that very day and never took another drop."

By then, though, his whole body was breaking down from the wear and tear of life on the road. In 1956, plagued by diabetes and high blood pressure, he came back to New Orleans expecting to die. A gallbladder infection nearly killed him three years later, but an emergency operation at Charity Hospital saved his life.

What really sealed Punch's recovery, though, was his return to music. Larry Borenstein had hired him as a handyman and coaxed him into blowing his horn at some of his early art gallery sessions. Punch soon got his chops back and formed a band, Punch Miller's Bunch, that became a regular feature at Preservation Hall.

Punch's return from the dead, almost literally, was repeated by dozens of the old musicians during these years. Time after time, we saw men who had been laid low by diabetes, strokes, emphysema, alcohol, and just plain old age climb from their sick beds, like Lazarus, and live to play again. Doctors and hospitals did their part, of course. But the real elixir was their music and the fact that, after years of neglect, people wanted to hear it again—and paid good money for it.

What we were witnessing was not just a revival of the old style of playing, but the physical and spiritual resurrection of the mens. My father, with his romantic and literary bent, said there was something epic, almost religious, about it. He saw the old men as keepers of a noble flame, like ancient warriors or high priests carrying on the rites of some lost civilization. "It's like watching *The Iliad* and *The Odyssey* unfold in front of your own eyes," he said.

I'm not sure what Punch would have made of all that. Music was his life. But as far as his health went, he put his faith neither in the healing power of jazz nor in doctors. No, Punch believed only in the patent medicines that filled the nooks and crannies of his battered trumpet case: chocolate-covered garlic pills, cod-liver capsules, Dr. Tichenor's antiseptic, Alka-Seltzer, milk of magnesia, Chap-Stick (he always called it "Chop-Stick"), and God knows what else.

Punch lived alone in a rented shotgun single on Fourth Street, just off Claiborne Avenue, not far from where the Superdome was built a decade later. It was a rough black quarter where break-ins, muggings, and even murders were common. Then, as now, New Orleans was the murder capital of the U.S., and neighborhoods like this one, Tremé, and the Eighth and Ninth Wards contributed heavily to the grim statistics. The vast majority of the victims, as well as the perpetrators, were black—not surprising, perhaps, in a city whose population was two-thirds black, and in neighborhoods where poverty, substandard housing, drug abuse, and high unemployment were the rule.

Sometimes my father and I would go there to visit Punch or drive him down to the Hall. White people almost never ventured into such neighborhoods, and we would get curious or hostile stares from Punch's neighbors each time we got out of the car and walked up to his front steps. They had no way to know about our sympathies on the race question, or my father's track record as a crusader for civil rights. We didn't have the word *liberal* tattooed on our foreheads. And it probably would have made no difference if we did. Punch was always glad to see us, but he warned my father, "Don't come 'round here after dark, Tom."

But it was not only on the streets outside that danger lurked. One day my dad and I knocked on Punch's door. "Who's that?" he barked from inside.

"Tommy," I said.

"Johnny? I don't know no Johnny. You get on way from here."

"No, Punch, it's Tommy."

The door opened a crack and a gun barrel emerged. "I done told you to get away from here 'fore I shoot your ass," Punch growled. Then he peered through the crack and recognized us.

"Oh, it's y'all," he said with a big grin. "Why didn't you say so?"

The old man laughed and welcomed us into his tiny living room. He had a stocking pulled tight over his head to keep his rebellious hair down, and held a nickel-plated .22 pistol in his right hand.

"Got to be careful in this neighborhood," he said as he put the weapon down on his mantelpiece. "Some of these boys around here be so cheeky."

I think Punch enjoyed our visits. He lived a lonely life, apart from the time he spent at the Hall. In his little apartment, he was surrounded only by memories—stacks of yellowed sheet music; a few of his own records, which he would sometimes listen to on an old Victrola; and pictures from his long life on the road.

One old publicity photo showed him in a matador's costume, flashing a toothy smile, his hair slicked down with pomade, a trumpet in one hand and an oversized sombrero in the other. He looked like a matinee idol from the silent movie era. He was still trim and handsome when I knew him, despite the physical grind of his restless life. Only his brow, furrowed like an old bloodhound's, bore the traces of the hard times he had lived through.

"Now you see that picture?" He tapped on the glass of a framed photo. "That's me with the Walter Barnes Orchestra. I used to play with them in Chicago. I had just quit that band in 1940 when they went down to Natchez and burned up in a fire at the Rhythm Night Club. All but two of those boys died. Ain't that a bitch?"

Another photo he pointed to with pride was the cracked sepia portrait of his mother that stood on the table by his bed. "That's my mama," he would say tenderly. "She was really somethin', my mama." Like George Lewis and so many other musicians—and like my dad, for that matter—Punch had been raised by a single mother.

His only remaining family was a twin sister, Judy, who lived out in the country in a town called Plaquemines. He used to take a Greyhound bus to visit her, and doted on her grandchildren. He would save up money to buy them Christmas and birthday presents. Punch had an estranged wife up North somewhere, but never had children of his own. What he called his "children" were the dozens of tunes he had composed, but nobody ever played them anymore.

CHAPTER ELEVEN

I had always done well in school. Good grades, lots of friends, a smattering of prizes and awards. I did have a bit of a "deportment" problem, meaning I talked too much in class and had a weakness for wisecracks that teachers did not always appreciate. By most measures, though, I was a successful student. Yet once I started to develop a passion for jazz in the summer of 1962, I realized that the world of school and the world of the mens did not mix at all.

First off, there was no place for blacks at Eleanor McMain Junior High. Despite the Supreme Court's landmark 1954 *Brown v. Board of Education* decision, integration had not yet gotten beyond the token level in Louisiana and was met with fierce resistance.

When Judge J. Skelly Wright ordered the state to begin desegregating the public schools in 1960, his courageous ruling had touched off an ugly backlash. Snarling, jeering mobs surrounded William Frantz Elementary School as six-year-old Ruby Bridges, accompanied by federal marshals, became the first black child to attend a white New Orleans school since Reconstruction. Whites formed "citizens' councils" and boycotted the newly integrated establishments. Some of my own schoolmates threw handfuls of rocks at passing black schoolbuses and chanted, "Two-four-six-eight, we don't want to integrate." The 1960 governor's race, in which a country-and-western singer named Jimmie Davis beat the certifiably insane incumbent Earl K. Long, had been all about keeping blacks out of the schools. On inauguration day, Davis (composer of the song "You Are My Sunshine") rode his horse right into the legislature to celebrate the victory of segregation.

Even at the tender age of eleven, I had followed that race with great interest. The reason for that was not that I was some sort of precocious political junkie, but that fact that my father covered the campaign with A. J. Liebling, serving as his "cicerone" and criss-crossing the state at the wheel of his rusty old station wagon. I rode in the backseat on some of their trips, all ears as my father explained the ins and outs of Louisiana politics to the great journalist. My father always felt he should have shared the byline when Liebling published his story, first in a long *New Yorker* series, and finally as a book, *The Earl of Louisiana*, which remains to this day an American political classic.

I don't know what arrangement they had about the byline, but I do know Liebling paid my father as a consultant and quoted him liberally throughout the book. And, as any reader can attest, my dad enjoyed a lot of free expense-account meals at some of New Orleans's greatest restaurants—Antoine's, Broussard's, Galatoire's, Commander's Palace. For if Joe Liebling was arguably the greatest American political journalist of his era, he was without a doubt the country's most unabashed epicurean. I was present at a couple of those feasts and remember watching Liebling work his way through a pile of boiled seafood with his sleeves rolled up and crab fat smeared all over his hands and forearms.

At a time when my dad was flailing around in the P.R. business, brimming with political insights but unable to publish them, his collaboration with Liebling was a welcome chance for him to ply his real trade. Liebling read his situation perfectly: "Tom is the last independent source of news left in New Orleans," he wrote in *The Earl of Louisiana*. "He is in the situation of the RAF hero who was 30,000 feet in the air, without an aircraft." In another passage,

Liebling offered this perceptive thumbnail of my father's career: "Tom is obsessed with the South, particularly with his littoral, where he was born. He went North once, in about 1940, as a Nieman fellow at Harvard and became an editor of *The New Republic*, but New Orleans drew him back before he could get it in perspective."

The subject of the book, of course, was not Tom Sancton but rather Governor Earl Long (Huey's younger brother) and his desperate bid to win reelection after a first term marked by scandal, a fling with a stripper named Blaze Starr, and a brief internment in a mental hospital. The main campaign theme was the race issue. And all the candidates—even the self-styled liberal, New Orleans Mayor Chep Morrison—strived to convince voters that they would be most effective in keeping blacks out of the schools. It almost didn't matter who won, because the result would have been the same on that central issue.

Not surprising, then, that black people and black culture had no place in my school. Moreover, there was no way to graft the music I was learning onto the music played by the school band. I could not read well enough to play the sheet music of the band's Sousa marches, and nothing remotely resembling jazz ever emerged from the second-floor band room where Prof. Longuefosse held sway.

I didn't talk much to my friends about my newfound passion for jazz. Musically, they were all into top-40 rock 'n' roll. Most were forbidden by their parents to set foot in the sinful French Quarter. And none of them would have understood my fondness for hanging out with a bunch of old black guys.

My one attempt to get a schoolmate interested in playing jazz ended disastrously. He was a Mexican-American kid named Tony Rodriguez, who played trumpet in the school band. I told him about my Saturday sessions with Punch and, after some coaxing, he agreed to come to one.

We took the St. Charles Avenue streetcar down to the foot of Bourbon Street and walked past all the lurid strip joints and transvestite reviews on the way to the Hall. The clubs were closed at that hour, but the eye-popping posters of the tits-and-feathers shows made quite an impression on Tony, a good Catholic boy who had never been in the Quarter before.

"You think the women take all their clothes off in there?" he asked.

"I don't know," I said. "I just come down here for the music."

"Your parents let you come alone?"

"In the daytime, yeah. At night, they bring me."

His black eyes grew big as saucers. "To the Quarter? At night?"

"Sure. What's the matter with that?"

Tony just shook his head. "Man . . . "

My friend didn't seem to take to the lesson. Punch had written out some harmony parts for us. Tony dutifully read the music, but there was no spark of enthusiasm. When Punch talked about "getting off," Tony just looked confused. The dusty old hall with its spooky paintings on the walls—and this old black guy telling him how to play—were not his thing.

When I asked him about coming back the next week, Tony shrugged and muttered something vague. I pressed him on it for a few days and finally he said, "Look, I told my mother about that place and she said she doesn't want me hanging around with niggers."

Tony wasn't the only one who found my jazz frequentations objectionable.

One morning the assistant principal at McMain, a brawny gym teacher, called me into his office. This usually meant some discipline was about to be meted out, and I was trying to figure out what I had done. I ruled out the usuals—chewing gum, talking in class, playing hookey, writing graffiti on the bathroom walls.

"What were you doing in Preservation Hall at midnight on a school night?" he asked sternly. He had caught sight of me from a bar across the street that was actually owned by another McMain gym teacher named Johnny White.

"Listening to the music," I said. "I go there with my parents."

"Your *parents* take you down to the French Quarter? What for?"

"I'm trying to learn to play the clarinet."

He frowned. "Why don't you play in the school band? Why do you want to hang around with all those old colored guys? Half of 'em can't even read music."

"Because I want to play jazz."

Thereafter, I resolved to keep the two worlds separate. I would go to school by day, play softball or go swimming with my friends after school, but at night—or at least several nights a week—I was off to Preservation Hall with my parents. Like Clark Kent, I had a double identity.

I did find a group of friends who shared my interest in jazz, but they did not come from my local white middle-class world. I called them the jazz pilgrims. New Orleans was like a Mecca of traditional jazz. Anyone who wanted to play the old style had to come drink at the source, learn first-hand from the old sages, practice the rites of initiation, and, in time, pass the flame along to others.

The pilgrims came from all over the world—England, Scandinavia, Belgium, Germany, Australia, and as far away as Japan. They were young men, for the most part, infused with a passion for jazz that made them borrow money, quit their jobs, abandon their studies (or at least take long vacations), and make their way to New Orleans. Some, like Sammy Rimington, passed through town only briefly; others settled down and became part of the scene. And they, too, with their exotic accents and their strange ways, became my friends and broadened my world.

Barry Martyn, a drummer from London, was one of the first foreigners I met at the Hall. The son of a Covent Garden green-grocer, Barry had a bushy mustache, beaver-like front teeth, and an addiction to cheap cigars the size of chair spindles. In addition to leading one of the best English bands, Barry later produced some important records and published a couple of books.

I soon met other young Englishmen: trumpeter Clive Wilson, the son of a country vicar; trombonist Mike Casimir, an antique dealer from London; and drummer Trevor Richards, a university student from Bexhill-on-Sea. Tom Bethell, an Oxford graduate, was a poor trumpet player, but proved to be a better writer, turn-ing out an excellent biography of George Lewis before he moved to Washington and became an ultraconservative political colum-nist. Another English trumpet player, John Simmons, married a local black woman, Dodie Smith, and settled down to raise a real New Orleans family.

Lars Edegran and Orjan Kellin had played together in a Stockholm trad band. Lars played piano and Orjan—whom the locals called "Orange"—played clarinet. The two were inseparable friends, later teaming up to create the successful musical *One Mo' Time* that made it all the way to Broadway. But at some point, they quarreled over money and stopped speaking to each other.

No one traveled further than Yoshio Toyama and his wife, Keiko, who came from Osaka, Japan. Yoshio was quickly dubbed "Claiborne" by trumpeter Kid Sheik, who could never remember his real name. Like a lot of young trumpet players, he had learned from Bunk Johnson recordings. But with his uncanny Japanese ability to copy, Claiborne managed to sound more like Bunk than anybody else I ever heard. Even Bill Russell, who had "discovered" Bunk, said it would have fooled him. Keiko, a diminutive, bright-eyed young woman, spoke rudimentary English and giggled a lot. But she played a hell of a banjo.

Claiborne and Keiko were smitten with New Orleans and wanted to stay, but they ran into immigration problems. Allan Jaffe saw a newspaper article saying that there was a shortage of "chicken-sexers"—specialists in determining the gender of newly hatched chicks—and that the State Department was offering green cards to foreigners who had this particular talent. Claiborne found somebody who offered to teach him the chicken sexing trade, but just couldn't get the knack of it. "So small, you know," he said.

Then they came up with a more complicated scheme: they would get divorced, Keiko would enter a marriage of convenience with a U.S. citizen, get her green card, then divorce the accomplice and remarry Claiborne. Bill Russell, of all people, offered to marry Keiko. Claiborne thought about it for a long while but finally decided against it; he wasn't sure Bill would agree to divorce Keiko once she had married him. Though the coveted green card eluded them, the Toyamas somehow managed to finesse their immigration problems and hang on for several more years.

Claiborne and Keiko once took a bus to New Iberia to take pictures of Bunk's hometown. When the prints were developed Claiborne almost fainted. On one photo, a blurry male figure is standing on top of Bunk's grave. His features are indistinct and it is impossible to tell whether it is a black or white man. Bill Russell, who had probably known Bunk better than any man alive, looked at it and said the figure had Bunk's height, build, and posture. Claiborne had a fancy Japanese camera on which it was impossible to make a double exposure. Was it Bunk's ghost appearing to his young apostle? No one could say for sure, but Claiborne went around showing the photo to everyone and, it seemed to me, played even more like Bunk after this bizarre experience.

Not all the pilgrims came from across the sea. There were a couple of musicians from Minnesota who came down from time to time. One was a tall, quiet guy named Butch Thompson, in his early twenties, who played the piano and clarinet and later went on to fame as a regular on Garrison Keillor's "Prairie Home Companion" radio show. The other was a trumpet player, Charlie Devore, who had first discovered New Orleans music while serving at a local naval base in the 1950s.

Charlie had made history of sorts by becoming one of the first white musicians to be arrested for playing in an integrated band. He had been sitting in on one of the early jam sessions at Larry Borenstein's art gallery in January 1957, when the cops swooped in and arrested him—along with Punch Miller, Kid Thomas Valentine, trombonist Eddie Morris, and two other white players.

The judge, a fierce segregationist, harangued the defendants with a combination of mockery and indignation. He told Kid Thomas that he was a good "yard boy," and could be forgiven if he didn't get "uppity" again. But as for Charlie and the other "baggy-pants" Yankees standing before him, he said they had "sunk to a new low" and warned them not to "mix your cream with our coffee."

The judge dropped the charges of disturbing the peace but warned the defendants never to do it again "if you know what's good for your health." It was to avoid precisely this kind of kangaroo court inquisition that Jaffe would often close the shutters of the Hall in the early days when white players sat in with the black bands.

All these aspiring players had come from afar to learn the music, and in many ways their experience was similar to mine. We formed a sort of fraternity of jazz apprentices—a group that meant much more to me than the teenage social club I belonged to but rarely frequented. But there was one thing that made my apprenticeship unique: I was about the only white middle-class kid of my generation who came from within the local culture.*

It was as if an Afrikaner boy from Johannesburg had moved to a black village to learn tribal drumming. A musician from Sweden or an ethnologist from England might go to the same village and learn a lot about its culture. But a white kid born within the system would see things differently—and be seen differently by his black teachers.

As for the young blacks of New Orleans, I never saw a single one hanging around the Hall or trying to learn from the old players in those days. Their absence had little to do with legal segregation. This was the 1960s, the dawn of the Black Power era, and even those young people who were not politicized sensed that the old ways and attitudes were passé.

To the younger generation, the music of the mens was degrading, servile, Steppin Fetchit stuff. They even scorned Louis Armstrong—one of the greatest cultural figures of the century—as a shuffling Uncle Tom playing for the white folks. So most of the young blacks played rhythm 'n' blues, funk, blues, bebop—anything but traditional jazz. For reasons that are as understandable as they are regrettable, they cut themselves off from their own heritage.

That's one of the reasons the old men appreciated the fact that people like Sammy and me, and all the other jazz pilgrims from around the world, were trying to learn their style. They'd tell us,

*I should also mention Bill Huntington, twelve years my elder, a talented New Orleans-born banjoist and bass player, who played and recorded with many of the old musicians in the 1950s before moving to Atlanta and abandoning traditional jazz in favor of more modern styles.

"Y'all got to keep this thing going." By default, perhaps, but with the fervor of converts, we became the anointed keepers of the flame. And by the time some young black musicians did begin to show an interest in traditional jazz, years later, most of the mens were long gone.

One thing that struck me about the foreign musicians was their absolute lack of racial prejudice. All the local white people I knew, even the so-called liberals, somehow defined themselves with respect to race. They were either racists, or prided themselves on not being racists. But race was always part of the equation. For the foreigners, who came from outside the system, race itself was not an issue—though they certainly observed and deplored the many instances of racial prejudice and discrimination that they observed in New Orleans.

My father, of course, noticed this too. And he had an interesting explanation. For the Brits, who made up the bulk of the visiting musicians, class prejudice was a fundamental feature of their society. My family had a glaring proof of this one night when we invited an upper-class British girl home to share a crab-and-gumbo dinner along with some young cockney musicians. We thought that they would get on famously because they were all English. They hardly spoke a word to each other all night. It was probably the first time in all their lives that any of them had sat at the same dinner table with someone from the opposite side of the class line. But both the aristocratic girl and the cockneys were perfectly at ease in the company of the old musicians—and vice versa. "It's because they're all outside their normal class structure," said my father. He went even further, saying that the English working people were the servant class in their society, the bottom rung of the ladder, and that they probably felt more kinship with New Orleans blacks than with upper classes in their own country.

That theory didn't work for all the foreigners, though. Clive Wilson and Tom Bethell were public school boys, Orange and Lars were middle-class Swedes, and the Toyamas came from a society where racial homogeneity and social conformity went unquestioned. Yet despite their different backgrounds, all of these people were united in their admiration and affection for the mens and their culture. I think it's because there was something so fundamentally human about the old players. Their music spoke to the heart, and the heart is neither black nor white.

CHAPTER TWELVE

Allan Jaffe liked to throw afternoon parties in the patio behind the Hall. There was always a lot of food there: jambalaya, red beans, and mufaletta sandwiches—those unctuous, multilayered confections of olive salad, salami, and ham on sesame bread that were the pride of the Central Grocery on Decatur Street. There was a galvanized washtub full of crushed ice, beer, and soft drinks. Everybody piled their paper plates high and sprinkled them with Tabasco sauce. Laughter and chattering voices reverberated through the sun-dappled courtyard.

But the real life of Jaffe's parties was the music. Perched on folding chairs in the shade of a big banana tree, the musicians took their turns jamming with each other. The first time my parents brought me to one of Jaffe's parties, Punch Miller was there, along with Jim Robinson, Kid Thomas Valentine, and Willie Humphrey. But one man who impressed me most that day was the banjo player, Creole George Guesnon, which everybody pronounced *Gay*-no. Since there were no drums, he was the man who laid down the rhythm, and he did it with a power and drive that fired up the whole group.

Guesnon was a big man, with a massive head and enormous hands that fluttered along the neck of his banjo with grace and ease. His face was the color of café au lait and his wavy, pomaded hair was plastered down and combed straight back from his broad ox-like forehead. He would close his heavy-lidded eyes and pump his banjo with a dreamy half-smile on his face and a cigarette dangling from his lips. Whenever somebody played a lick he liked, he'd grin and say, "Oh, man, that's some pretty stuff." And that included his own single-string solos.

Hearing Kid Thomas in that setting was a revelation. At the Hall, he always played with his own band, the Algiers Stompers. Dark, wiry, and bright-eyed, Thomas indulged in a lot of corny show-biz shenanigans with his band. He would put on a wig or a top hat, stand up on his chair for the final chorus, and jump down on the final note—all of which used to drive Guesnon crazy. "That cat make such a fool out of himself," he'd mutter. "They ought to put a plunger on the ceiling when he stand up on that chair—catch him by his head and hold him up there till he get some sense." At this jam session, though, deprived of his band and his bag of silly props, Thomas's sparse, staccato phrases came through for what they were: the reduction of melody to its most powerful broad-brush essentials.

All the holes that Kid Thomas left in the ensembles were eagerly filled in by Willie Humphrey's clarinet. Willie had broad shoulders and twinkling eyes and wavy salt-and-pepper hair that came down to a point just above his thick eyebrows. He liked to stand up for his solos, cheeks bulging out as he danced around and blew endless cascades of notes with his clarinet pointed up in the air. Willie was dazzling with his funky mix of flowing arpeggios, bluesy slurs, and complex counter-rhythms that bounced around inside his phrases like Ping-Pong balls. When I first heard him, though, I was too smitten with George Lewis's lyricism to fully appreciate Willie's artistry.

After a while, most of the older musicians had gotten tired and there were some empty band chairs. Creole George saw me sitting there with my clarinet case and he said, "Well, I done heard what Willie Humphrey and Kid Thomas got to say. I'd like to hear what this young man can do on his horn."

I panicked. I had half-hoped for a chance to play that day, but after hearing all those great musicians I thought I wasn't up to it. But Sally Fellon was sitting at my side, and prodded me. "Go on, Tommy," she said, nudging me on the shoulder and sending shivers up my spine. "This is your big chance. I want to hear you play."

I put my horn together and took an empty chair next to George. "Now what do you want to play, young man?" he asked me. "You know 'Basin Street Blues'?"

I nodded. That was one of the tunes I had worked on with Punch Miller—and Punch happened to be right next to me on the trumpet.

"Well, let's go then."

Punch played the first figure: dot-dot-dee-daaah . . .

I answered on the clarinet: deee-doodle-la-daaah . . .

Then our horns locked in together on the tight harmonies Punch had taught me. Guesnon's gold-capped front teeth gleamed in the sunlight. He was looking right at me all the time, nodding and chuckling and churning out those beautiful chords of his. As soon as we hit the last note, he said, "Aw, you dogs, if that don't get it."

We played two or three more tunes—all things that I had learned with Punch or George Lewis—and they went like gangbusters. But the beer and red beans finally ran out and the men started packing up their instruments.

My father came over and thanked Guesnon for inviting me to play.

"Aw, man," said George. "That boy got a gift. He really got the feelin' for this music."

"Well, he's had some great teachers," my dad said.

"Oh yeah? Who you studyin' with?"

"I take clarinet lessons with George Lewis," I said proudly. "And Punch teaches me a lot of things at his jam sessions."

"Unh-huh." Guesnon nodded his head and wiped down the strings of his banjo with his handkerchief. "Well, George Lewis don't read no music," he said, after a long pause. "I mean, George play real nice, but he don't *know* no music. What you need to do is find you a real music teacher. I'd send you to Professor Manuel Manetta across the river, but he's about retired now. He don't take no new scholars these days."

"Can you suggest anybody else?" my father asked. "This boy really wants to learn."

"Tell you the truth, Tom," he replied. "The best music teacher in this town is Creole George Guesnon. You bring that boy around my house. I'll teach him things he ain't gonna learn nowhere else."

George handed my dad his business card: "Creole George Guesnon, Musician and Composer, Music for All Occasions, 1012 North Roman Street, New Orleans, La. 944-5573."

"You come over and see me, young man," said George with his solid gold grin. "I'll make a real jazzman out of you."

CHAPTER THIRTEEN

I went to George Guesnon for music lessons, but I wound up getting much more than that. For if George was one of the world's best tenor banjo players, he was without a doubt the greatest talker in New Orleans. He talked endlessly about the long-lost good old days, the great bands he had played with, and the kicks he'd had shooting pool up in Harlem with Jelly Roll Morton—probably the only man from New Orleans who could out-talk him. But most of all, George Guesnon talked about George Guesnon. He was the center of his own universe. To his brilliant, embittered and tortured mind, everything else fell into place around the iron core of his ego.

George Guesnon knew who he was. It was written right there on his red mailbox the first time I knocked on the door of his shotgun house on North Roman Street: "Creole George Guesnon," it said, in crudely painted letters, along with a few notes of music. Creole *and* musician. Those were the fundamental, inseparable, pillars of his identity. And no visitor ever entered his door without learning that.

"Take a seat, young man," he said, directing me to a stool in his front bedroom. "Now, look, before we talk about music, you got to know who you dealin' with. You know why folks call me Creole George?"

I shook my head.

"Cause I was born a Creole, right here in the Tremé district. You know anything about the Creoles?"

I told him what I had learned in my Louisiana history classes in school: the Creoles were the descendants of the original French and Spanish settlers.

"That's a lie," George said. "I'm talkin' about the *real* Creoles, the Creoles of color. That's *my* people, the *gens de couleur*. We're a race within a race, a mixture of French, Spanish, and Negro. See, in the slavery times, the Creoles were free people. They weren't no slaves. They *owned* slaves, some of 'em. Among them were some of the richest, best-educated people in the city—doctors, lawyers, musicians, artisans, cigar-makers, plasterers. They didn't teach you that in your Jim Crow school, did they?"

"No. I never knew that."

"And we had the most beautiful women in the world," George went on. "Aw, man, they were something to see. They were all colors—white and coral and brown. You never saw such beautiful women in your life. Here, look at this picture."

George picked up an oval-framed photograph from his bedside table and handed it to me. It was the sepia portrait of a pretty, light-skinned girl, with wavy hair, shining black eyes, and a sweet smile.

"That's my daughter, Velma Margaret," George said, with just a trace of tenderness in his voice. "The light of my life. She died in 1940 at the age of fifteen. And you should have seen my mother when she was young. Man, you talk about a beautiful woman! Her people came here from Haiti—that's where a lot of New Orleans Creoles come from."

"But, like I say," George continued, "everytime you got somethin' good goin', look like somebody got to fuck it up. See, it was the envy on the part of the whites that wound up pushin' the Creoles into the same ghettos with the blacks. They kept pushin' 'em in with that Buddy Bolden gang from uptown. That's where the real race mixin' come in at, man."

I had never heard any of the other musicians talk about race as openly as George Guesnon did. But race was central to Guesnon's universe. And, as I was starting to learn, it was a complicated, passionate issue.

To most people on the white side of the color line, Negroes were Negroes and that was that. But on the other side, as George explained, there was a hierarchy—a caste system—with the Creoles at the apex and the "Africans" below them. Which explained a lot about the attitudes some of the musicians had toward one another. I once asked George Lewis if he was friends with the great Creole clarinetist Alphonse Picou. "Picou didn't talk to people like me," he said matter-of-factly. "Picou didn't like you unless you had silky hair."

But Creole George wasn't just giving me an idle history lesson. Knowing about his ancestry was vital to understanding who he was; unless a person grasped his superiority as a man and an artist, he believed, there was nothing he could teach them about music.

"I ain't no phony. I'm for real," he told me. "I'm a Creole. I'm a composer. I'm a musician. I've written more than three hundred musical compositions, four or five short stories, two complete full-length novels and a book of poems. I've worked harder to gain more, and I want a little more."

In fact, George had gotten less than a lot of the other musicians who were better at getting along and going along. Guesnon was proud, hot-headed, and sharp-tongued. There were few musicians he had not locked horns with over the years, and few bosses he had not told off. Like his friend Jelly Roll Morton, who would talk himself into a job and then talk himself out of it, Guesnon's tongue was his worst enemy.

As a result, Guesnon's career was a litany of missed opportunities, busted-up bands, and dashed hopes. He'd made a few good recordings along the way, won some critical acclaim, and impressed a lot of people with his rhythmic drive and his intricate single-string solos. But at the end of the day, here he was living alone in half of a shotgun double—he called it his "bird cage"—with his banjo and his manuscripts and his memories. One night a week at the Hall barely paid his rent. So he supplemented his income by taking on "scholars" like me.

George's best and most loyal friend was Harold Dejan, a fellow Creole, who played saxophone and was the leader of the Olympia Brass Band. Harold, who was the world's most easygoing man, put up with George's bluster because he respected him so much as a musician. "George is a giant of a man, strong as an ox," he said. "Hold the whole band together. Some people say he's contrary, but he just don't like no bullshit."

Dejan, who had a good day job with the Lykes shipping line and plenty of work with his brass band, was always bringing George "a little something"—a taste of whiskey, a bag of fried chicken, a jar of red beans. Once Harold really splurged and gave George a tape recorder.

Guesnon was enthralled. He made hundreds of tapes of himself talking and playing alone, or occasionally with other musicians who would stop over to visit. He would turn these taping sessions into mock-radio broadcasts, speaking into the mike with his smooth-est cadences: "Hello, jazz lovers. This is Creole George Guesnon, jazz banjoist, guitarist, and composer of worldwide renown, speaking to you from New Orleans, Louisiana."

That was how I first heard my own playing on tape. George turned the machine on during that first lesson, and captured every note we played, every instruction he meted out, every word of praise or criticism he uttered. It was humbling to hear it back. But there were some nice moments, especially when George picked his filigree phrases behind me on the blues, or when I played soft fill-ins behind his vocals.

"That's beautiful, man," he said. "I mean, that's some pretty stuff. But let me tell you one thing, young man. You tryin' an awful lot to sound like George Lewis, am I right?"

"I sure hope I do," I said. "I really like the way he plays."

"Now listen at this well," George said, leaning forward in his chair and looking at me sternly under his half-inch thick eyebrows. "George Lewis has a wonderful tone. George Lewis is a big star. But do not copy George Lewis. Hear what I'm sayin'? Do *not* copy George Lewis."

I was perplexed, and a little angry. Copying George Lewis seemed to me like the obvious path to becoming a great jazz clarinetist. "Why not?" I asked.

"For two reasons. First, George play pretty, but he don't know no melodies. George know half a tune. George fake a tune. Second, you got to play your own style. See, jazz is primarily a state of mind. What you make on that horn must come from *your* mind. Every jazz musician who's worth a damn has his own sound, see what I'm sayin'? So don't copy George, don't copy Louis Cottrell, don't copy Willie Humphrey."

"So how am I supposed to learn?" I asked.

"You gonna learn by doin' like *I* tell you," said George, picking up his banjo and plucking a single-note phrase. "Now make that!"

I duplicated the phrase.

George played two more bars. "Make that."

I executed the notes he showed me. After we had worked our way through twelve bars in that call-and-response fashion, George leaned back in his chair and announced, "Now, you string all that together and you got my famous solo on the 'Tin Roof Blues.' That's real jazz. You play it just like that and make them people go crazy."

After a few lessons, George told my father he'd like to make a tape of me playing with him and his friend Emile Barnes. Better known as "Milé," Barnes was a real old-fashioned clarinet player with a gutsy, bluesy, primitive style. George said it would do me a lot of good to get together with Milé, because he could show me how to get "right to the heart of a tune—no frills and no bullshit." Milé, a taciturn man who let his horn do his talking, was also one of the few musicians George got along with, even though he was very dark-skinned and in no way a Creole. In the back of his mind, Guesnon probably thought that playing with Milé would help wean me away from copying George Lewis. Milé's sound was as earthy as George's was celestial.

So one Saturday morning in January 1963, my father and I picked Milé up at his house in the lower Ninth Ward and drove him over to George's "bird cage." He didn't say much during the trip; he just chain smoked through a little red plastic cigarette holder. He was a tall man, and powerfully built. People said that in his youth he had a hot temper and had laid many a man low with his fists. Now, well into his seventies, he was slowed by age and had trouble breathing, but you could still sense the raw power deep inside him. It came out through his horn in his punchy, percussive phrases and penetrating tone. He had long since switched to plastic reeds, which lasted longer and didn't require as much fussing with as the cane variety. That gave him kind of a wailing sound, which my father compared to "some ancient Elizabethan woodwind."

When we got to George's house, he was chomping at the bit to get started. Milé had a funky old horn, a simple system with only twelve keys, held together with rubber bands, scotch tape, and wads of chewing gum to replace the leaky pads. But he made it do what it had to do. I had to pull my barrel way out to get in tune with him.

Guesnon told us to stay in the lower register, "'cause all that screechin' gonna screw up the tape." I think the real reason was so his banjo would come through loud and clear. After a short warmup, he took us into "Just a Closer Walk with Thee." We followed that with "Saint James Infirmary," "Milé's Blues," and "Corinna." George was in great form. He sang and played single-string solos on all the tunes, grinning all the while. Sometimes, he would shout out things like, "Aw, that's beautiful cats, that's beautiful," or "What are you doin' Mister Barnes? I like that!"

I mostly played simple melody. Milé weaved around it, filling in the holes with rhythmic, staccato phrases. What struck me about his playing was that he did not waste a single note on embellishment. It seemed like his whole purpose was to make the band sound good, even if it was only a trio. And I never heard anyone play the blues better than Milé, with a growling, moaning sound that went right to the heart. When the session was over, George printed the names of the tunes on the box and handed me the tape.

I was lucky to get that face time with Milé. He did not play much in public in those days and soon stopped playing entirely. Both his horn and his body had broken down. Dick Douthwaite, a visiting English clarinetist who idolized Milé, thought he could jump-start his hero back to life by getting his horn fixed. He took it over to Benny the repairman and had it completely overhauled. When it was ready, Dick and I went out to Milé's house along with some other young musicians, including Clive Wilson and Lars Edegran. Milé was like a kid with a new toy. I had never heard him sound so good. We took out our instruments and played a jam session that went on all afternoon. When we left, he begged us to come back.

Those were probably the last notes that Emile Barnes ever played. The next day, his wife phoned Clive and told him, "Y'all got Milé so excited he can't even sleep. He was up pacin' the floor all night. Doctor say he got to quit playin' that horn. So, please, don't come back here no more." So ended a musical career that had begun in 1908. Not long afterward, Milé died at the age of seventy-seven.

My father found a kindred spirit in Creole George Guesnon. What most other people saw as hubris, arrogance, and bluster, my dad recognized as the railings of a superior intelligence trapped in a situation he could not control. He never said it in so many words, but I sensed that when he looked at the massive head of George Guesnon (which he likened to "the bust of Beethoven") he was also looking at himself. Not that Daddy had a shred of musicianship in him. "I have no musical talent whatsoever," he told George, "but I'm a hell of a writer."

Both were proud, wounded men, frustrated artists who believed that the world had slighted them and cheated them out of the success they deserved. Still, they both talked on and wrote on—George hand-printing his short stories and poems and musical compositions; my father typing and jotting endless notes that accumulated into piles without ever producing anything tangible.

Daddy once told me that George Guesnon made him think of a Dylan Thomas line, "I sang in my chains like the sea." I thought the same words could apply to Tom Sancton. George's chains—poverty and racial prejudice—were external; my father's were in his mind.

My father usually dropped me off at George's for my lessons and picked me up later. When he came back to get me, he liked to sit on the edge of George's bed and chat with him while I packed up my horn. And sometimes, when there was no lesson, he would go over and see George alone. In a kind of reverse psychoanalysis, he would stretch out on the bed—my dad was always a great one for naps—and just listen to George talk.

Guesnon would rant and rave and remake the universe, convinced that he finally had an interlocutor who understood him and appreciated his genius, a man who judged him and his culture without prejudice or condescension. His common-law wife, Corinne Monroe, later told us that George had given her this instruction: "If you ever get into trouble, call Tom Sancton. He is the one white man who does not hate Negroes."

"You know somethin', Tom?" he told my father one day. "If the cops come around here and catch an ofay cat sittin' here talkin' to a spook, they gonna throw both our asses in jail."

When it came to race relations, Guesnon knew what he was talking about. He knew it from experience, of course, but he also knew it from books. For George was a reader as well as a writer. He had a collection of well-thumbed paperbacks on his shelf, and a lot of them had to do with slavery and race.

One day he grabbed a book off his shelf and flipped to a passage he had marked in Herbert Aptheker's *History of the Negro People*. Guesnon read me the details of a horrific lynching in Duck Hill, Mississippi, where a white mob had burned a black man alive with a blow torch.

"You see, Tommy," he said. "That's what I'm talkin' about. That's what we up against. And it ain't just a bunch of rednecks up there in Mississippi. Right here, in your own hometown, we had things goin' on you wouldn't believe. You ever hear of the Robert Charles race riot?"

I had not.

"Well that happened in 1900. It was a little before my time, but my parents lived through it. So did Papa John Joseph. He'll tell you about it. See, there was this cat named Robert Charles got tired of the cops messin' with him, so he got him a gun and shot some of 'em. Man, that made all the white folks go crazy. So they come rampaging through our neighborhoods beatin' and killin' all the colored people they could find. People were afraid to go out their house. Down at the French Market, you could take you a ham right out the butcher shop, 'cause there wasn't nobody left around to stop you. And a whole lot of colored people died."

"That's incredible," I said. "But I don't think anything like that could happen today."

"That ain't true"—George wagged a finger at me—"That ain't true. This town is like a pressure cooker that can blow at any moment. People say things are better today, but I disagree. I say they *worse* today, and I'll tell you why."

George proceeded to lay out his vision of the Golden Age of New Orleans, and how it was destroyed by greed and modernity and political reform. It was a theme he returned to, over and over, for as long as I knew him. The story was essential to his sense of self, I think, for if the Golden Age had been destroyed by the folly of others, then the poverty and mediocrity of his current condition were not his fault.

"In the old days," he'd say, "the bosses knew how to run a city. They spread a big table for themselves, and put all the fine things they wanted on that table. But they always let a few crumbs fall for Old Mose. In those days, man, we black folks never wanted for no crumbs. Everybody had their kicks, and all the people got along. Oh, it was a rough, tough city, don't get me wrong. But didn't nobody bother you as long as you were carryin' this"—he patted the top of his banjo case.

"Then a lot of country Cajuns come in here and screwed everything up. Used to be the air smelled of magnolia and jasmine, everybody had work, there was plenty of good food, you could walk right out your house and catch you a mess of fresh fish in the old basin. Now they paved the basin over. Shit, man, they don't want you to have nothin' no more. Today, this is just another big crimeridden city with concrete and skyscrapers and neon lights and pollution from all the cars. And there ain't no more crumbs for Mose."

One of Guesnon's proudest possessions was his scrapbook. It was a thick bound volume into which he had pasted photos of himself from childhood to the present, along with pictures of various musicians and bands he had worked with and press clippings about him—all accompanied by captions and commentary that he printed out in meticulous block-roman letters. He had a habit of writing people's names right on the photograph and invariably drew arrows pointing to himself in group pictures. In some photos, he had scratched out the faces of musicians he didn't like.

George's scrapbook also contained a handwritten list of reasons why he considered himself a superior man. Reason number one: he was a Creole. Reason number two: he was a banjo virtuoso. Reason number three: "Looks—you can see for yourself." Reason number four: "I got enough dick hanging on me to satisfy any woman."

There was a gamey side to George. He loved to tell stories about pimps and whores and all the kicks he'd had in the brothels and cabarets of old New Orleans. In fact, that's how he got into the music business in the first place. "When I was still a teenager," he recounted, "a friend of mine took me over to the old Humming Bird Cabaret on Bienville and Marais. Boy, they had a show like I had never seen before! I looked at all them long-legged dancing girls with their asses hanging out and the fifty- and hundred-dollar bills stuffed in their stockings and I didn't ever want to go home again. I started hanging around there doing odd jobs and got to know all the musicians in the band—Kid Clayton's Happy Pals. That's how I came to take up the banjo, and when their regular banjo player took sick at the end of 1927, I got his job. The rest is history."

I admired Guesnon and wanted to please him, even if I resented his scorn for my idol George Lewis. As for his blatant racial prejudice toward the darker musicians, I found it distasteful, but at the same time there was something fascinating about it. Through George, I was learning new things about the complex fabric of New Orleans culture and society. It was not all pretty. But it was rich, dark, and deep. And I wanted to be part of it all.

CHAPTER FOURTEEN

My sisters and I used to dread the first day of school every year. Not for the usual reasons—fear of new teachers and schoolmates, the return to homework and exams. No, our reason was different. We dreaded having to fill out the "father's occupation" line on our attendance cards. It was rarely the same from year to year, and more than one of our teachers remarked that our father seemed to change jobs a lot: "Reporter, New Orleans *Item*," "Author," "Self-employed public relations consultant," "Publicist, Louisiana Heart Association," "Associate Vice-President, Walker-Saussy Advertising Agency," "Self-employed public relations consultant (again)." Some years, we didn't have a clue what to write in that space because he wasn't doing anything at all as far as we could see.

My sisters feared the judgment of their friends, whose dads all seemed to be lawyers, doctors, businessmen, contractors—or at least plumbers with steady jobs. What bothered me most, though, was that I wanted to admire my father, wanted him to be a hero, but what I mostly saw in him was the confused drift of a depressed and defeated man. None of this was really clear in my fuzzy adolescent thoughts, but I sensed that something was not quite right with my dad. And I grieved over it. I wanted desperately for something to put him back on the pedestal, where he belonged.

From time to time, there were glimmers of hope. Once a New York publisher named Harris Lewine called him out of the blue and said he had greatly admired *Count Roller Skates*. Would my father be interested in writing another novel? My dad wrote him a long letter describing the kind of book he wanted to write—and the kind he wouldn't write. Lewine's brief answer: "I have tried and tried, but I don't see how I can make this work." Another time, an editor at the *Times-Picayune* called and offered to put him on staff and even give him his own column. My father's reply—laying out all sorts of conditions—succeeded in torpedoing the offer. "Sorry, Tom," the editor wrote back, "but there's no place at the *Times-Picayune* for a prima donna."

Another time, a big magazine asked him to write a splashy travel piece about French Quarter hotels. He spent several free nights in some quaint establishments and interviewed a few owners. But the article never got written. Then there was the powerful Louisiana congressman who asked him to ghost write his autobiography. The Great Man put Daddy on his congressional staff payroll and paid him good money. My father ran around for a few months taping interviews with the congressman and his friends. Then at one point, he suddenly announced, "Hell, I'm a major American writer. I can't do a hack job like this." He put his tapes and notes in a suitcase and left them outside the door of the congressman's office.

As much as I longed for things to be different, I came to realize that something was broken in him. "He can't help it, darling, he just can't help it," my Aunt Pat would tell me when I confided to her my distress and grief over my father's situation.

He was always talking about writing, and spent hours locked in his room typing. But nothing ever came of it. He was like a musician who played scales all day but never showed up for a gig.

The real musicians in my life, the mens, had also gone through a season in hell. Since the Depression, most of them had known nothing but hard times—sickness, poverty, Jim Crow racial discrimination, the declining popularity of their music. Like my father after his failed novels, they were derailed and marginalized as artists and human beings. But when the jazz revival took off, they got off the canvas. Despite advanced age, health problems, loss of teeth, and lack of practice, they did show up for the gigs. They played long hours at the French Quarter jazz halls and marched in all-day parades through the sweltering back streets. And when the touring started, they caught the planes and rode the buses and showed up on time with their shoes shined and their instruments at the ready. I admired their courage and energy as much as their musical genius.

Daddy also marveled at their return to active life. He even said it reminded him of the Biblical passage where God tells Ezekiel to "breathe on these dry bones that they may live." He could see, and cherish, the miracle of the men's revival. But he could work no miracles on himself.

My dad had a lot of time on his hands. He spent hours at his desk typing letters, shuffling papers, and supposedly working on his third novel. He was always scrawling notes to himself and typing and throwing it all into cardboard boxes once his filing cabinets had overflowed. Then he would decide to move all the boxes up to the attic, or down to the basement, or out on the porch and back again.

Mother referred to all this activity as "making Gosky patties." I asked what that meant and she said it came from a nonsense recipe by Edward Lear: first, you make a paste of sour cream, Cheshire cheese, quinces, black pins, and foolscap paper, then you beat a live pig with a broom until he squeals; if the paste does not turn into Gosky patties after several days, "it never will."

Once, when she was fed up at having her living room and dining room submerged under Daddy's boxes, she unleashed a brutal
and uncharacteristic remark: "Tom, when you die, I'm going to
make a bonfire and burn all those files. Nobody cares what's in
them and no one will ever read them." She also vowed that she
would burn the threadbare couch in which he would spend whole
afternoons taking naps—and where he slept at night because his
antique four-poster bed was covered with papers.

But my mother rarely complained overtly, even though it was
unheard of, among her generation of Jackson debutantes, for a
married woman to have to go to work to make ends meet. They
might do church work or charity work, but never a paying job.
Mother would sometimes drop a remark, in passing, about "declining expectations" or mutter that "*some* people" had things easier.
At the same time, she always declared her devotion to Daddy and
said they were "made for each other." Theirs was a strange, but
very real, symbiosis.

Did she ever regret the privileged life she would have had as the
wife of her old medical student-turned-wealthy surgeon? If so, she
never said it. But as the years wore on, she developed a pronounced
taste for bourbon whiskey. She joked that she took it for "medicinal
purposes," but I suspect its real function was to dull the pain. My
father, with his compulsion to control the lives of everyone around
him, kept the bottle under lock and key. He poured out one jigger's
worth every morning and evening like a strict father doling out candy
to his child. And, who knows, maybe that was for the best.

When he was not typing letters and notes, or sleeping on the couch
with a pillow over his head, Daddy read. He read voraciously—
magazines like *The New Republic*, *Commentary*, *The Nation*, *Time*,

Newsweek, and books on every subject imaginable. His reading was well served by my mother, who worked in the gifts and exchange department at the Tulane University library and brought home cartloads of discarded duplicate books. They filled the shelves and closets and piled up on the living room floor.

His reading was eclectic. He loved poetry, and in his younger years, probably in school, he had learned dozens of verses by heart. I remember one poem that particularly moved him was Walt Whitman's "Prayer of Columbus," the confused meditation of "A batter'd, wreck'd old man,/Thrown on this savage shore, far from home . . ." He particularly liked the last part, in which the old navigator asks himself: "Is it the prophet's thought I speak, or am I raving?/What do I know of life? what of myself? . . . And these things I see suddenly, what mean they?/As if some miracle, some hand divine unseal'd my eyes,/Shadowy vast shapes smile through the air and sky,/And on the distant waves sail countless ships,/And anthems in new tongues I hear saluting me." Why did these lines touch him so deeply? Perhaps he saw something of himself in the combination of self-doubt and megalomania.

As for books, he preferred the old classics—Greek and Roman history, Plutarch, Saint-Simon, the Russians, Dickens, Balzac, Thackery. But he didn't like everything he read. Apart from his early idol Thomas Wolfe, there were very few twentieth-century writers he admired. In fact, he voiced contempt for almost any writer who was even close to being his contemporary: Nabokov, Mailer, Beckett, Updike, Philip Roth, even his old New York friend Saul Bellow, were all denounced as frauds and charlatans. My mother's friend Eudora Welty was, in his view, a quaint but shallow local writer. The one exception to this strange, sweeping condemnation was Henry Roth, whose classic novel of Jewish immigrant life, *Call It Sleep*, he regarded as one of the greatest American books ever written. Apart from its literary merits, I think Roth's book inspired him because it had gone unnoticed for thirty years before it was republished to widespread acclaim. For a disappointed novelist like my father, perhaps, Roth's experience held out the hope of redemption.

CHAPTER FIFTEEN

My dad actually did publish something during those years. The music producer Nesui Ertegun came to town in the summer of 1962 to record some local bands for Atlantic Records. He had known my father in New York and asked him to write the liner notes for the Eureka Brass Band album. Daddy threw himself into the project with a kind of manic enthusiasm, sweeping everything else aside to concentrate on this brief text—for which he was probably paid $100.

He spent several weeks hunkered down in a Toulouse Street apartment loaned to him by Larry Borenstein. Larry had also sold him a second-hand hi-fi with an enormous speaker—"a real deal"—on which he listened to the test pressings over and over on sticky summer afternoons and evenings, drinking in the music, lost in thought, pecking away paragraph by paragraph on his old Underwood No. 4, the same machine he had used years earlier to write his novels.

It had been years since the byline "Thomas Sancton" had appeared in print, but he wrote the best description of a New Orleans parade I had ever read:

> To be swept by sheer luck and accident into the second-line of a New Orleans brass band is an experience that can fill the heart with a sense of joy forever. The surging power of the music—the incredible drumming, the feathery gamecock wildness of the dancing, the unrehearsed, lost, backstreet freedom of the whole parade and all the

neighbors, swaying and shouting from splintered porches, and sagging window sills—set the heart pounding and all life's juices flowing, and the stranger grasps at some vanished ritual grandeur of humanity that has been lost in the stones, the jungle and the dust, yet lies only lightly sleeping in our blood.

The brass band he described was the oldest and best of the city's marching groups—a New Orleans tradition since before the Civil War. I had heard the Eureka in the street many times, starting with Papa Celestin's funeral when I was five years old. When Preservation Hall opened, Allan Jaffe hired them for Sunday afternoon parades that would start in front of the Hall and meander through the French Quarter attracting huge crowds in their wake. As soon as the bass drummer kicked off the first tune, the whole neighborhood resonated with excitement. People would come out on their balconies and cheer—some of them still in pajamas and bathrobes. Tourists and local residents would jam the sidewalks, dancing, shouting, clapping.

In the middle of it all, the ten musicians played with the power and exuberance of men half their age. The horns had a way of working together by sections—trombones, reeds, and trumpets—that produced rich voicings, unison riffs, and punchy counterpoints behind the strong melody line. The tempos were moderate—as Bunk Johnson used to say, no New Orleans band plays faster than it can walk—but they swung all the more for it. The walls of the old buildings that lined the narrow streets echoed the sound and amplified the power of the music.

Percy Humphrey, who played first trumpet, had the word *Leader* written in gold letters on the crest of his white parade cap. He would march along with military grace, his head hunched down and his trumpet pointed straight ahead over the bulging paunch of his belly. Slung over his shoulder was a canvas pouch full of sheet music. The band used the arrangements only for funeral dirges, but the bag had become part of Percy's uniform. Sometimes, when he was feeling frisky, he would hold his horn with one hand like a big cigar. You could hear his high, clarion trumpet leads from blocks away.

Percy was the scion of a great musical family. His grandfather, Jim Humphrey, an ex-slave-turned-music professor, had taught several generations of kids at the Magnolia Plantation, downriver from New Orleans. He also turned his three grandsons—Percy, Willie, and trombonist Earl—into first-rate musicians.

Percy wasn't given to bragging. But one night, after a Eureka concert in Washington, he grabbed my father's arm and told him he had something important to say. My dad had accompanied the band up there for some reason, and they were walking across the moonlit Mall on the way back to their hotel. Percy had had a few drinks and wasn't too steady on his feet. "Listen here, Tom," he said in his gravelly voice. "People always talkin' about who invented jazz. I'm fixin' to tell you. It was my granddaddy. He's the one started breakin' up the leads." Breaking up the leads—getting off the written melody—was the key that opened the door to all the jazz music that followed, said Percy.

The French Quarter marches were actually tame affairs compared to the parades and funerals in the black neighborhoods. Out on the back streets, the dancing became freer and wilder, and the shouts and whoops were sometimes punctuated by gunfire. The "second-liners," those who danced behind the band, bumped and gyrated with pelvic thrusts that no white person could imitate, though some pathetically tried.

The Eureka was the best known of the marching bands, but there were a bunch of others. Each band had its own personality. John

Casimir's Tuxedo Brass Band was the best one to hear at a funeral. The reason for that was the banshee wail of Casimir's tiny E♭ clarinet, a chilling sound that seemed to come from another world. When they played numbers like "Westlawn Dirge," "Eternal Peace," or "Flee as a Bird to the Mountain," with Casimir floating above the brass like a lone swallow at dusk, it would bring tears to your eyes.

Casimir had another specialty: he had what he called "the sight," meaning he could look at someone and tell when they were going to die. "It's like I can see through 'em," he explained. "When I can see the wallpaper behind 'em, they done for." People would call him in when relatives were ailing—not to heal them, but to determine whether they would live or die. If he left two quarters on the mantelpiece on the way out, it was a bad sign: the coins were meant to cover the dead man's eyes.

Casimir always said he wouldn't be able to tell when he himself was about to go " 'cause when somebody fixin' to die, the sight leave him and go to somebody else." I don't know if anyone left quarters for Casimir, but he died shortly after that conversation, in January 1963.

The Onward Brass Band was another great one. Its leader was Louis Cottrell, an elegant Creole clarinetist and the no-nonsense president of the colored Musicians' Union. (When I joined that local in 1964, Cottrell was the man who swore me in.) The snare drummer was the great Paul Barbarin, who had played with Louis Armstrong and would later die the ideal musician's death, collapsing in the street during a parade. And the lead trumpet player was Ernie Cagnolatti—Little Cag, they called him—the shortest, and most powerful, member of the group. Sometimes there would be so many second-liners crowded around the band that you couldn't even see Cag. But you could hear him soaring up in the upper register and hitting blue notes that gave you goose bumps.

Cag was a great storyteller. I was talking to him at a funeral while waiting for the church service to end. He'd had a few pops from his silver hip flask and was reminiscing about his childhood across the lake in St. Tammany Parish.

"My daddy worked at a saw mill," he said. "My mama would send me over there every day with his lunch. One time I went over there and—boom—something fall on the floor right in front of me. I look down and I see it's somebody's hand. Then I say, 'I know that hand. That's my daddy's hand!' I ran up the stairs where they had the buzz saw, and sho' nuff, my daddy up there screamin' and hollerin' and they wrappin' rags around his stump. And I say, 'Oh Daddy, it's okay, I found your hand right down there on the flo.' He look at me an' he say, 'Ain't no good to me now, son. That hand gone!'"

Cag was standing on the sidewalk with his legs spread apart, rocking a little on the balls of his feet as if he were on the deck of a boat. The black parade cap was pulled down low on his forehead. His beady eyes were bloodshot and brimming with tears. He cocked his head to the side and looked at me.

"You don't believe me, Tommy? You don't believe me?"

"Yes I do," I said. "I believe you, Cag."

"Why should I lie to you? Why should I lie?" Cag went on, oblivious to my reply. "If you pay me ten dollars to tell you a lie, okay, I'll tell you a lie. Otherwise, shit, I might as well just tell you the truth and . . . and get it over with."

By far the funkiest of the marching groups was Harold Dejan's Olympia Brass Band. Harold had a day job as a driver and delivery man for the Lykes shipping line, but his real love, and genius, was running the Olympia. Harold had a favorite saying—"Everything's lovely"—and when you hung out with him and his band, everything *was* lovely and life was fun.

Harold was one of the younger jazz musicians, probably in his late fifties when I met him. He was short, broad-shouldered—he used to be an amateur boxer—and a bit paunchy. He had a smooth, gentle voice and a ready laugh that always made you happy to be around him. People called him the Duke.

He played an alto sax with a transparent red plastic mouthpiece. To tell the truth, Harold was not a dazzling instrumentalist. In fact, he never played anything but straight melody. That was surprising, since he had played with some famous bands in his youth—reading bands that required high-level musicianship. So I couldn't figure why he never ventured past the melody line or displayed any kind of technique.

He explained this to me one day when I asked his advice about clarinet playing. "Tommy, I'm a tell you how it is," he said with a loud sniff. I think he had some kind of allergy, because he wore reddish-tinted glasses and was always sniffing and blowing his nose. "You take me—I can run scales and arpeggios all up and down my horn. But you'll never hear me do that. You know why? Because you gotta let the people know what you *playin'*. Out on the street, folks don't want to hear all that fancy stuff. What they loves is the melody."

"Yeah, you right, Harold," said George "Kid Sheik" Colar, the Olympia's second trumpet player, who was standing nearby. "They say one good note is better than a thousand bad notes."

Sheik was a technically limited trumpet player who stuck close to the melody, never played high notes, and used only the most basic fingering. Like Harold, Sheik communicated more through feeling and personality than through any prowess on his instrument. One English record-jacket writer observed that Sheik was "the outstanding example of the average New Orleans trumpet player."

Sheik was well aware of his own limitations. "You know, I don't play that much on my horn," he told me one day, sitting in the courtyard behind the Hall. "But most people likes me, see, because of the way I conduct myself. If you ain't playin' much and you got a good disposition, people 'preciate you more than if you playin' plenty with a dirty disposition."

The Olympia musicians were the most unselfconsciously funny people I had ever met. They were always kidding each other, bragging about their sexual prowess, their drinking capacity, or their luck at the race track, or telling hilarious stories about one another.

Harold saw humor in almost every situation—even death. "This here gonna be a short one," he announced one day as his band gathered in front of Blandin's Funeral Home on St. Claude Street. "The widda didn't want to pay us enough money, so guess what? She gettin' a two block funeral."

Harold was a man of his word. When the pallbearers brought out the flower-covered casket, the Olympia launched into the mournful strains of "The Old Rugged Cross." Once the hearse started rolling, the band marched ahead of it for about a hundred yards, then Harold suddenly stopped playing and waved his arms like a football referee signaling a bad kick. "That's all she wrote, boys," he said. "Time to cut the body loose."

As the hearse moved past the musicians and headed on toward the cemetery unaccompanied, Harold kicked off an up-tempo chorus of "I'll Be Glad When You Dead, You Rascal You."

The Olympia had a bass drummer named Henry "Booker T" Glass. He was up in his eighties, slender and sinewy with a dark, bony face like an African mask. Book could play an all-day parade with the heavy bass drum strapped to his chest and never miss a beat.

Everybody was always teasing him about his age—Harold once told him if he died during a funeral they'd bury him for free—and Book would laugh louder than the rest of them.

"Shit, Harold," he said. "I'm a bury *you*. I'm a bury *all* you black bastards."

"That's all right," Harold shot back. "You just get a plumber to run two pipes into my grave—one for Scotch and one for bourbon—then everything *still* be lovely."

Booker T had a son named Nowell, a jovial, gum-chewing, pie-faced snare drummer that everyone—including Book—called Pa-*pa*. One day Book was late for the start of a parade, so Papa strapped on the bass drum and prepared to hit the pickup beats to launch the first tune.

"Hold everything!" Somebody shouted. "Don't you hit that drum!" It was Book, running up the street from the bus stop. Huffing and puffing, his large nostrils flaring like an enraged bull, he charged right up to Papa and grabbed at the straps with his powerful, bony hands. "Gimme that drum, sombitch," he demanded. Papa dutifully took the harness off and gave the drum to his father. After he had adjusted the straps and snatched the stick from Papa, Book glared at him under bristly white eyebrows and said, "Boy, if you waitin' for *this* drum, don't hold your breath."

Book could be feisty. Once the tuba player Anderson Minor said something he didn't like, so he confronted him with the big drum strapped to his belly and his drumstick raised high in the air like a club. At his age, he knew he couldn't physically fight anybody but he could not contain his rage. "Sombitch, Minor," he shouted, "you better take that back or I'll, I'll . . . I'll *sue* you."

The real powerhouse of the Olympia Brass Band was trumpeter Milton Batiste, better known as Bat. He was one of the rare players from the younger generation, probably in his mid-thirties at the time, and had a head full of rhythm 'n' blues riffs. But what he lacked in old-time authenticity he more than made up for with his volume, his stratospheric high notes, and the raucous, swinging jive of his playing.

Batiste was built like a football player, with a bull neck and shoulders as wide as an icebox. When he got to strutting down the street, dancing sideways with his trumpet held in one hand and a big white towel around his neck, the second-liners, especially the girls, would shout out his name like a rock star. "Bat! Bat! Ba-TEEST!"

Batiste gave the music everything he had. He played so hard that he had blown all the pigment off the front of his lips. He had a little coral-pink circle in the middle of his embouchure. The other striking thing about Bat was that he had no hair on one side of his head, the result of a childhood brain operation. For this reason, some of the neighborhood kids called him "half-head," but never to his face.

Harold was as proud of Batiste as if he were his own son. "Yeah, man," he'd say with a sniff. "Soon as Bat hold that horn up, all them womens go crazy."

I asked him how he had come to hire a young guy like Batiste.

"I heard him playing with Anderson Minor's band over by Shakespeare Park one day," he said. "Man, he had all that power, hittin' all them high notes. So I walk up to him after the parade and I tell him, 'How you like to play with the Olympia?' He say, 'The *Olympia?* You kiddin'!' I say, 'No, I ain't kiddin'. I want you to join my band.' He say, 'Okay.'"

"I bet Minor didn't like that," I asked.

"I'm fixin' to tell you," said Harold, savoring his story. "I seen Minor at Buster's the next day. He'd been drinkin' that Sweet Vino all afternoon, and his eyes was all bloodshot. He come up to me and start blubberin', 'Harold, you son-of-a-bitch, you done stole my trumpet player! You done stole my trumpet player!' I say, 'Shut up, Minor, or I'm a steal you, too.' He say, 'What you mean?' I tell him, 'Your little ole raggedy-ass band don't get no jobs anyhow, so I'm a bring you in the Olympia, too.' Boy, that shut him up! No jive. He's been playin' the bass horn with me ever since."

Joining the Olympia was a big deal, because it was the most active marching band in the city and gave its members plenty of work. Some people said that was because Harold was not really a Dejan (pronounced *Day*-zhawn) but the natural son of somebody connected with the Blandin Funeral Home, one of the city's best-known black undertaking firms. I don't know if there was any truth to that, but the Olympia did seem to have a lock on the best funeral jobs—not to mention the frequent parades put on by the black social clubs like the Door Poppers, the Tremé Sports, and the Jolly Bunch.

Those marching societies could be rough. The members, dressed to the nines, would get to drinking and dancing and twirling their feathery, sequined umbrellas in the air. Fights would often break out and bullets would fly. But Harold said he never had any trouble on those parades because his music made people happy.

"When my bass drummer hit that drum, it look like everybody's heart open up. I guess some of the people be out there, they don't have a loaf of bread to eat. But when that band strike up, they get to jumpin' down the street like they rich, like they own half the world. Yeah, Tommy, that New Orleans music do somethin' to 'em."

Harold loved to encourage young musicians. He would often invite me, along with Clive Wilson and other visiting foreign players, to sit in with the Olympia on parades and funerals. That was how I got my first real experience playing with a New Orleans jazz band. My father accompanied me at first, proud and happy to see his son playing his horn with the mens. But when I got a little older I would go alone.

Not only were the all-day parades great for building up my chops, they also gave me an experience that very few local white people could have in those days: marching, playing, and watching from the inside of a brass band as it wound its way through the heart of the old black neighborhoods. I would find myself surrounded by a writhing sea of people, hearing their whoops and shouts, marveling at their supple, sensual dancing, occasionally dodging brickbats and gunshots when tempers flared and violence erupted on the hot streets. This was more than music. This was life. I wanted to drink it all in.

CHAPTER SIXTEEN

One day, as we sat soaking up the air conditioning at Buster's bar after a long, hot parade, Harold slid a brown paper bag across the table.

"What's that?" I asked.

"Look inside," he said.

I opened the bag and found a black-and-gold Olympia hat band.

"I want you to play regular with the Olympia, Tommy," he told me. "I ain't got no usual clarinet player now. I can use you out there on the street."

I was thrilled. "But I'm still in school, Harold. I can't make all the jobs."

"That's all right," he sniffed. "Make the ones you can. You're always welcome in the Olympia."

It wasn't long after that that Harold called me for my first official job, and I soon realized that marching with the Olympia could be hard and dangerous work.

It was an all-day parade for the Tremé Sports, one of the city's wildest, baddest marching clubs. The weather was hellish—98 degrees and humid as a pot of simmering gumbo. When I got to the meeting point, a rough bar called the Caledonia Club at the corner of St. Claude and St. Philip, there was already a huge crowd milling around it. The Tremé Sports had about a hundred members, all dressed in identical iridescent green pants cut high above the waist, baggy in the legs, and tight at the top. They wore green-

felt derbies with green feathers in the hatbands and two-tone alligator shoes. Each man carried a brightly painted umbrella in one
hand and a flower-covered basket in the other. Most of the bas-
kets contained bottles of Old Crow or Jack Daniels.

Clustered around the marchers were neighborhood dudes in dark
glasses and backward baseball caps, talking jive and swilling beer,
fat women with bandannas tied around their sweaty brows, little
kids in short pants and T-shirts, and young girls in tight jeans with
their shirttails tied in knots over their flat black bellies.

The musicians were hunkered down inside drinking beer and
chatting up the ladies. Cigar smoke was as thick as fog in the dark,
air-conditioned grotto of a barroom. "There's my clarinet man,"
Harold chuckled. "Boy, I'm a work your ass today."

The crowd outside was getting restless and people were shouting for the music to start. "Arright, mens," said Harold, giving a
toot on his alto, "Let's hit it."

We pushed our way through the crowded doorway and lined up
in the sun-drenched street. Fats Houston, an enormous hulk of a
man dressed in his black suit and tails, white gloves, and a black
derby, took up his Grand Marshall's position at the head of the
band. Book pounded his bass drum and off we went, trailing a raucous throng in our wake.

The crowd stretched for three blocks behind the band. Garish
umbrellas began to wave and bob. People were hanging out of their
windowsills and doorways and sitting on their front porches. Children spilled out of the alleys and into the street. The old folks grinned
and nodded from their rocking chairs. Batiste eyed the girls and
strutted sideways, holding his trumpet in one hand. Sweat trickled
down his cheeks and into the collar of his open-neck white shirt.

Everybody was getting his little "taste" to cool off in the sweltering heat. Silver flasks, bottles and beer cans glinted in the sun

like fish scales. Mannie Paul had a can of Dixie wedged in the bell of his tenor sax. Even teenagers were sipping from foaming bottles held in one hand as they danced, heads back, eyes closed. The second-line dancing got looser and wilder and better.

Suddenly I heard a muffled "Pop!" Then three more—Pop! Pop! Pop! I turned around. A young woman was splayed out on the ground right behind me.

Kid Sheik ran over to the other side of the street when he heard the gunshots. I followed him.

"Shit!" he grunted as we crouched behind a car. "Every time we parade for them Tremé Sports look like some dude want to play cowboy."

The initial stunned silence gave way to shrieks and screams. Everybody stampeded away from the spot as if the gunman had gone berserk. Two or three hundred people—men, women, kids— were running down the street at full speed. Sheik and I ran with them. I heard another shot. Two. Three. More screams. Then the stampede stopped and people began to cluster around the wounded woman again. From their gestures, I supposed that the assailant had run down a side street that angled off North Rampart.

A police car, siren wailing and red lights flashing, jerked to a halt. A fat sergeant jumped out and ran toward the crowd with his gun drawn. Another car drove up. Two officers leapt out and ran in the same direction. Then came two motorcycles, two more cars, another motorcycle, an ambulance. Ten or fifteen policemen were running down an alley after the gunman.

By now the panic had subsided and the crowd was buzzing with excitement.

"They call him Shorty. I know him."

"He just done got out of jail las' month."

"Shorty always been a bad dude. Look like they got him, now, though. He goin' back in the joint."

"That girl hurt bad?"

"I think she hit in the leg. I seen blood all over the road."

The band had moved down the street and was starting to play again. I tried to catch up, but the crowd was too thick. I was falling behind, swallowed up in a mass of black faces and flame-painted umbrellas. Then I saw a parade cap just in front of me. It was Sam Alcorn calmly oiling the valves of his trumpet.

"Hey, Sam!" I said. "I'm gonna quit this parade. I don't like this stuff."

"Don't worry about all that foolishness, man. They never bother with musicians."

"Yeah, but it's different with me. You know what I mean."

He looked at my white face and blue eyes, a frightened sixteen-year-old kid trapped in the wrong part of town. "Don't worry about that, man. This is just folks fightin' among themselves, know what I mean? See, they got these little gangs, they always fightin' each other. The guys from the Ninth Ward always splittin' skulls with the cats from this housing project here, you know? Now, prob'ly the dude that did all the shootin' was from the projects and he seen one of these Ninth Ward cats who just beat him up last week, something like that. So he go home and get his gun."

"Well, he could have hit me or you just as easily."

Sam shrugged. "Me, I'm used to this shit. You'll prob'ly see two or three more shootouts before this gig's over. I grew up with this, man. It's just part of my life."

"Well, it's not part of mine," I protested. "I feel like a target in a shooting gallery. If some guy wants to pop an ofay, I happen to be the only one around here."

Sam smiled and put his hand on my shoulder. "You scared, ain't you?"

I shrugged.

"This ain't no race thing, Tommy. Least I don't think so. But if you want to hang out in the streets, man, you just gotta accept these things. For me, bein' shot is a chance I got to take every day in my neighborhood. Now *you* startin' to learn how it is. You just gotta take your chances, baby."

We had caught up with the band by then. Sam started to blow his trumpet again and the music went on. Everybody seemed so cool about the thing. Duck your head, run your tail out the way, make sure the dude's not coming after you, then go on about your business.

Today, their business was music, dancing, and good times, and the good times went rolling right along. The second-liners re-formed. They shouted, they danced, they drank and they laughed. The trumpets blared, the clarinet sang, the bass drum throbbed, the trombones moaned.

Fats Houston, his black derby cocked under his left arm, led the band through the surging crowds like the prow of a ship. He also gave those Tremé Sports a run for their money in the fashion department with his pink satin sash and yellow-ribboned epaulettes topped with artificial carnations. Block after sweltering block, this sweat-drenched, melon-faced ex-football player set the pace and cleared the way.

It was Fats who decided where and when the band would stop for refreshments, and the stops became more frequent as that hot day wore on.

At one neighborhood bar, a foxy chick pushed up against me. Her nipples stuck out like baby's thumbs under her braless T-shirt.

"Hey, white folks," she said. "I got three girls with me. Don't you want to buy us a beer?"

I told her I didn't have any money.

"Don't you want to do things with us, baby?"

"All I'm doing today is playing music," I said.

"Well you come back here when the parade's over, baby. We'll be waitin' for you."

Before I could answer, Fats blew his silver whistle and we were off again. We hadn't gone far before a rumble broke out just in front of the band—pushing, shoving, name-calling. "I'll call the *po*-lice if you don't stop that shit, boy," I heard Fats say. "They'll put your ass in jail so fast."

Just then another loud crack rang out and the crowd scattered again. I pushed some people out of my way and dived behind a car. Sam Alcorn was right behind me. "I told you the bullets were gonna be flyin' again, Tommy. You still scared?"

What I felt at that point was not fear but a hot and cold sensation in the gut, a kind of numb, breathless excitement. Maybe that's what it felt like on a battlefield.

"Don't worry, baby, I got my eye on you," Sam said.

I was drained by the time we got back to the Caledonia. Kid Sheik slid me a cold Dixie across the wooden counter. I was underage, but nobody checked ID's in the Caledonia Club.

Harold was eying me, though. "You better watch it, Tommy. I done promise your daddy I wouldn't let you drink with my band. You go home drunk, and we *both* gonna be in trouble with your old man."

"I just need one, to cool me off." My white shirt was soaked through and stuck to my hairless chest like Saran Wrap.

"Man, you look whipped," Sheik chuckled.

"Yeah, Sheik, I'm beat." I greedily chugged the chilled, stinging beer then pressed the can to my forehead. "That was a long one."

"Long, short, don't matter. Got to play the whole gig, Tommy. If we stop playin', we lost."

As soon as Harold paid us, Sam Alcorn stuffed the bills into his back pocket and buttoned it up. "Take it easy, Tommy," he said with a tap on my back. "And look, don't hang around the bar when the musicians leave. You go on home, you hear me? This ain't your neighborhood."

I had another beer with Sheik then took Sam's advice and headed out the door. As I was leaving, a couple of young guys were leaning on a car, smoking fat cigarettes and glowering at me with bloodshot eyes.

"What you got there?" said one.

"Clarinet."

"What you know about the clarinet? My uncle play the clarinet. I bet he play better than you."

"What's his name?"

"Israel Gorman."

"I know Israel Gorman," I said. "I've heard him play at Preservation Hall. I even have one of his records."

I thought that would mollify the guy. I was wrong.

"You lyin'," he snarled. "You don't know nothin' about no motherfuckin' record."

"Yes I do, and I'll show you."

Gorman was not my favorite clarinet player—he had a kind of screechy sound like a snake charmer—but for some reason I had learned his "St. Louis Blues" solo from a record he had just made with Punch Miller's Bunch. I put my horn together and played the solo note for note, doing my best to imitate Gorman's shrill, eerie tone.

The man's scowl turned to a grin.

"Yeah, you right, brother! You proved yo'self, man. You sure did. Ain't gotta say another word." He gave me a high five. "You my soul brother, baby—even if you *is* the wrong color."

As violent as things could sometimes get in Tremé, it paled in comparison with the brutal rape of that historic neighborhood at the hands of the city fathers. Tremé, right next to the French Quarter, between North Rampart and North Claiborne, was the heart of the city's jazz and Creole culture. George Lewis was born there, along with other jazz greats like Jimmie Noone and Chris Kelly. A lot of the famous black dance halls were there—Hopes Hall, the San Jacinto club, the Gypsy Tea Room, Funky Butt Hall, and Artisan's Hall. Every jazz musician in the city cut his teeth playing in those places. The centerpiece of this historic neighborhood was Congo Square, where the slaves used to dance to drum music on Sundays and where, legend has it, the rhythmic pulse of jazz was born.

In the late 1960s, ten square blocks of Tremé were flattened to build—irony of ironies—a cultural center, which was later incorporated into a park honoring Louis Armstrong. That project put millions into the pockets of contractors and corrupt politicians, but did little for the city residents or the tourists it was supposed to attract. The park, which looks like a Disneyland stage set with its cutesy fountains and bridges, quickly became a venue for muggings, murders, and drug deals—a strange way to honor Armstrong, whose own childhood home on Janes Alley, by the way, was demolished in the 1950s over the protests of jazz lovers who wanted to turn it into a museum.

Then there was the long, grassy strip on the so-called neutral ground between the two lanes of North Claiborne Avenue, just on the edge of Tremé. Though it was not an official city park, it was a green and pleasant place, shaded by quadruple rows of century-old live oaks, in the middle of a poor black neighborhood. Generations had used it for picnics, touch-football games, impromptu jazz concerts, and brass band parades. The colored Musicians' Union, local 496, had its hall along that strip, as did many black-owned shops and businesses.

In the late 1960s, a city planner sat at a drawing board and decided to run Interstate Highway 10 down the neutral ground and put an abrupt end to all that. No wonder the young kids in that neighborhood turned to stealing hubcaps and selling drugs after one of the few places where they could congregate with their friends and families fell victim to progress.

My father, ever the old radical at heart, watched all this and railed. "These neighborhoods were a hundred years in the making," he said. "Then came progress, and all these blocks, and the life they contained, were gone in an instant. The earth-devouring greed is in all of us, Tommy, but it becomes terrible when it's backed by government power and demagoguery. It gets into City Hall, then moves into the funding phase, the cutting in of contractors, suppliers, bond lawyers. The next thing you know, a whole layer of culture is stripped away."

My father had to admit that he himself had contributed indirectly to this process: his main P.R. client was a big architectural firm whose projects, including the Louisiana Superdome, replaced many acres of the old urban fabric.

CHAPTER SEVENTEEN

Chester Zardis was one of the best bass players in town and he knew it. He had little patience with people who couldn't play right. "You can't put music in somebody if they don't have it," he'd say. Chester had made some great early records with George Lewis in the 1940s, then got fed up with the music business and moved across the lake to Mandeville, where he worked a farm and raised pigs. Finally, Allan Jaffe rode out there on his Vespa and convinced him to come back to New Orleans and play.

Chester took an interest in me after I started sitting in with him at the Hall, and invited me over to his house on North Robertson for lunch one day. His wife, Bernadette, daughter of Olympia drummer Booker T Glass, fixed us red beans and rice with cornbread. Then Chester sat me down in his living room and started talking.

He told me all about how he had started out in music, secretly taking lessons with old man Billy Marrero because his mother didn't want him to be a musician. On his first job at the old Perseverance Hall, when he wasn't but fifteen, his mother came to the dance and saw him up on the bandstand. "Man," he told me with a chuckle, "she look up there and she like to die, seeing her little boy playing all that sinful music with the mens. She start shakin' her fist at me. When it was over, I told her, 'Mama, I'm sorry.' And she say, 'Poor little Chester, if you keep playin' that jazz, them womens gonna kill you.' But the next day, she took me down to the Tremé market and introduced me to all her friends. 'This my boy Chester, he play the bass.' Turn out she was proud of me."

Now that I was starting out in the same sinful business, Chester said he had some important advice for me. His main message was not to play like a white man, but to try to absorb the rhythm and the feeling of the black players. "A black man is playin' music 'cause he gotta learn," he said. "And he gonna try to learn it like it's sup-posed to be. He gonna try to find some kind of way to put a *touch* to it—swing, you know what I mean? Because a black man is al-ways swingy. I don't know why, but it look like that kind of music just *get* to them black people. They got the taste for it and they puts more into it, and it makes that music come out big."

The problem with a lot of white musicians, Chester said, was that they just didn't have the feeling—"and if you ain't got that, you might as well just forget about it." So his advice to me was "get together with the colored players so you can get that feeling that they got. I'm tellin' *you* that, now. You got to be with a black man often and take notice of him. And once you have learned *his* ways, you can make it."

I told him that's what I was trying to do by hanging out at the Hall, studying with George, and playing street parades. "Yeah, I see what you doin'," he said. "And you got to keep it up. Don't let all them race attitudes keep you from learnin'. That shit's been goin' on too long in this town. It's got to stop."

Chester was kind to me, but I sensed he could turn feisty and even violent when provoked. He stood five foot two and was built like a fireplug, with close-cropped white hair, powerful shoulders, and arms toned up by a half-century of plucking bass strings. By day, he worked as a guard at the Jefferson Parish prison, and rumor had it that more than one troublesome inmate had gotten his skull cracked by Chester's billy club. By night, he played the bass in

Preservation Hall, where the other musicians had learned from experience not to mess with little Chester.

"Chester's a bad dude, man," the piano player Sing Miller once told me. "You cross Chester and he'll kill you. He even drawed his gun on me one night. He was just sittin' there playin' his bass, all full of liquor and 'bout to fall off his stool. So I give him a little push to straighten him up, you know what I mean? And he drawed his automatic on me. Pulled the trigger, too, but it just make a snap. Didn't go off. Shit, man, I took that pistol away from Chester so fast. I don't play no more jobs with Chester. I don't care how much they pay me."

Chester's aggressiveness had developed early. He told me he had knocked the teeth out of a ticket taker in the old Avalon movie theater when he was fifteen and got sent to reform school. "That's where I met Louis Armstrong," he said. "Louis told me we'd start a band when we got out, but we never did get together."

I suspected Chester's violent side was rooted in the survival instincts of a man who was born short and black in a crime-ridden city. He was obsessed with protecting his house from burglars. He had a closetful of weapons—pistols, shotguns, automatics—and turned his mutt, fittingly named Bullet, into a snarling, snapping attack dog. Chester would even sprinkle gunpowder extracted from his shotgun shells on Bullet's food to "make him bad." And he was mighty pleased with the result. "Yeah," he'd say with a chuckle, "Bullet a hellfire dog. You break in this house, man, Bullet gonna take a chunk out of you."

My suspicions about Chester's survival instincts were confirmed by a story he told me that day.

"I was workin' at the Astoria down on South Rampart with the Kid Rena band," he said. "I would come home late at night, and them white boys, man, they run the hell out of us. So I said to myself, 'Man, I'm tired of this. I'm gonna start doin' a little dirt.' I used to carry a long-handled razor. So when I come home from work that night, I miss that damn 2 a.m. trolley car down Claiborne Avenue, and I say, 'Well, I done missed my car. I'm gonna walk down Claiborne and I hope I don't meet no son of a bitch and have to kill him.' I was just talkin' to my own self, and I takes my razor, and I open it, and put the handle up my sleeve."

Chester leaned forward in his chair and made a flicking motion with his wrist. I could picture him, perhaps forty years earlier, slipping that blade up his sleeve and sauntering down the grassy Claiborne Avenue neutral ground in the dark of a steamy New Orleans night. Little Chester would have looked like an easy target walking alone on that deserted thoroughfare.

"Boy," he continued, "I got to Claiborne and Canal, and two sombitches drive past me in an automobile. 'Hey, nigger, where you goin', you bastard?' I didn't say nothin', just kept a walkin'. 'Hey, you black motherfucker. Where you goin' at?' That's a hard pill to swallow, you know what I mean? But I just kept walkin'.

"When I get to Conti Street, one son of a bitch—big tall fella— get out the car and the other man keep the engine runnin'. He say, 'Hey, you motherfucker, don't you hear me talkin' to you?' I say"— Chester's voice became deeper and softer, almost a whisper— "'Man, why don't you go on 'head home . . . while you *can* go.' He take a swing at me. Well, I ducked and hit him right here with that straight-handle razor." He traced a line across his midsection with the flat of his hand. "And all that, man, was open. So he say, 'Johnny! Oh Johnny! That motherfucker done cut me!' Well I hauled ass, me. And the next day in the paper, they wrote that a Negro held up a white man and kill him. It wasn't like that at all. That white man was meddlin' *me*. See what I'm talkin' about?"

I was astounded. "He actually died?"

"Shit yeah, the motherfucker died. It was him or me."

It was an old story, but it said a lot about the environment of racial fear and conflict that the musicians had grown up with. It had shaped their world and confined their horizons, but it forced them to focus their talents and energies on one of the few domains open to them: music. Which is one reason they became great jazzmen.

But there was something chilling about Chester's murderous white-black confrontation. It continued to work on my mind long after I had told him and Bernadette good-bye and returned to my parents' home uptown. Sure, the white boy had provoked the fight, but you couldn't exactly say he asked for it—he didn't ask to have his guts spilled on the sidewalk. And I thought about his mother, waiting up for him and, finally, getting a dreadful phone call from the police: "Ma'am, I'm sorry to inform you that your son was robbed and murdered by a nigger down on Conti Street."

The story was ugly, brutal, tragic. It reminded me of another racial clash I'd heard about involving Sweet Emma's late husband Ricard Alexis. He had been a great trumpet player in the 1920s until a group of white boys beat him up and broke his jaw while he was waiting for the streetcar. He could never play the trumpet again; he played bass instead. My father told me he knew who did it: some "old line" society kids, who bragged and laughed about it the next day. I took comfort in the thought that these dreadful incidents were buried in the distant past. But if there ever was a race war in New Orleans, as Guesnon predicted, which side would I be on?

CHAPTER EIGHTEEN

On November 22, 1963, I sprained my ankle in gym class and decided to check out of school. My mother was working at the Tulane library and couldn't pick me up, so I called Aunt Pat. She drove up shortly after lunchtime in her metallic gray Cadillac.

On the way to her house, we turned on the radio and heard a breaking news bulletin: "President Kennedy has just been shot while traveling in a motorcade through Dallas, Texas. He was rushed to Parkland Memorial Hospital. We have no word on his condition at this point."

By the time we got home, all the TV networks had switched to blanket coverage of the events in Dallas. Nobody seemed to know anything for sure. It was just a nick on the shoulder; no, a shot in the neck; no, a serious head wound. Then CBS anchor Walter Cronkite, looking distraught, wiped his eye, looked into the camera and told the nation: "From Dallas, Texas, the flash—apparently official—President Kennedy died at 1:00 p.m. central standard time, 2 p.m. eastern standard time, some thirty-eight minutes ago."

Aunt Pat and I stayed glued to the TV set in the den, joined by her cook Mary Jiles.

"I know why they shot that boy," Mary sobbed. "He was tryin' to help the colored people."

I thought Mary might be right. I knew what had happened in Little Rock, Selma, and Birmingham—church burnings, lynchings, Southern cops attacking little black schoolkids with dogs and clubs.

The rednecks said they'd die fighting before they'd see a colored child sitting on a white school bench. They had just gunned down a civil rights worker named Medgar Evers in my mother's home town of Jackson. Kennedy was pushing hard for civil rights, so why wouldn't they shoot him in Dallas?

But as the coverage continued, that theory seemed less likely. By late afternoon, they had arrested a suspect named Lee Harvey Oswald in a Dallas movie theater. The TV flashed a police mug shot of him, his right eye swollen and puffy from blows he had received during his capture. It turned out he was from New Orleans and had recently been arrested for handing out pro-Castro leaflets on a local streetcorner. Ex-Marine, Russian wife, Communist leanings . . .

"I just can't get over it," said Aunt Pat, who always wanted to believe the best about everybody. "A nice-looking boy like that. I wonder what ever got into him?"

Oswald's picture kept flashing on the screen. It looked strangely familiar. And then it clicked: the face in the window. I had seen him one night peering through the window of Preservation Hall, not three feet from where I was sitting in the corner seat by the drummer. I had looked at him and he glared back. He had short brown hair, blazing eyes, a challenging stare. The kind of stare that says, "You got a problem?" I was glad there was a window between us.

My mother picked me up after work and we returned home to watch more news coverage. My father hated TV—he had once left our broken set unrepaired for six months—but this night he watched it with us.

"Daddy," I told him, "I think I saw that guy in front of the Hall."

"I saw him," said my father. "He was hanging around the Quarter. I saw him pick a fight in front of the Bourbon House a couple of weeks ago. He threw some guy up on the hood of a parked car. It was him all right."

I was mortified to think that my city had produced such a monster, that Lee Harvey Oswald had attended our public schools, walked our streets, heard our jazz, eaten our food. And as the investigations unfolded, it became apparent to many observers—if not to the Warren Commission—that Oswald was not just a deranged loner. He was linked to a whole New Orleans-based network of plotters, freaks, and criminals. They were all around us. They were part of our world. Somehow, I thought, the city bore its share of guilt for the horrible thing that had happened in Dallas.

Kennedy left a legacy that would soon change the lives of everybody in the South: a Civil Rights Act that his successor Lyndon Johnson pushed through Congress in 1964. With one stroke of the new president's pen, it put an end to legal segregation throughout the fifty states.

It seemed like the culmination of everything my father had fought for as a young man. He always said that Jim Crow had reenslaved the blacks, that as long as you had laws saying they couldn't drink from the same water fountains as us, go to the same restaurants, use the same toilets, or send their kids to the same schools, mutual hatred and violence were inevitable. To his generation of civil rights advocates, integration would solve all that. That was the thrilling message of Martin Luther King Jr.'s 1963 "I Have a Dream" speech.

Integration wasn't the magic wand they had hoped for. Discrimination, inequality, and racial frictions hardly disappeared overnight. But a lot of things changed. The "white only" and "black only" signs were taken off the public water fountains and restrooms. Hotels opened their doors to all races. Black kids took their places in our classrooms. At the Hall, Allan Jaffe could legally hire white musicians like the great clarinetist Raymond Burke, composer of the haunting ballad "City of a Million Dreams." And blacks finally had the legal right to enter any bar or restaurant in town.

Of course, there were still a lot of establishments that they would be wise to stay out of. Not long after the law passed, I was jamming with some young European musicians in a rough working-class bar downtown. At one point, the owner asked us to stop playing so he could make an important announcement. "I got good news for y'all," he said. "Today we filed papers to make this place a private club. So there ain't no niggers comin' in here." Before the cheers and rebel yells had died down, my friends and I had started playing a chorus of "We Shall Overcome." Then we packed up our horns and walked out.

CHAPTER NINETEEN

My dad always said racial harmony would begin when blacks and whites could eat and drink together. And there was no better example of that than Buster Holmes's restaurant on Orleans and Burgundy. That was the place where the musicians gathered to eat, drink, socialize, and womanize.

It was rare—and technically illegal—to see a white person in Buster's before 1964. After that, as word about Buster's great food and funky atmosphere got around town and into the guidebooks, the musicians and locals were joined by uptown folks, hippies, and tourists eager to soak up some local color along with their red beans, turnip greens, and cornbread. Buster welcomed them all.

His real name was Clarence but nobody ever called him that. He was a big, round-faced, cigar-chomping ex-longshoreman from Plaquemines Parish who had been serving up food in the French Quarter since the early 1940s. He didn't play any music himself, but he loved having musicians around his place, especially when they pulled out their horns and played.

"Restaurant" was a big word for Buster's place. It was really a one-room bar with some formica-topped tables, a concrete floor, and a big open kitchen next door with a lunch counter running around it. The main room had a ceiling fan and dingy walls covered with photos and yellowed newspaper clippings. There were a couple of fluorescent tube lights on the ceiling and a blue neon Pabst beer sign over the jukebox.

Behind the oak bar there was a smoky, pitted mirror flanked by shelves stocked with various brands of bourbon, Scotch, vodka, and L&J Sweet Vino, a syrupy concoction that was the cheapest way to get drunk—and the surest way to get a hangover. The walls behind the bar were plastered with pictures of musicians, including one of Louis Armstrong mugging over a heaping plate of Buster's red beans.

The main man around Buster's—apart from Buster himself—was the trumpet player Kid Sheik. He was one of the most popular guys I ever met; everybody just loved to be around him. When he wasn't playing at the Hall, parading, or prowling for women, you could always find Sheik holding court at the bar. He would stand there for hours at a time, smoking his King Edward cigars, drinking Dixie beer, and filling the room with his rapid-fire chuckle. In the Musicians' Union directory, Sheik had two numbers listed by his name: his home phone and Buster's.

Buster wasn't a fancy cook, but everything that came out of his kitchen was down home. His menu, which he posted on a chalk board each day, was likely to include such fare as garlic chicken, barbecue ribs, ham and turnip greens, and shrimp jambalaya. But his most popular dish was the most famous New Orleans staple, red beans and rice, which he sold for twenty-six cents a plate in those days. For sixty cents, he'd add his gut-scalding hot sausage.

The tables in the main room were always jammed at meal times, but the best place to eat was at the lunch counter next door in the kitchen. There were half a dozen big iron pots simmering on the stove, filled with mustard greens, cabbage and ham, gumbo, turtle soup, red beans, and shrimp. It all mixed together in a warm cloud of vapor that bathed the room in a pungent, spicy, meaty smell. Blown out onto the street by a big rickety window fan, the aroma of Buster's kitchen filled the whole neighborhood.

It was the same smell that wafted out of all the splintery shot-gun houses behind Congo Square, from the brick windows of the housing projects, from the shacks and shanties along the levee, from the sprawling black-and-white checkerboard of houses in the working-class Ninth Ward. It was a smell that was unmistakably New Orleans. And here, mixed with beer, fresh coffee, cigar smoke, sweat, and cheap perfume, it was unmistakably Buster's.

The Olympia Brass Band would often go to Buster's after a pa-rade or funeral to drink, eat, and sometimes play more music. I re-member one parade that wound up there and turned into a marathon jam session. When we got there, horns blaring and drums pound-ing, there was bedlam at the front door. The rhythm-drunk second-liners were trying to jam into the barroom along with the band, but the swinging butts and shoulders and umbrellas and bass horns just couldn't make it through the narrow entrance at the same time. Blowing furiously on his silver whistle, Fats Houston started grab-bing people by the scruff of their necks and throwing them out of the doorway. "Get outta there, you!" he shouted. "Let them *musicianers* in there, goddammit!"

Buster's was jammed. Dozens of second-liners had followed the musicians inside expecting to hear some more music. But the band had scattered, some drinking and schmoozing with women at the bar, some sitting around the tables, some back in the kitchen eat-ing Buster's red beans.

Fats was sitting next to me with his eyes closed and his head tilted back. Big drops of sweat formed on his forehead, rolled down his cheeks and dropped in little puddles on the concrete floor. He was still wearing his black derby and had his plumed, sequined um-brella propped up against his chair. The harsh light that came in from the doorway glistened on his dark, sweat-slick face.

Louis Armstrong's "Bye and Bye" was playing on the jukebox, barely audible over the laughter and chatter. Manuel Paul, the tenor sax player, had a buxom woman sitting on his lap. "Aw, baby, I been waitin' for you to come by me all afternoon," he said, grinning under the close-cropped white mustache that made him look like an otter when he played his horn.

Sheik stood at the bar with his parade hat cocked on the back of his head. Booker T was sitting in a corner by the jukebox sipping Scotch. He looked up at me with red-rimmed eyes and smiled.

"Get your horn out, junior," he said. "You and me gonna play some music."

"Aren't you tired?"

"Me?" he said. "Shit, man. I'm only eighty-five, and I ain't countin' the years I went barefooted, neither."

I was still exhausted from marching in the hot sun, but before I could say so a woman in a tight pink dress sauntered over and grabbed my arm. "Oh bay-*bee!* Ain't you gonna play some more music for us?"

Other voices chimed in from every corner of the room.

"Give us some second-line music, baby, second-*line!*"

The old man stood up and began to strap on his bass drum. Harold had left and Book was running the show now. "Papa! Oh, Papa, come on over here, boy." Papa picked up his snare drum and stood next to his father. Sheik pulled his trumpet out of its purple velvet carrying bag.

"Manuel!" Book shouted. "Get your horn." Someone handed Mannie his tenor. He reluctantly let his ladyfriend slide off his lap as he attached his neck strap and blew a deep-throated note—*Tzonk!*—that triggered a volley of whoops from the crowd.

"All right, Book," said Sheik. "We'll give 'em 'Joe Avery'." Booker T thumped out the intro—*Boom!* Ba-doom-*boom!* Ba-doom-*boom-boom!*—and the whole room erupted with sound and movement. Shreiks and shouts. Clapping hands. Twirling umbrellas.

The walls throbbed with the lashing syncopation of the music. Even though there were only five of us playing, the reverberation of the small barroom with its hard walls and concrete floor made it sound like a whole brass band.

People were coming in off the streets in threes and fours—off-duty maids in their crisp white uniforms, shoeshine boys, quarter-hustling tap dancers, toothless old men in straw hats, and fine young girls with tight jeans and round, pulpy rumps.

Fats was leaning up against the wall, chewing gum and cooling himself with his feathered grand marshall's fan. A short, skinny woman slinked up and began to dance belly-to-belly with him.

After about ten choruses, Sheik signaled the end and we brought the tune to a delirious climax. I plopped down in a chair, unable to play another note.

Book was standing next to me, still strapped to his bass drum. "Heh-heh-heh. You tired, ain't you? Get that horn again, boy, you gonna work now. Come on, me and you. Let's go!"

Before I could protest, I was besieged by women begging me to "play just one more, baby, just one more." Book hit the drum and off we went for another number, then another, then another.

Suddenly Booker T announced that the show was over because he had to keep "a very special appointment." No amount of sweet-talking was going to keep *him* there. "Papa!" he called out as he unstrapped his drum. "Go get your truck and drive by here for me."

Papa shook his head and grinned at the old man as he disappeared through the front door. No doubt who the papa bear was in that family.

After a little while Book picked up his drum and headed for the door. "Come on, junior," he said. "We'll give you a ride."

Fats waddled up to him, out of breath and sweating like an ox. "Give me a ride to my car, Book. I'm too tired to make it."

"You big fat lazy bastard," the old man snapped. "You ought to lose some weight."

Fats laughed so hard he had to sit down. He had been in a near-fatal automobile crash some years earlier, and one knee was badly injured. With all the weight he carried—some three hundred pounds—every step was painful. But as long as the music played, he couldn't feel it.

The sun was still bright outside and the late afternoon air was hot and humid as a Turkish bath. Papa drove up in his rattletrap green pickup and groaned to a stop. Booker set his drum down in the back, then climbed nimbly over the side and sat up on the tailgate. "Let Fats get inside, junior. He take up three places all by himself. You sit back here by me."

After we dropped Fats off by his car, Book and I got inside with Papa. "Say, Book," Papa laughed. "You seen that girl dancin' up on Fats, huh?"

"Yeah. They like them big mens. Heh-heh-heh-heh."

We drove down North Claiborne Avenue, then turned onto one of the side streets. It was lined with wooden shacks and shotgun houses with long, narrow alleys and rusty iron fences. Old people sat on the front steps, trying to cool off. Scruffy dogs barked at the passing truck. Children were playing on the mossy brick sidewalks, eating popsicles, roller-skating, twirling their hula-hoops. There were rusty old cars parked on the side of the street, some of them missing wheels and jacked up on piles of bricks.

Papa pulled over to the curb and Booker hopped out. "Take my drum home, Papa," he ordered. "And drop this young man by his streetcar stop. You take it easy, junior."

The old man opened a gate and vanished down a long, dank alley.

"Is this where your dad lives?" I asked Papa.

"Oh, no, man," he said. "This his girlfriend's place."

I thought Papa had been kidding me. There was no way an eighty-five-year-old man was getting frisky with a woman, especially after that long day of playing.

Not long afterward, I saw Kid Sheik and pianist Sing Miller sitting together in Buster's and decided to ask them about it.

"Say, Sheik," I said, pulling up a chair. "Papa told me Book's got a girlfriend. Is that true?"

"No, Book ain't got a girlfriend," Sheik grinned. "He got *three* girlfriends."

"That's right, man," Sing volunteered. "Plus his wife."

"At his age?" I protested. "How is it possible?"

"Book might be old, but he's still a hell of a man," Sheik said. "Nobody mess with Book, man. He be carryin' a .45 in his bosom and he ain't afraid to use it."

Sing nodded. "That man save my life one day."

"With his gun?" I asked.

"Naw, man. With his bare hands. Book used to be a pipelayer's foreman, and they put him in charge of a big job on the docks. He hired me to work with him. Treated me like his own son, man. That's what got me into doin' construction work, back in the forties."

"Shit, man, that's *hard* work," said Sheik. "Break your back."

"That's what I'm tellin' you. But it ain't the work that like to kill me—it's Book tellin' all those funny stories. He said something one morning that tickled me so much I took to one of those laughin' spells. I laugh so hard I fell right in that river with my overcoat on. I thought I was gone, man, I thought I was fixin' to leave away from here. When I went down for the third time, Book draw up alongside me in a skiff. He grab me by the back of my hair and pull me out the water. And when they got me back up on that dock, boy, I drank a whole *pint* of Old Quaker all by myself. *Gloug-gloug-gloug-gloug!* If it wasn't for Book, I wouldn't be sittin' here talkin' to you today."

I never knew whether to believe Sing. He never let the strict truth get in the way of a good story.

"Yeah, Book a hell of a man," said Sheik. "You know he got three balls?"

"What?"

"For true, man. Book got three balls. Ask him. He'll whip 'em out and show 'em to you. He's prouder of that than a medal or somethin'."

"Yeah, that's true," Sing chimed in. "But men like that, you only run into a handful of 'em."

CHAPTER TWENTY

My own amorous instincts were beginning to stir in those years. At the time I discovered the jazz world, I was still at the hand-holding and peck-on-the cheek stage with my girlfriends in school. And then I met Sally Fellon and fell tragically in love, the way adolescents do the first time they meet a beautiful woman and get close enough to feel her breath on their cheek and smell her perfume. I think Sally loved me, too, in a certain way. She once told me I was "a lovely boy." But there was no way anything could happen between us given the age difference. Besides, by the time I was sexually mature, Sally was long gone.

She told me the news as we sat together in the carriageway on a summer night in 1964. "I'm leaving town, Tommy," she said. "I'm going out to San Francisco to stay with my sister."

"Will you be gone long?" I asked.

"Who knows?" she said. "I might stay there for good."

The reason for this sudden departure was not clear to me. Sally was evasive when I asked her to explain. I gathered it had something to do with her domestic situation. She was still living at home with her parents and had several other siblings. Or maybe it was that her sister needed her to help with her kids in San Francisco. Or maybe she had boyfriend trouble. I didn't know for sure. I just knew that her news jolted me and made me very sad.

"But how can you leave New Orleans?" I asked. "You don't like the music anymore?"

"Oh, I love the music. I love coming here. I love talking to you. I love it all. But sometimes you just have to do things."

I offered to see her off at the Greyhound bus station on Canal Street, but she said her parents were taking her and it might be awkward. So I said good-bye to her that night with a kiss on the cheek. She gave me a hug and a pat on the back, and she was off.

Ten days later, I got a letter from Sally, the first of many. Just the sight of her slanted, elongated handwriting made my heart jump. I sniffed the envelope, but it was the unscented dime-store variety. The letter recounted her long trip across the country— two days during which her ankles swelled up like "eggplants"— and her first impressions of San Francisco. To my dismay, she seemed charmed by the place. She described the wharves, the bay, the Golden Gate Bridge, the chilly wind that came in from the Pacific at night, the cable cars, Chinatown. It seemed so far away.

I wrote back, telling her all the stuff that was going on at the Hall. I also mentioned that my father seemed really fascinated by this guy Rockmore, a New York artist who had recently started hanging around the Hall, but I thought he was "creepy." And I told her, in my childish way, that I missed having her as a friend.

Sally replied promptly, saying I was wrong about Rockmore. She found him "really interesting," with his painting and his classical music and all his stories about the art scene in New York. I was horrified at the thought that Sally might know Rockmore a lot better than I had imagined.

I hated the idea that she was five years older than I, that she was a woman while I was still a boy, that any romantic ideas I might have had about her were doomed by the gap of time—and distance—that separated us. I thought of the lyrics to "Telephone Me," Sweet Emma's favorite tune: *"If life should divide us, from Frisco*

to Maine, I'd walk a million miles to see your sweet smile again." And
I cried a little.

Before too long, though, I found girls my own age to lust
after. At sixteen, full of hormones and romantic yearnings, I fell
head over heels in love with a girl from my high school. Her name
was Cathy. She had transferred in from out West, and all the
guys thought she was the most beautiful girl they had ever
seen. She had pale blue eyes, dazzling white teeth, honey-colored
hair, and smooth, slightly tan skin that glowed with health and
youth. She was slender but shapely, athletic, and brilliant in class.
Every one of my schoolmates had a crush on her, but somehow
she and I gravitated toward one another with the kind of mag-
netic attraction and passion that only the hunger of first love can
engender.

Cathy and I dated through our junior and senior years at Benjamin Franklin High. A typical outing consisted of a movie, followed by hamburgers and Brandy Alexanders in the parking lot of
Ye Olde College Inn on Carrollton Avenue. The College Inn featured drive-in service, with waiters who would attach metal trays
to the driver's side window and never checked ID's.

They also did not ask any questions about what young couples
were doing inside their cars, which was usually "making out" and
heavy petting. It was there, in the backseat of my father's old VW,
that I first explored the secrets of a woman's body.

One fine night we parked under a moss-draped oak tree in
Audubon Park. At the critical moment, a police car pulled up and
shone its searchlight on us. "I don't care what you're doing in there,
son," a cop barked, "just get your car off the golf course."

But for all her physical beauty, this lovely girl seemed to be tor-
mented by demons. Her behavior was erratic and marked by mood
swings. She frequently appeared jealous and competitive.

None of this sat well with my father, who knew a troubled soul when he saw one. He strongly disapproved of the relationship. Furthermore, the girl totally rejected the musical side of my life. She didn't like to go with me to Preservation Hall because she felt intimidated by my friendship with the old musicians. And, frankly, I felt uncomfortable about taking her there because the Jaffes teased me about having a girlfriend and said they'd tell Sally.

The Hall wasn't the only place I couldn't take her. One Sunday my father organized a jazz party at my Aunt Pat's house. One reason for the choice of venue was that Aunt Pat had a piano and we didn't. The other was that Uncle Buck loved old-time jazz and wanted to show his clarinet-playing nephew off to his friends. Besides, he was always ready to party.

There was a strange mix of people there that afternoon: Uncle Buck's pals and drinking buddies, my parents, some of my European friends, and three old black musicians—pianist Octave Crosby, trombonist Eddie Summers, and drummer Alec Bigard.

It would never have occurred to Uncle Buck to invite blacks to his home socially. But musicians are often considered like hired help, so they must have occupied the same place in his mind as his cooks and cleaning women. As for the fact that his nephew was playing alongside them, well, that was cute. After downing a few Scotch-and-sodas, Uncle Buck took out his snare drum and played along with them himself. He had a ball.

The real odd-person-out was Cathy. She spent the whole afternoon hiding in the kitchen with the maid, Azurine, who plied her with Scotch and got her quite tipsy. The girl boycotted the living room, refused to say hello to my family and friends, and glared at me silently and angrily when I drove her home. Later that night, she phoned me and said, "There's no room in your life for anything but your clarinet, your father, and your old men."

I often think of what Cathy said on the phone that night. And I wonder if she wasn't right. Was there room in my soul for music and something else? Yes, I went to school, danced at teenage parties, played baseball and touch football with my friends. But my heart and mind were always anchored in the music. I spent hours alone in the closet practicing my clarinet and many more hours at the Hall, playing in parades and jam sessions, hanging out with the old men, eating red beans at Buster's.

In fact, I lived in two different worlds. Which path would I follow when I grew up? Could I be a musician *and* a student? A musician *and* a lawyer? It's true that most of the mens had day jobs. George Lewis had been a stevedore, Harold Dejan was a driver, Kid Thomas was a house painter, Narvin Kimball was a postman. But that's not who they were. They may have done other things to pay the rent, but when they woke up in the morning and looked in the mirror, I'm sure they thought of themselves as "musicianers" and nothing else. I knew I could never be a full-fledged musician unless my dedication was as total as theirs. That was impossible as long as I was in school. But someday I would have a choice to make.

French Quarter
NEW ORLEANS

CITY OF A MILLION DREAMS

Courtesy of Joan Marian Peyton Jones collection

© Leo Touchet

CAFÉ DU MONDE

Seta Alexander   *Thomas Sancton*

Mississippi debutante Seta Alexander before her marriage to the dashing New Orleans newspaperman Tom Sancton. At left, I am nestled in my father's lap, flanked by sisters Beth and Wendy on Easter Day 1951. Three years later, my mother accompanied me on my first day of school at McDonogh No. 10.

John Kuhlman, courtesy Louisiana State Museum

One of my earliest music memories was the 1954 jazz funeral of the great trumpeter Oscar "Papa" Celestin. It was about that time that the street vendor Dora Bliggen, pictured at right in front of our house, recorded her haunting "blackberry" call and a hymn in our living room. I had never heard singing like that.

Frederic Ramsey, Jr., courtesy The Estate of Frederic Ramsey, Jr.

PRESERVATION HALL

André Clergeat

William Carter

Grauman Marks

This former art gallery on St. Peter Street
became the world's traditional jazz Mecca,
and our favorite hangout. My father forged
close friendships with the musicians and
with the Hall's Philadelphia-born owners,
Sandra and Allan Jaffe, pictured with him
above. The Jaffes lived in the former slave
quarters at the back of the courtyard, where
they often held impromptu jazz parties.

Unknown photographer, Preservation Hall Collection

LARRY BORENSTEIN

Unknown photographer, Preservation Hall Collection

BILL RUSSELL

© T. A. Sancton

ALLAN JAFFE

Unknown photographer, Preservation Hall Collection

FRANK "THE DUDE" AMACKER

Dan Leyrer

The Hall was full of strange and wondrous people, like Larry Borenstein, who started the whole thing in his French Quarter art gallery; Bill Russell, who made historic recordings and lived amid his disheveled jazz archives; Allan Jaffe, who played tuba and built the kitty hall into a lucrative business; and the ex-pimp Frank "the Dude" Amacker, who didn't play there but filled the carriageway with his "God-given voice."

ROLE MODEL

From the first time I heard the angelic sound of George Lewis' clarinet, I wanted to make music like that. He became my friend, my teacher, and my idol. In the early '60s, I could hear him two or three times a week at Preservation Hall, as pictured below with (left to right) Cie Frazier, Dede Pierce, Chester Zardis, Billie Pierce.

Grauman Marks

GEORGE LEWIS
and the NEW ORLEANS ALL-STARS
IN TOKYO 1963

GEORGE LEWIS
with
KID SHOTS

© John Daigle

Thomas Sancton (Sr.)

Dan Leyrer

After my first few lessons, George decided it was time to put me on the bandstand, so he invited me to sit in with his quartet, backed by Joe Watkins, Papa John Joseph, and Dolly Adams. On Saturday afternoons, trumpeter Punch Miller (left), an early friend and rival of Louis Armstrong, taught me and other aspiring young jazzmen down at the Hall.

STALWARTS

JIM ROBINSON

Among the regulars at the Hall, these three were standouts: trombonist Jim Robinson, a self-proclaimed "man amongst men," who counted on my father to buy his "groceries"; and the Humphrey brothers, Willie and Percy, scions of a famous jazz family and the mainstays of the Eureka Brass Band. All three men were members of Sweet Emma's Bell Boys and of the Preservation Hall touring band, which took the jazz message around the world.

WILLIE AND PERCY HUMPHREY

Creole George was a great banjo player and world champion raconteur. During my lessons at his "bird cage" of a house, he talked endlessly about music, race, history, money, sex and, mainly, about himself and his proud Creole ancestry. When he died in 1968, he left me his scrapbook as a "legacy." It remains one of my most treasured possessions.

(CREOLE GEORGE GUESNON
=COMPOSER = MUSICIAN=
OF NEW ORLEANS LA.
FEATURED ON PAGE 51)

LOUIS ARMSTRONG AND CREOLE GEORGE GUESNON NEW YORK CITY (1955)

THE GEORGE LEWIS TRIO = 1963

T. A. Sancton Collection

On parade with Harold Dejan's Olympia Brass Band. From the middle of the band, I plied the back neighborhoods, marveled at the supple, sensual dancing, and occasionally dodged brickbats and bullets as tempers flared on the steamy streets. During one parade rest, at left, I gave an impromptu clarinet lesson to a young second liner.

T. A. Sancton Collection

Lee Friedlander, courtesy Fraenkel Gallery, San Francisco

The hot streets of New Orleans echoed with the throb of bass drums and the blare of trumpets. Grand Marshals Slow Drag Pavageau and Fats Houston lead the Eureka (above). The Preservation Hall touring band (below) took the jazz message around the world: left to right, Jim Robinson, Cie Frazier, James Prevost, Percy Humphrey, Willie Humphrey, Sing Miller, Narvin Kimball.

Ralph Cowan, courtesy Pat L. Cowan

SWEET EMMA BARRETT

Grauman Marks

ALBERT BURBANK

William Carter

JOE WATKINS

Edward G. Marks

The first time I saw Sweet Emma Barrett, she reminded me of Marie Laveau, the legendary Voodoo Queen; clarinetist Albert Burbank preferred giving me fishing lessons to music lessons; Joe Watkins climbed off his sickbed to make a great final recording; bassist Chester Zardis advised me to "get together with a black man and learn his ways" if I wanted to play jazz right.

CHESTER ZARDIS

William Carter

John Simmons

John Edser

This funky bar and restaurant on the corner of Orleans and Burgundy is where the musicians gathered to eat, drink, and socialize. Many parades wound up here, and the music and fun would continue over cans of Dixie beer and heaping plates of red beans and rice. For Harold Dejan and Kid Sheik, shown here with youthful admirers, Buster's was practically a second home.

Courtesy John Simmons

BUSTER HOLMES

William Carter

Courtesy John Simmons

MASTERS AND APPRENTICES

T. A. Sancton Collection

Dan Leyrer

T. A. Sancton Collection

Along with the young "jazz pilgrims" from overseas, I learned the musician's trade at the side of the old masters. At one wedding reception, pictured above, trumpeter Punch Miller and trombonist Eddie Summers spearheaded a group including, left to right, Lars Edegran, Orange Kellin, myself, Trevor Richards, and Clive Wilson. At left, Punch gives a lesson to me, Yoichi Kimura, and Allan Jaffe. Above, a backyard party with Kimura, Edegran, Wilson, and myself.

DANNY BARKER

John Chiasson

ERNEST "SING" MILLER

© T. A. Sancton

GEORGE "KID SHEIK" COLAR

Lee Friedlander, courtesy Fraenkel Gallery, San Francisco

Danny Barker came home after years on the road and made his peace with the "hamfat" locals; Ernest "Sing" Miller was a bluesy piano man who never let the strict truth get in the way of a good story; trumpeter George "Kid Sheik" Colar made up for his technical limits with a sunny personality and rapid-fire chuckle; bassist Papa John Joseph, the son of an ex-slave, was pushing 90 when he dropped dead in the Hall on New Year's Eve 1964.

PAPA JOHN JOSEPH

Dan Leyrer, Preservation Hall Collection

Leo Touchet

Leo Touchet

The day we buried George Lewis, January 3, 1969, marked the end of an era for me. As I marched in his funeral with the Olympia Brass Band, I knew that the world would never see the like of him again. My father (right) was also gripped by the day's somber mood. "I beat and pound for the dead," wrote Whitman, "I blow. . . my loudest and gayest for them."

Grauman Marks

CHAPTER TWENTY-ONE

Any hopes I had of getting my classmates interested in traditional jazz ended on February 9, 1964. That was the night that the Beatles made their American debut on the Ed Sullivan Show. It is said that 73 million people tuned in to watch these four mop-headed Brits perform the hits that were already topping the charts in the U.S.— "All My Loving," "She Loves You," "I Want to Hold Your Hand." The girls who screamed and swooned on our black-and-white TV screens that night gave voice to the mass hysteria that soon swept like a wildfire through the ranks of America's youth. I was among them.

Like all my friends at school, I listened to the Beatles on the radio, bought their records, danced to their music at parties. We knew the words to all their songs and sang them in the halls between class, even in the showers in gym. Some went further than that. A friend of mine, George Welch, asked me to join a band he was forming to play Beatles tunes—a four-man group called the Blazers. I eagerly accepted.

There was no room for a clarinet in the Beatles' repertoire, so I did what all the other kids were doing those days: I got a guitar and learned half-a-dozen chords. Soon I was strumming and singing along with the Blazers at school functions and parties. I even let my hair grow long, but it was very curly and looked more like an Afro than a mop-top. My sisters tried to straighten my hair with a steam iron, but my bangs just stuck out like an awning.

Later that year, the Beatles themselves came to New Orleans on their first American tour. They played in City Park stadium, the same place my dad used to take me to watch the New Orleans Pelicans baseball games before the team folded in 1959. I was there in the bleachers that night, shouting and cheering and snapping pictures with my Brownie camera. There was no chance of getting a decent photo, though, since the stage was fifty yards away and the Beatles looked like fuzz-topped matchsticks in the viewfinder.

Halfway through the concert, a bunch of kids broke through the police barricades and rushed the stage. They were soon followed by hundreds more. It was bedlam. Cops were running after hysterical girls, grabbing them by the collar, ripping their skirts, and even tackling them, to prevent them from getting to the Beatles. A girl managed to climb up on the drummer's raised platform, nearly toppling Ringo Starr off his perch. One of the group's gorillas grabbed her at the last moment and threw her roughly off the stage.

The Beatles seemed amused by it all. After the last number, Paul McCartney voiced his special thanks to "all you football players who came out to support us tonight." Then the four lads disappeared into a black limousine and drove off through a sea of shrieking fans.

"It was so great," I told my father, when he came to pick me up. "Even if I didn't see them from up close."

"I did," he said. "My car was parked by the exit road when they drove by, not six feet from me. They were soaked with sweat, like they had just come in from the rain."

I was awestruck and jealous that my father had been close enough to the Beatles to see the very sweat on their brows. It was totally wasted on him, since he didn't care a damn about their music and said all the fuss over them was ridiculous.

The powerful magnetism of the Beatles, the pull of peer pressure, and the desire to be part of my generation briefly eclipsed my fascination with the mens and their music. I still went to the Hall. But for a while, I put more time into guitar practice and Blazer rehearsals than woodshedding my horn. I thought no one would notice. I should have known better.

After a long hiatus, I went to see George Guesnon for a lesson and he really chewed me out. "I don't know what the hell got into you, Tommy," he said sternly. "You done forgot half the things I taught you. I mean, one time you come over here, you blowin' like a house on fire. You come back and you can't make it no more. I ain't gonna lie to you, son. You ain't cuttin' it."

I was mortified. I felt like I had failed Guesnon, failed George Lewis, failed my clarinet. The worst part was that I knew he was right. I mumbled something about being distracted by the guitar.

His eyes suddenly lit up. "Oh, yeah? You playin' the guitar now? That's a good double. It'll help you learn your chords and arpeggios. But don't you put down that clarinet, you hear?"

A couple of weeks later, my father came home from one of his soul-to-soul visits with Guesnon and plopped a thick spiral notebook down in front of me. I flipped it open and saw page after page of handwritten chord notations. "Guesnon made this to help you learn the guitar," my father told me.

The old man had put a lot of work into it. Of course, I could have bought a standard guitar chord book at Werlein's. But I treasured the one written in Guesnon's own hand. And this way, Guesnon wound up with the "crumbs" instead of Mr. Werlein: he had charged my dad twenty dollars for the book. Even with his friend and kindred spirit, Creole George was always looking for the angle.

CHAPTER TWENTY-TWO

It was one of those hot, steamy nights that can make New Orleans unbearable for tourists. The locals don't like them much, either, but at least we're used to it. Tonight, though, the soggy air that drifted in from the river and the lake and the bayous carried with it something that can ruin many a summer evening and, in the old days, infected the whole city with yellow fever: mosquitoes. They swarmed around you in the street, then they followed you indoors to torment you with their incessant buzzing and stinging. Inside Preservation Hall, the band could hardly play because the musicians were slapping so much at the pesky insects.

But George Lewis didn't slap. "Mosquitoes don't bother me none," he said. "I got bitter skin."

"Bitter skin?" said Joe Watkins. "George got bitter everything."

That bit of bandstand banter said a lot about the relationship between George and his long-time drummer. For all his soulfulness, George had a mean streak and Joe was his favorite whipping boy. Whenever George felt something was not right with the band—even if he himself had just hit a bad note—he would wheel around and glare at his drummer. Sometimes he growled out of the corner of his mouth: "Come on, Joe!" or "Pick it up, Joe!" Joe would turn sullen and shake his head with a hangdog look. If anybody else in the band told George to take it easy on Joe, he'd snap back, "I don't ride Joe hard. Joe ride his *own* self hard."

We could hear those exchanges clearly from our favorite seats near the drums. It was like being right in the middle of the band. You could see every gesture, hear the asides between the musicians, and catch their funny looks, scowls, and winks. Above all, the corner seats were a great place for watching the drummer.

We felt a special bond with Joe. He was such an endearing soul that Mother never talked about him without referring to him as "precious Joe." Joe sensed our affection for him. He always looked for us when he arrived and asked about us if we were not in our usual seats.

Joe had a dark, mournful face, with large, sad eyes, and flaring nostrils. He was a sweet man, gentle and good-natured, and had a smile that could light up the whole room. As soon as the first number kicked off, though, Joe was all concentration, counting measures in his head, keeping the tempo steady, carefully placing each woodblock and cymbal lick so as to drive the band without getting in the way.

His face brightened up when he sang, though even there his concentration was total. Some musicians made up half the words as they went along, but Joe prided himself on getting all the lyrics right. He always brought a stack of well-worn notebooks in which he had neatly printed the lyrics to hundreds of tunes in block capitals. You could hear the sweetness of Joe Watkins's soul in the sound of his voice.

Joe had been with George Lewis for twenty years, and his flawless time-keeping was a key ingredient of the band's phenomenal drive. Joe had all the moves—rim shots, tight press rolls, and lashing cymbals—but he never let fancy technique get in the way of the old-time drumming style that he had learned as a young man and never changed. That's why George hired him in the first place. And for all his self-effacing manners, Joe had influenced hundreds of young drummers around the world through his records and concert tours. The Beatles' Ringo Starr, who heard the Lewis band in Liverpool in the 1950s, later marveled over Joe's "incredible" playing in a *Billboard* interview: "He only had two drums—a snare and a bass drum—and a high hat and ride cymbal. And for any tom-tom work, he just ducked down and played the bass drum. It was just like, 'Wow!'"

Joe was delighted when George asked him to come along on his big tour of Japan in 1963. He hadn't been on the road with George in years and this seemed like a return to their glory days of international globe-trotting. The three-month tour was a huge success. The band played to packed concert halls all over the country—Tokyo, Osaka, Nagasaki. At every stop, they were mobbed by autograph-seeking fans, showered with flowers and gifts, catered to by beautiful geishas. Strange as it seems, George was a big hero in Japan. Scores of Japanese musicians modeled their playing on him and his band. Tokyo had at least two Swing Cafes that featured huge posters of George and his band mates, and played their records nonstop.

But it was also a grueling tour, involving strange food, late nights, and thousands of miles of travel. All the while, George seemed to ride Joe harder than ever. Joe was exhausted when he got back to New Orleans, and the task of taking care of his invalid wife Edna weighed him down even more. His strength just seemed to sap away from him.

Joe played at the Hall for a few months after his return, then his appearances became less and less regular. And by the time Edna died the following year, he had stopped playing altogether. Stricken with arthritis, malnutrition, and high blood pressure, he finally took to his bed and became a virtual invalid himself.

I could hardly believe my eyes the first time I saw him in this condition. He had become so thin that he looked like some African famine victim, with hollowed cheeks, stick-like legs, and blank, empty eyes. He would just lie there day after day, sweating into his dirty sheets and staring at the cracked yellow wallpaper while the summer heat, mosquitoes, and traffic noise drifted into his window.

But Joe never complained. "Hello, Tommy," he would say when I went to see him in his upstairs apartment on North Galvez Street. "How you makin' out, pardner?" He would ask for news from the "mens" at the Hall, talked about getting back on his feet and returning to work. His taxi-driving friend Pickles Jackson came by once in a while to help him walk a bit, for he could not even sit up by himself. "I'll be coming back down there one of these days," he vowed, "if God spare life." I thought Precious Joe was not long for this world. But Joe would surprise us all a few years later.

CHAPTER TWENTY-THREE

In my junior year at Ben Franklin High School, I had to write a research paper on some aspect of Louisiana history. I asked my father if he had any ideas for a topic. "Why don't you do it on the Plessy case?" he suggested. "That started in Louisiana and affected the whole history of race relations in this country. It was a landmark decision."

He gave me a quick fill-in: a group of New Orleans Creoles had mounted a legal challenge to the state's new segregation law in the 1890s; their case went all the way to the Supreme Court, which ruled against them in the *Plessy v. Ferguson* decision of 1896. "What the court decided," my father explained, "was that it was constitutional to separate the races as long as they got 'equal' treatment. So the 'separate but equal' doctrine became the law of the land, and the Supreme Court wound up condoning the most brutal treatment of southern Negroes since the end of slavery."

That sounded pretty interesting to me, but I was afraid the research would be limited to a bunch of dry legal texts and law review articles. I said I would prefer to do something on jazz history. "This case will teach you more about the roots of jazz in this city than anything else you could do," said my father. "And if you think it's dry, I'll take you around to meet Antoine Plessy. His cousin, Homer Plessy, was the one who started the thing. Son, this stuff is still living and breathing on the streets of New Orleans." As I often did during these years, I dropped my objections and followed my father's lead.

The next day, armed with a tape recorder and a notebook, I jumped into the front seat of my dad's VW and off we went to Antoine's house at 2528 Havana Street in the heart of the downtown Creole neighborhood.

My father had interviewed Antoine Plessy years earlier for an article he wrote in the New Orleans *Item* marking the sixtieth anniversary of the decision. Plessy, now up in his seventies, remembered him and received us warmly.

Light skinned, tall and trim, with scholarly looking glasses, Plessy was a retired carpenter and contractor who proudly told us he had built his own house and several more in the neighborhood. His father and grandfather had been contractors before him. The grandfather, in fact, had been a wealthy free man of color who owned slaves, "threw his lot in with the Confederacy," and was wiped out by the collapse of Confederate money.

Homer Adolph Plessy, which he pronounced French-style as "O-*mer*," was Antoine's first cousin once removed. Homer had been a member of the local committee that tried to fight the new segregation law. He was arrested on June 7, 1892 for refusing to ride in the Jim Crow train car, and thus became the plaintiff who lent his name to the famous case. (Ferguson was the lower court judge who initially ruled against Plessy before the case went to the Supreme Court on appeal.)

Antoine remembered him as a "beautiful man, almost as light-skinned as a Caucasian." Homer's grandfather, he said, was a French aristocrat, du Plessis, who fled to Kentucky after the Revolution. Homer himself spoke Parisian French and made a good living as an insurance collector. Antoine described him as "a proud, fearless man who would not take nothing off nobody." That would explain why he had wanted to fight the Jim Crow laws, perhaps, but it became clear that the motivation of Homer Plessy and his fellow committee members was to defend their own rights—not those of the colored population in general.

"Homer felt superior to the American-speaking colored because they had been slaves and were from a lower social level than him," Antoine explained. "See, all the Creole families thought they were better than the ex-slaves. And to keep us from going with these people—you know, there was prejudice—they established their own social clubs and dance halls all through the city. They had the France Amis Hall, the Jeunes Amis Hall. Sometimes you would go in those places when they were holdin' a soirée and you wouldn't see a dark face. Well, they done that purposely."

The old man's memories of Creole society led him away from the Plessy case and into a long discussion about the dance halls and the musicians who were a central part of that culture. Without any prompting from me, without even knowing that I had any interest in the subject, he started telling me about all the jazz musicians he had grown up with. He had gone to the O. O. Robertson school with Freddie Keppard, one of the city's great early trumpet players, described by Antoine as "the most careless, triflin' boy I ever knew, tie always on crooked, nose running, hair messed up." He was also close friends with two famous Creole clarinetists, Alphonse Picou and Lorenzo Tio Jr. Tio, in fact, had taught Antoine's son to play the saxophone.

Many's the night, he said, that he had danced to the music of A. J. Piron, Manuel Perez, and Buddy Bolden—all legendary names in the jazz pantheon, but just good local musicians to Antoine Plessy. They were part of his world and Homer's world. I was starting to understand how this music, which would later have such a huge impact on America's cultural history, had coalesced like a rich gumbo on the back streets of New Orleans.

Next, my father sent me to talk to a man named A. P. Tureaud, a prominent local civil rights lawyer and an authority on the Creoles. Tureaud had brought one of the suits that was ultimately bundled into the 1954 *Brown* decision, which finally overturned the separate but equal doctrine. A short, round, café-au-lait-colored man with a bald pate and graying hair at the temples, Tureaud was an inexhaustible font of Creole lore. One of his ancestors was a French army officer who had fled Haiti during the 1803 black uprising and moved to New Orleans with his black concubine.

"There were some 15,000 free persons of color in Louisiana around the time the battle of New Orleans was fought," he explained, referring to the 1814 clash between the Americans and the British just south of the city. "And they were mixing with Indians, some were mixing with the Cubans and the Mexicans. But the large number of them who were from Haiti came over here identified with either white or Negro, according to their own appraisal of their racial identity."

Many passed for white, or tried to, he said, and even those who were considered colored did not want to mix with the blacks. "There was a certain amount of pride that these old Creoles had in their ancestry," Tureaud said. "They wanted to make a distinction between them and the slaves. They were a stratified group of their own." He went on to tell me about Creole cooking, voodoo practices, music and social clubs—in fact we barely even got into the legal battle against segregation, although Tureaud himself had played a key role in it. Such is the flow of a New Orleans conversation: somehow it always comes back to food and music.

The next day, I was in the Louisiana Department of the Public Library on Loyola Avenue delving into books and articles on the Creoles—not the so-called white Creoles from French and Spanish backgrounds, but the *gens de couleur* of mixed white and African blood. They were the ones who had brought the Plessy case and ladled their culture into the jazz gumbo.

I learned that the origins of this class, really a caste, went back to the eighteenth century. Many of these French-speaking mulattoes were descended from the offspring of white slaveholders and female slaves in the French colony of Louisiana. There was also a large influx of mulattoes from Haiti after a black uprising led by Toussaint Louverture and Henri Christophe ousted the French in 1803 and turned that Caribbean island into the first independent republic run by former black slaves.

In the teeming, freewheeling Mississippi River port of New Orleans, these *gens de couleur* enjoyed a special status. The *Code Noir* of 1724, while very severe on the Negro slaves, had provided for the freeing (with the owner's consent) of mixed-blood offspring and their enjoyment of property rights. Many of these freed people were provided for in the wills of their former masters and became wealthy property owners in their own right. Some of them, like Antoine Plessy's grandfather, became slave owners themselves.

As Creole George Guesnon had already told me during my very first music lesson with him, this privileged and talented class thrived in that wide-open city and many of its members—not a few of them educated in France—distinguished themselves in the arts, music, business, liberal arts professions, and skilled trades such as carpentry, shoemaking, cigarmaking, upholstery, barbering, and tailoring. The fairest of the young Creole girls attended the famous quadroon balls, where they would meet wealthy white suitors eager to set them up as their mistresses.

But the privileged position of the Creoles of color deteriorated steadily after the Civil War and the abolition of slavery, which suddenly created a large free colored population dominated by rough, poor, uneducated blacks. The Creoles were gradually eased out of their prominent position in business, the professions, and local politics and increasingly had to turn to the trades—and music—to make a living.

The Creoles responded to the new situation by trying to wall themselves off from the blacks. But their attempts to maintain a separate and superior social status received a devastating blow in 1890, when the Louisiana state legislature passed Act 111, a law "to promote the comfort of passengers on railway trains" by requiring separate train cars for the white and colored races. Anyone with any trace of African blood was now officially considered colored and treated accordingly.

It was the opening wedge of a series of Jim Crow laws that soon spread through the other Southern states and eventually extended segregation to every kind of public facility from schools, restaurants, and theaters to toilets, drinking fountains, and graveyards. Foreseeing the danger of Act 111 as a precedent for systematic, state-sponsored discrimination against them, the New Orleans Creole community decided to challenge the law before the courts.

Now that I understood the historical background, I was ready to delve into the legal aspects of the Plessy case. Again at my father's suggestion, I went to see Judge John Minor Wisdom, a well-known liberal jurist and then head of the U.S. Fifth Circuit Court of Appeals in New Orleans. Wisdom's chambers were in a big, white, neocolonial court building on Royal Street, just a few blocks away from Preservation Hall.

Judge Wisdom, it turned out, was fascinated with the Plessy case and had collected all sorts of documents about it. He told me that

Plessy and the other members of the Creole citizens' committee were right to fear the new law, because it sealed the process of returning power to the former slave owners after the end of Reconstruction. "*Plessy v. Ferguson*," he said, "was all part of this great surge back to the establishment in the South of the whites as the dominant race."

Wisdom lent me a stack of books, articles, and documents relating to the case. Among these treasures was a French-language pamphlet called *Nos Hommes et Notre Histoire*, by a certain R. L. Desdunes. It recounted the history of the Louisiana Creoles and, in particular, the story of their legal challenge. The *comité des citoyens*, I learned, included relatives of many of the Creole musicians. Among them were famous jazz names like Piron, Bocage, Baquet, and Desdunes. The pamphlet also contained biographies of Creole writers, poets, artists, classical musicians, and opera singers. It was increasingly clear that the music and the Plessy case were all part of the same history.

From the Desdunes pamphlet and the other documents Judge Wisdom lent me, I learned that the citizens' committee had hired a passionate and colorful lawyer from upstate New York named Albion W. Tourgée. A chunky, one-eyed Union army veteran, failed novelist, and former carpetbagger judge in North Carolina, Tourgée deeply believed in equal rights and was embittered over the betrayal of the blacks after the Civil War. His arguments before the Supreme Court were brilliant, and went right to the heart of the case: the real goal of segregation was not to "promote comfort," as the Louisiana law put it, but to subjugate the Negro population and deprive them of their civil rights. Separation, he insisted, was inherently unequal. "Justice is pictured as blind," he declared, "and her daughter, the law, ought at least to be color blind." Tourgée was right, of course, and when the court reversed itself in

1954, Chief Justice Earl Warren's decision was couched in almost identical terms.

The irony was that Tourgée was trying to protect the rights of all African-Americans. But the committee of Creoles who had organized the legal challenge and paid his bills had a different motivation: they didn't want to be thrown into the Jim Crow car with the dark-skinned ex-slaves. They themselves were anything but "color blind." They were in fact fighting for a kind of segregation—the right to maintain their own separate social status. They lost that fight and were forced to cohabit, despite their own prejudice and pride, with the darker, rougher population. But in cultural terms, there was one positive result of all this: it mingled the Creoles' refined European musical tradition with the more visceral, rhythmic, and emotional approach of the blacks. And that was a powerful catalyst for the birth of New Orleans jazz.

I didn't get into the jazz history in my high school research paper on *Plessy v. Ferguson*. But what I learned about the Creoles and their history helped me understand a lot about the complex world of the mens. I had a better idea now why the proud Creole trumpet player Peter Bocage had such a precise, almost polite, style of playing—and why he always insisted on pulling out his violin in the Hall. (When Sandy Jaffe once asked him to play more trumpet and less violin, he snapped back, "Who do you think knows more about jazz, young lady, you or me?") I realized why Louis Cottrell had such a clean, fluid technique and elegant harmonies, why George Lewis still fumed over the Creole dance halls that wouldn't admit him because he didn't have "silky hair." And why George Guesnon always insisted on being called "Creole George." History was present in every note, every word, every glance exchanged on the bandstand.

CHAPTER TWENTY-FOUR

Unable to draw my attention away from jazz, my girlfriend began to attack it with all the power of her superior intellect and the fury of her troubled soul. She was aided in this by ten years of piano lessons and the fact that her real father, whom she idolized but rarely saw, played first violin in a symphony orchestra up North. Few people her age, certainly in New Orleans, could boast such a classical music culture.

"You realize, of course, that all your jazz stuff is retrograde music," she said. "It's like some dusty museum display. Old music for old men."

"Old music? If you want to talk about old music look at Beethoven and Mozart."

"*You* should look at Beethoven and Mozart. It would do you a lot of good. If you really want to impress me with your stupid clarinet, why don't you learn the Mozart concerto? Sorry, I forgot, you can't read music."

I knew Cathy was trying to hurt me. She was in one of her aggressive moods and there was no point trying to reason with her. But I did. "Beethoven and Mozart are great, but they represent a totally different time and culture. Jazz is twentieth-century music, and the guys I'm learning from practically invented it. It's living, moving, real."

"Ha! When your old men were inventing jazz, Debussy, Satie, and Poulenc were pushing back the boundaries and rewriting all the rules. That's the real twentieth-century music."

I didn't have the arms or ammunition to fight her on that turf. "Look, this isn't classical music. It's folk music. It's primitive, instinctive, spontaneous, like a conversation."

"Conversation?"

"Just listen to it. There are all these different voices that speak and answer one another. The trumpet plays the melody, the clarinet answers with harmonies and fill-ins, the trombone chimes in with counterpoints and bass lines, the piano adds the chords, the drums keep the time. There are six or seven voices, but one conversation. They're all playing together, listening to one another, answering one another."

"Call it whatever you want, that music still depresses me. It's whiny and emotional, and guts-out. Especially those treacly hymns and blues you're always practicing. It's a real bummer. It all reeks of death."

"Yeah, you're right. There is sadness in it. There's also love, compassion, exuberance, humor, and fun. But there's no point analyzing it. Either you feel it or you don't. I guess you don't."

Cathy was so stung by the suggestion that she couldn't feel anything—and so competitive by nature—that she finally decided to take up the clarinet herself. I was delighted that she seemed at last to share my interest in jazz. But it wasn't that. She just wanted to become better than me on the clarinet. It was a kind of revenge. So I lent her Sammy's old horn and showed her some basic fingerings. Then she began practicing obsessively in her basement room at home.

For a long time she refused to play for me. One day, shortly before our graduation, she did agree to play a tune. It was "Closer Walk with Thee," just the melody with no embellishment, no vibrato, no "guts." But she got around the horn nicely and had somehow discovered an alternate way of making a C-sharp. (I took note of her unorthodox fingering and have used it ever since.)

I let Cathy keep the clarinet, but sensed that I would never see her or the horn again once we graduated and went to separate colleges. Several years later, after she had married and divorced one of my old high school rivals, she showed up at my mother's office in the Tulane library and dropped off a package for me. It was Sammy's clarinet.

CHAPTER TWENTY-FIVE

I didn't know what to make of Danny Barker when he showed up in New Orleans in 1965. A guitarist and banjo player with strong opinions and a sharp tongue, he was one of the many local musicians who had gone North years earlier and somehow he didn't seem to fit in with the mens anymore. He had toured for years with the Cab Calloway band, recorded in New York with Louis Armstrong, played with big jazz stars like Benny Carter and Clark Terry, and lived the fast-paced life of the Harlem jazzman. Danny finally got tired of life on the road and moved back home, where he'd been offered a job as assistant curator of the New Orleans Jazz Museum. But he arrived with some trepidation. "New Orleans is a place where, if you leave here, don't come back," he told me some years later. "If you do, it looks like you couldn't make it."

Danny hit town with a huge chip on his shoulder, trying to prove that he was superior to all the "hamfat" local musicians because he'd played with famous bands up North. He even looked different from the other players I knew, with his shiny-black conked toupee and his dapper, pencil-thin mustache. He had a glib speaking style that was more Harlem hip than down-home New Orleans. I instinctively disliked him at first.

But Danny's attitude finally mellowed. He never claimed to be a virtuoso musician. "I'm just a journeyman rhythm guitarist," he said. But he was one of the world's great time-keepers. And nobody cut him as a raconteur. He was a natural comedian who could

break up a house with his nonstop jive and his hilarious compositions like "Don't You Feel My Leg" and "Save the Bones for Henry
Jones."

The lyrics to most of Danny's songs were heavy with sexual in-
nuendo. And he was said to have more than verbal talents in that
domain. When I met the trumpeter Buck Clayton in New York
some years later, he told me to give his regards to "the Stallion"
when I got back home. "You don't know who the Stallion is?" he
laughed. "That's Danny Barker, man. That's his nickname—and
it ain't got nothin' to do with horses."

In the end, Danny's hometown roots proved stronger than his
Harlem sophistication. He got active in his community and did a
great service to the music by organizing a brass band for the kids at
his Fairview Baptist Church in an attempt to put the younger
generation—including future stars like Wynton Marsalis and Leroy
Jones—in touch with their jazz heritage. He was also a rich re-
pository of anecdotes about the early days of jazz and finally put
them into a highly entertaining autobiography, *A Life in Jazz.*

Perhaps because of his broad experience of the world, Danny
could look on New Orleans culture and society with a shrewd and
critical eye. "I'm a Capricorn," he said. "Like a goat, I look around
and try to figure out why."

I knew Danny thought and talked a lot about his life as a musician, so I asked if I could drop by for a chat. He agreed, and invited me out to his house at 1514 Sere Street, between City Park
and the Industrial Canal, where he lived in a one-story white bungalow with his blues-singing wife, "Blue Lu." The tiny house was
jammed with Danny's instruments, manuscripts, and momentos,
and Blue Lu was ailing, so we sat out on his screened-in front porch
and talked over the drone of a lawn mower. I took it as a sign that

times had gotten better for musicians when they could pay someone else to cut their grass.

Danny agreed. "Yeah, Tommy," he said, "this is a wonderful
town. Musicians are starting to be able to make a living with their
talent. Folks are starting to give you money. In this city, the potential has no end to it. Here you have a million people raised with
the habit to celebrate. Ain't no curfew here. Most people, when
they give parties, they go on till six o'clock in the a.m. Ain't no
good-time, get-down city in the world like New Orleans. In this
town, folks even throw a party for the dog's birthday. Somebody
goin' to jail? Give 'em a party. Somebody died? Give 'em a party.
This is the only city in the world where they bury a person with a
brass band."

Danny needed little prodding to share his views on race. He'd
had plenty of time to think and talk about it with fellow bands-
men in his years on the road. One of the reasons he had decided
to return to New Orleans, he said, was that race relations had
become so hostile in the North in the 1960s that he figured he
might as well go back South where at least the people were "less
hypocritical" about discrimination.

"From my perspective as a black man," he told me, "I learned to
go with social scenes everywhere I've been. I learned from my
grandfather years ago, let the bear sleep, don't shake him. That's
my philosophy. When I was growing up, my family insistently
demanded of us to stay out of trouble. 'What don't concern you,
leave it alone,' they'd say. 'Go on about your business.' Or they'd
tell us, 'That's white folks' business. You don't want to get involved
in that.'"

That lesson was hammered into Danny's head from his first day
of school at a private establishment run by a multilingual black

scholar and former seminary student named Medard Nelson. "Professor Nelson would tell us, 'Those people—the whites—they control everything. You have to calculate your ideas to keep them to a certain level. Don't have too much ambition. You must use special tactics. You shouldn't be overaggressive.' You know, we couldn't even play in this school. They didn't want the noise to annoy white neighbors. At 3 p.m., Prof. Nelson would tell me, 'Master Barker, go home. Don't stop and wait for your friends.' He didn't want to attract attention to the school. There was a lot of fear among whites at that time about teaching blacks."

The only other musician I knew who talked so explicitly about race relations was George Guesnon. As it turned out, Guesnon was also a student in Prof. Nelson's school. "Yeah, Guesnon was in my class," said Danny. "He was a pretty boy. Smart aleck. He used to talk in class all the time with Emile Labat. The teacher didn't like that."

"Was Guesnon a good student?" I asked.

Danny smiled. "He talk too much."

Coming from the Danny Barker, that was almost a compliment. In fact, Barker and Guesnon were the most indefatigable talkers in the city. They were rival talkers and rival banjo players from the same part of town, and educated on the same school benches. But their takes on the race question were slightly different. Guesnon, with his Creole pride, had not heeded Prof. Nelson's warnings about not pushing too hard or seeming ambitious. But the harder Guesnon pushed—the more he talked about wanting more because he'd "done more"—the less "crumbs" he got.

Danny, like an old goat who had figured out the system, was shrewder at getting along by going along. In the end, he wound up with a nice sinecure at the jazz museum, lots of music jobs, and even a certain acclaim as a writer—exactly what Guesnon most aspired to be. And while Guesnon continued to issue dire warnings of race wars even after the Civil Rights Act was passed, Danny Barker had a rosier view of the future. "Things have gotten better," he told me. "They're getting better all the time. The more people get educated, the less friction you will have. New Orleans today is not the New Orleans of the 1920s. Black people pay taxes just like everybody else."

They also vote. Once the legal and extralegal impediments were removed, the city's black majority began to assert its political clout. Ever since Ernest "Dutch" Morial was elected mayor in 1978, New Orleans has had nothing but black mayors and mostly black police chiefs. That dramatic power shift hardly put an end to local corruption and crime—*au contraire*—but at least democracy was functioning as it was supposed to. Danny Barker lived to see that revolution; Guesnon did not. I wonder what the old Creole would have made of it?

CHAPTER TWENTY-SIX

The amazing thing about the mens is that they never gave up. Old, sick, down on their luck, they were always looking for the next gig, the next break. And when they got a chance to play again, they grabbed at it. None of them quit trying. I think that's one reason—along with his deep love of black folk culture—that my father was so enthralled with the whole scene around the Hall. He desperately wanted to believe in phoenix-like revivals and Hail Mary comebacks, so he rejoiced when he saw the old men pick themselves up and play again.

The musicians sensed this, and they reciprocated his affection and respect. As the bass player Joe Butler once told me, "Me and your daddy, we admires to be 'mongst one another." None of them, except maybe Guesnon, knew anything about his torment as a frustrated writer. To them, he was just Tom Sancton, a decent-hearted white man, an avid jazz fan, and a faithful friend who was there when they needed him. He was always helping them out—driving them home, taking them to the hospital, slipping them a few bucks when they were having hard times. They all knew they could count on him. One time, he even saved George Lewis's life.

It happened in the fall of 1965. My dad drove me across the river for a clarinet lesson. George's daughter Shirley came to the door in a panic. "Daddy's dyin'," she sobbed. "Daddy's dyin'."

We found George in his bedroom lying flat on his back and struggling to breathe. He was suffering from a severe asthma attack and could only talk in short spurts. Shirley showed my father to the phone so he could call for an ambulance, leaving me alone with George.

George gasped and wheezed and stared blankly at his young visitor. I wasn't sure he recognized me, but suddenly he whispered, "You the one now, Tommy. You the one. I had a good life. I made history."

We couldn't wait for the ambulance, so my father carried George out to our car and sped off in the direction of the Mississippi River Bridge. Shirley sat in the back seat, cradling George's ninety-nine pounds in her arms. "Oh, Daddy, don't die," she cried. "Don't leave me, Daddy, don't leave me."

When we finally pulled up at the emergency entrance to Touro Infirmary in uptown New Orleans, George was hardly breathing. I thought he might be dead, but the doctor revived him with an injection. "If you hadn't brought him in when you did," he told my dad, "I don't think he would have made it."

We visited George the next day and found him lying comfortably under crisp white sheets in a semiprivate room. He was looking quietly out of the window with his bony hands folded over the covers. The crisis seemed past.

No sooner had he greeted us than George started complaining about his treatment. A young resident had picked him up physically, held him upside down, and told him to cough in order to dislodge the phlegm and fluid that had built up in his lungs. George, a small man with a lot of pride, regarded this upending as a humiliation in front of the other patient in his room. He was still seething when he recounted this to us. "We ain't gonna do *that* again," he said.

The phone rang on his bedside table. George leaned over and picked it up. He muttered a few words, then hung up and lay back in bed with a big smile on his face. He told us he'd just won money on some prizefight he'd bet on.

George had always followed the fights. Boxers and jazzmen were the great folk heroes of the culture he grew up in. In George's youth, long before black men were allowed into other fields of professional sports and entertainment, the fighter and the musician had been regarded by their community with an almost reverential respect. George, with his slight frame and sensitive nature, had taken the musical path. His son, George Zeno, had become a boxer and for a time was a promising middleweight. But too many blows to the head had prematurely ended his career. My father once asked George if his son was a contender. "Not anymore," George said simply. "He been punched out."

Before we left him that day, George asked my father to keep his wallet for him until he got out of the hospital. "If I give it to Shirley," he said, "she'll go through this money like water." George scooped under his pillow, pulled the wallet out and handed it to my father. They were counting the bills together—some $200— when a photo fell out. It was a snapshot of a white woman dressed only in stockings and a slip, pulled down low on her breasts.

We instantly recognized the woman: it was the wife of a well-known jazz record producer from South Carolina. During one of George's later illnesses, she moved down to New Orleans on the pretext of overseeing his health care and never went home. She became his final companion. "Women came to George, and he took it as a matter of course," my father said. "No talk, no boasting. It was just a part of his life."

During all the years I knew George Lewis, he was in and out of hospitals, tottering at death's door one minute, back on the bandstand the next. He suffered from emphysema, the result of a lifetime of heavy smoking, which grew steadily worse as he aged. Now that he was well up in his sixties, he was starting to have heart problems, too. Any doctor would have said his prognosis was grim. But George kept blowing those shimmering notes through his horn, singing an old, plaintive song whose deepest roots were still planted in the black earth of Senegal.

He lived on intimate terms with death. On the night that Evan Thomas's lifeblood spattered all over his shirtfront, George had learned how sudden and violent the end could be. And his mother's gentle passing taught him how easily and painlessly the boundary could be crossed. And so he was serene in the face of his own mortality.

George never let up or took it easy. He had played hard all his life. Percy Humphrey told me that George would "wear me out" when they played all-night jitney dances together in the 1930s and '40s, calling one tune after another without a break—"that little man never did take down, didn't know nothin' but work." In the years that I knew George, I was amazed how little concession he made to his own failing health. Retirement was not an option for him.

Retirement wasn't an option for any of the mens as long as they could still play their instruments. The bassist Papa John Joseph was nearly three decades past retirement age when I met him, but he was still appearing regularly at the Hall.

Papa John was the oldest man I had ever seen. People said he was close to ninety, but no one seemed to know for sure. He was tall, slender, and straight as an arrow, with skin the color of a pecan-shell and impeccably trimmed white hair. He and his brother Nelson Joseph ran a barber shop on First Street, in the same block where the trumpeter Buddy Bolden, the mythical "first man of jazz," had lived before they carted him off to the insane asylum in 1907.

Born about the same time as Bolden, Papa John had played with him before the turn of the century. In fact, Bolden used to hang around Joseph's barbershop; in those pre-telephone days, it was the place he used for messages and rendezvous concerning his band jobs. The shop was still in business in the 1960s. Papa John had quit barbering by then, but he would still come there during the day and swap stories with the neighborhood regulars. Or rather listen to stories. He didn't talk much.

Papa John was one of the first men in New Orleans to play a saxophone. He had also played the clarinet and guitar in his youth, gigging around with his brother Willie in the red light district. But by the time I heard him in the Hall, he only played the bass. Blowing a horn took too much wind out of him.

He had another problem that made it hard for him to play reed instruments: a mule had kicked him in the face when he was little and fractured his jaw. There was still a big lump on the right side of his chin. I guess nobody had bothered to set the bones.

In spite of his age, there was nothing feeble about Papa John. He walked slowly but always with grace and dignity, and never used a cane. He would stand erect in the back corner of the Hall, pulling at the strings with a sinewy right arm. He always wore a white shirt with suspenders and sleeves rolled up to the elbow. Papa John rarely took a solo and never clowned around like some of the other musicians. But once in a while, he would pluck the strings with a kind of bouncy rhythm, giving just a hint of friskiness.

Between sets, Papa John never drank in the back courtyard with the others. He sat in the carriageway on the long wooden church pew that served as a bench, quietly watching the people come and go like a wise old village elder sitting on a log and observing the marketplace. There was something timeless about him.

Once a fan came up and showed Papa John a newspaper article that mentioned him. The old man stared at it for a moment, then handed the clipping to me. "Read it to me, son," he said. "I don't have my glasses." Another time someone asked him to autograph a record he had just purchased. "Oh, my hand still shakin' from the bass. I'm gonna let this young man sign my name for me." He never told me he couldn't read or write. A black man born in the South in the 1870s was not likely to have spent a lot of time in school.

Louisiana was still under Yankee occupation when Papa John was born. He told me proudly that his father was "the best blacksmith in St. James Parish" and that he had "fetched a high price" when he was young. "You know," he explained, "they used to sell fellas in them days."

My father often drove Papa John home after the Hall. It was quite a sight. Our little VW had a sunroof, and my dad put the bass in the back seat with the neck sticking up in the air. Papa John sat in the front and my mother and I squeezed into the back on either side of the instrument. Crowds would gather on St. Peter Street to watch while we loaded the bass into the beetle—but then it never took much to draw a crowd in the French Quarter.

Papa John lived in one of the endless rows of Depression-era brick housing projects on Simon Bolivar Avenue not far from Shakespeare Park, one of the city's biggest black playgrounds. Whenever we pulled up in front of his building, we'd see a comely young woman sitting in a rocking chair on the front porch waiting up for him. She always gave us a timid little nod. Papa John told us it was his "niece," but we found out later that it was his common-law wife. I thought it must be a platonic relationship, but Harold Dejan told me that the woman had once confided to him that Papa John was "a good man—and I mean a *good* man."

On December 31, 1964, Papa John helped ring in the New Year with Punch Miller's Bunch. The audience was in a festive mood, and called for an encore when the last set ended at 12:30. Punch stomped off a fast-tempo rendition of "The Saints." They played chorus after chorus, with solos all around, building the excitement up to a feverish climax.

As the audience whooped and shouted at the end, Papa John leaned over to the piano player Dolly Adams and whispered, "That last number just about did me in." Then he keeled over.

Papa John was dead when he hit the floor. The bewildered audience was quickly cleared out of the hall. The other musicians just sat on the bandstand looking at the old man while Dolly repeated over and over how it had happened. "And then he went down—boom—just like that." Nobody said it, but they all knew it could happen to any one of them. And it might not be the worst way to go.

Somebody called the police from the pay phone on the wall of the carriageway. But before they got there, my father ran over to Pat O'Brien's next door and came back with the photographer who made a living taking souvenir pictures of tourists. He gave the guy twenty bucks and asked him to shoot a picture of Papa John on the floor.

"What for?" the guy asked.

"Because this is history."

The photographer was about to shoot the picture, when my father suddenly held up his hands. "Wait a minute! Hold it! Hold it!"

He went and got Papa John's felt hat and coat off the wall rack behind the piano and carefully placed them on a chair next to the body. He stood the bass up behind him, "like the shield of a fallen warrior," he said. Then he gently turned Papa John's face so people could recognize him.

Dramatizing the death scene was a trick my father had learned as a reporter for the old *Item*. One photographer he worked with, Jerry Arnold, would even carry around a pair of shoes in the trunk of his car; every time he had to shoot some horrific automobile accident, he would throw the shoes down next to the victim as if they had been knocked off by the shock of the collision.

I later came upon that black and white photo in my dad's files. It is a strangely beautiful image. It captures the old man's serene dignity and nobility—and the finality of the last set. The most painful thing about it, though, is that it makes me think of that young woman waiting on the porch.

Papa John's death confronted me with a depressing reality: the old musicians I had come to know and love were starting to fall like ranks of soldiers under enemy fire. Already the list of departed friends was long: Chinee Foster, John Casimir, Kid Howard, Papa John. Others would follow all too soon. Before I was sixteen, I had marched in dozens of funerals for friends and unknowns, played hundreds of hymns and dirges along the mournful road from church to cemetery.

Those trips touched me with sadness, especially if the deceased was a musician I was close to. But the pageantry also filled me with a sense of something noble and exalted in the New Orleans way of sending off departed souls, first with lamentations, then with jazz.

"This is the only town in the world where funerals make people happy," Harold Dejan said while we were standing outside a church and waiting for a long-winded preacher to finish his eulogy. "That's the way it's supposed to be—it's like the Bible say, 'Cry when you born, rejoice when you die.' That's why we pick up the tempo comin' out the graveyard. That New Orleans music make *everybody* happy, man. I done seen some of the family make the damn limousine stop so they can jump out and dance."

But when the music stopped, the joy wore off. Especially for those musicians who had just bid one of their buddies farewell.

"You know, this music world is a funny thing," the pianist Sing Miller told me not long after Papa John died. "You take somebody you worked with every night, and you looked at 'em every night, and you're sittin' close to 'em—and then you don't see 'em no more. And the worst thing is when you got to grab that casket and bury 'em in that hole, man. That's where the *sad* part come in at—when you tote your brother to the cemetery. I mean them kind of things, you know, it makes you think, man. All the guys I used to like to play with, they gone. They gone."

"They must have a pretty good band up there in heaven," I said, trying to lighten the mood.

"Aw man, they got a *bunch* of bands. But we don't know where they at—heaven or hell." Sing chuckled a bit, then turned reflective again. "And when you singin' them hymns, man, make *hair* rise on your head. Then you got to come home, get your union book, scratch his name out. You say, 'Looka here, this one gone. That one gone. Can't call 'em no more.' Yeah, Tommy, that's where the sad part come in."

What a strange thing, and strangely beautiful, I thought, for youth to encounter old age and death and feel their haunting majesty. When I was in high school I came across a line by Thornton Wilder that summed up my feelings about all this: "There is a land of the living and a land of the dead and the bridge is love, the only survival, the only meaning."

CHAPTER TWENTY-SEVEN

Jazz alone did not fill all my summers. I always spent a couple of weeks visiting my mother's people in Jackson. My family would also spend a few days at my Uncle Julian's vacation house at Pass Christian, on the Gulf Coast, swimming and fishing and sailing a little single-mast Sunfish loaned to us by Beth's boyfriend and future husband, Brother Villeré.

My father had done a lot of sailing in his youth and taught me the basics, which didn't prevent me from capsizing the dinky fiberglass craft whenever I took it out with my sisters. The water was so shallow in the Mississippi Sound, though, that there was little danger of drowning. If you flipped your boat, you could practically walk it in to shore.

I once saw my dad do an amazing thing in that shallow water. We were out on the end of the pier crabbing, and something kept taking our bait. My father finally identified the culprit. "Sand shark," he said. "I'm going to catch that sucker before he eats all our chicken necks."

He went back to the house and returned with one of my uncle's deep-sea fishing rods and a heavy steel hook that looked about big enough to snag a whale. He skewered a whole chicken neck on it and dropped the hook near the crab nets.

Within minutes, the shark had grabbed the hook and began thrashing around furiously in the water. Daddy tried to reel it in, but the fish was too strong. Suddenly, he jumped into the waist-deep water.

"What are you doing?" I cried. "The shark's going to get you."

"He can't bite me with that hook in his mouth," my dad said, and waded toward the shore, pulling the enraged beast behind him.

I thought he was crazy. I ran along the splintery wooden pier toward the beach, some fifty yards away. There I waited and worried while my father slowly dragged the shark in.

Five minutes later, huffing and puffing, he pulled it up on the beach. It was about three feet long—small for a shark, but no less scary to look at with its rows of pointy, razor-sharp teeth. The hook had gone all the way through the left eye, and blood streamed down its side. The fearsome creature looked strangely beautiful, and fragile, with its streamlined form and smooth, glistening skin.

The shark flopped around on the beach, gasping for air. After a couple of minutes, its movements became less vigorous, and finally ceased altogether. As flies began to buzz around the fresh carcass, my father silently contemplated his catch. Then he sighed, "Now, why did I do that?"

The shark was not edible, except by the flies that swarmed around it and the fiddler crabs that attacked its soft, white belly with their stubby claws.

But we did eat a lot of other things we caught on the coast: perch, catfish, and blue-claw crabs, along with the shrimp and minnows that we trapped in a ten-foot seine and dragged up on the beach. My dad had another trick: prying oysters off the big drainage pipes that jutted out into the water and disgorged their contents some twenty yards offshore. I wasn't sure how sanitary that was, but Daddy fried them over a driftwood fire right on the beach and said the boiling oil would kill whatever germs they might be carrying. He always seemed to know what he was doing.

I'm not sure Mother would have approved of the drainage-pipe oysters, but she was busy painting watercolors on the beach and paid no attention to our fishing methods. Neither did my sisters. They preferred the swimming pool at my uncle's place, and spent most of their time hanging out with the local boys in nearby Bay St. Louis.

Nothing lasts forever, though. One day Uncle Julian told my parents he'd prefer for us to rent his place rather than just ask for the key. Mother was hurt and Daddy was furious, and that was the end of our Pass Christian idylls. Anyway, the house blew down in Hurricane Camille a few years later.

Apart from those Gulf Coast interludes, we almost never took family vacation trips. My father did drive us all to Destin, Florida, one time. But the gas, hamburgers, and motel bills proved too expensive, so we drove back the next day with my sisters and me bitching all the way about the powder-white beaches and turquoise water we'd left behind. My dad always financed everything on a shoestring. "Never enough, but always just enough," was his motto. I still have a souvenir I bought in Destin: a cedar box with a re-production of *The Last Supper* on the lid, dedicated, I suppose, to the one and only meal we had there.

One trip I took every summer was to Camp Hardtner, an Epis-copal Church retreat in north Louisiana. It was sort of an ecclesias-tical version of my dad's beloved Camp Salmen. Apart from the morning Communion service, though, there wasn't anything very religious about it. Even the counselors told dirty jokes—and the priests topped them. One of the young women counselors had enor-mous breasts and wore a red bikini at the pool and we all fantasized about her in our bunks at night. And the used condoms we some-times found in the woods suggested that the male and female coun-selors were up to something other than sanctification after lights-out.

My first summer there, I was so reluctant to part with my music, even temporarily, that I lugged along a huge reel-to-reel tape recorder and a dozen tapes. I also took my clarinet, and practiced in the woods during my free time. My cabin mates didn't care much for my jazz tapes, but they dug the Beatles, the Animals, and the Rolling Stones that I had also brought along.

My counselor asked me if I would play my clarinet on "amateur night." I told him I couldn't do that. "I'm a professional. I belong to the Musicians' Union."

"Don't be an asshole, Sancton," he snapped. "This is a summer camp, not Carnegie Hall."

One night in August 1964 we were listening to the radio just before lights-out. A news bulletin announced that a North Vietnamese torpedo boat had attacked a U.S. naval ship in a place called the Tonkin Gulf. We had no way to know it then, but that incident would have a major effect on all our lives. It transformed a so-called police action into a full-scale war that sent half a million troops to Vietnam, spawned a generation-devouring antiwar movement, and killed fifty thousand American boys. Among the future victims were some of the young campers who shared the cabin with me that night.

The Vietnam War would become the curse and the obsession of my generation. As much as I might like to take shelter in my music, and in the reassuring routines of high school, the steady drumbeat of news and the brutal TV images from Southeast Asia made it clear that I could not isolate myself from the bigger, uglier world out there. I dreaded the approach of my eighteenth birthday, when I would have to register for the draft. I knew that going to college would give me a student deferment, but after that? Would Tommy Sancton trade in his clarinet for an M-16 and die in a rice paddy? Who would play the dirges for me in that godforsaken corner of the world?

CHAPTER TWENTY-EIGHT

My father took the lead in our Preservation Hall expeditions, but
Mother was very much present. Of course, she was no more of a
musician than my father, even though she would play fragments
of a childhood recital piece, "On the Ice at Sweet Briar," any time
she got near a piano. She also had Dede's banjo repaired after he
died and took a few lessons on it. But she had little ear for music.
When she tried to hum the melody of "Burgundy Street Blues," it
came out sounding like "There She Is, Miss America," as sung by
Bert Parks.

Mother loved all the musicians, and they got a kick out of her
Mississippi accent and her jokes. Sandy Jaffe thought she was hys-
terically funny. She'd break into a big smile as soon as my mother
walked through the gate. Mother had an amazing gift for talking
to anyone on their own wavelength. She could chat with a visiting
English aristocrat one minute and Jim Robinson the next, and
never miss a beat.

Were my sisters jealous of all the hours I spent with our parents at
the Hall? I didn't think so at the time. But Beth told me many years
later that they had "hated" me for it. Not because we went to the
Hall and hung out with a bunch of old black musicians, but because
I got all the attention from my parents and they felt neglected.

It's funny how something that seems so clear in retrospect did
not even cross my mind in those days. I thought my sisters just
preferred to be off in their own world. They spent all their free

time out on dates or hanging around Valencia, the teenage social club they belonged to. In fact, they got pretty wild, getting drunk and sometimes staying out all night, which sent Daddy into angry tirades. Once he grabbed a pair of scissors and cut off Beth's painted fingernails—he called them "needle nails"—in a fit of rage. He even plunged her head under water in the bathtub to wash off the spray-net, shouting, "Don't grow up! Don't grow up!"

What my father called their "wildness," though, might look to a psychologist like a classic call for help. I must admit my sisters didn't get much adult supervision. Mother went to work at the library when they were young teenagers, so she wasn't at home much during the day. And when our father was not meeting with his P.R. clients or wandering around the French Quarter, he was locked in his room typing, moving files around, or whatever. If ever anyone asked when he planned to publish something, he'd say, "How can I be expected to finish a book when I'm always having to deal with my kids' crises?"

That's a big word for the kind of routine problems most teenage kids have. The only real crisis involved Beth. She was madly in love with the son of one of the old-line families, a hot-blooded, impetuous boy who was fascinated with fast cars. Well, they jumped the gun, as Mother put it, and got married. She was seventeen, he was nineteen. Six months later, the boy crashed his car in a south Louisiana canefield, leaving Beth a widow and soon-to-be single mother.

I guess you'd have to call that a crisis, but Daddy couldn't do anything to "save" Beth from it. She's a tough girl. She saved herself. She inherited a little coal business, ran it well, made some shrewd real-estate investments, and put together a small fortune. In fact, my father could have learned a lot from her about how to pick up the pieces and move on. But maybe he did the best he could.

When he wasn't "saving" us, it seems he was saving everybody else in town. He was always going out of his way to help other people—perfect strangers, most of the time. He once brought an ex-convict home for a meal because the guy had expressed an interest in writing and my dad wanted to encourage him. When one of his fellow *Item* reporters had a nervous breakdown and spent a couple of weeks in a mental hospital, my dad volunteered to look after his three-year-old son (the burden of which, of course, fell on my mother). Another time, he brought home a Hungarian refugee he had interviewed for the newspaper, a former art dealer who had fled after the 1956 revolution with nothing to his name but a few paintings. Of course, my father bought one "to help him out," even though he could hardly afford to fill the refrigerator. The canvas depicted a European circus. It later burned up in a fire.

It all reminded me of that Tennessee Williams line about the "kindness of strangers." They practically had to be strangers, since he had so few real friends. He kept in touch with a couple of guys from his newspaper days—Phil Johnson and Jerry St. Pé, two younger men who had looked up to him as the *Item*'s ace reporter and still revered him. But he had long since burned his bridges with most of his contemporaries. In fact, he lived pretty much like a recluse in these years, and he wouldn't be caught dead in a fancy New Orleans restaurant for fear of being recognized and scorned by his former Tulane classmates or fraternity brothers. For as much as he might scoff at the trappings of bourgeois society, deep down he craved the respectability that had eluded him.

Apart from Phil and Jerry, his only real friends were the mens and the people who hung around Preservation Hall—safely nonestablishment types like Larry Borenstein and Allan Jaffe. And that suited him just fine.

CHAPTER TWENTY-NINE

My father had a complex relationship with Larry Borenstein. Deep down, they genuinely liked one another. Daddy was fascinated by Larry's wheeling and dealing, his acid wit, his relentless pursuit of his objectives. Larry probably saw my dad as a rare and curious bird—a southern liberal, a dreamy writer and romantic, but also a shrewd observer of the New Orleans scene who knew where a lot of skeletons were buried and had access to the press, all of which could be useful to him. And of course, both men shared a deep respect for the music and the culture of the mens. Yet they were forever going at one another in verbal sparring contests that Larry often won by the quickness of his tongue—but not always.

They almost came to blows over the Vincent Price incident. My father had breezed into Larry's shop on Royal Street one afternoon and found him sitting in front of a canvas next to a gaunt, sinister-looking man with a mustache and an affected English accent. Larry was in the middle of a big sale, and did not want to be distracted at this critical moment. But he nodded in my dad's direction and introduced him to Vincent Price, star of countless horror movies and a noted art collector.

My father, trying to be pleasant, told Price, "Oh yes, I've read about your art collection, it gets a lot of attention." For some reason, he could not stop there. He added: "Edward G. Robinson's collection gets a lot of attention, too."

He had unwittingly blundered into the killing field that can exist between two vain character actors—and rival art collectors. Price glared at him like Dracula preparing to draw blood. Larry gave him the cold stare of a commissar who has just made the silent decision to starve a province. Sensing that further conversation was pointless, my father said a quick good-bye and left the shop.

That night at the Hall Larry was livid. "Tom, you blew the deal," he said, choking and sputtering in exasperation. "You blew the deal. He walked out on me." Had my father not been an ignorant fool, Larry informed him, he would have known that Vincent Price and Edward G. Robinson hated each other, and it was all about their competing art collections. "I could have killed you."

Fortunately, they had their better moments. Shared jokes, easy banter, and serious conversations about music, art, politics, and business. And Larry even showed a magnanimous side on occasion. At one critical moment, he fixed my dad up with free office space.

My father had quit his Heart Fund job to join an advertising agency run by some high-society guy he'd known in college. With his patent lack of team-player skills, and his erratic work habits, he soon ran afoul of the boss and walked out in search of his own P.R. clients. He had no place to hang his shingle, so Larry lent him an apartment he owned on Toulouse Street to use as a temporary office.

This was not philanthropy on Borenstein's part; he was investing in a relationship that he thought might help him where he had no clout—with the middle-class establishment of New Orleans. It was in fact a rather poor investment, considering my father's radical past and his personal scorn for all things bourgeois.

Larry was no bourgeois, but he was a man of means. He owned a lot of French Quarter property and was always on the lookout for promising new acquisitions. There was one particular building, a dilapidated old mansion near Preservation Hall, that he had his eye on for a long time. But it hung by a thread—the life of a little old woman who lived there and, it seemed to Larry, just would not die.

Louisiana was still governed by the Napoleonic Code, according to which the building was divided equally among six heirs. Larry went to each of the heirs with an assignment contract and a cash offer representing only a fraction of what the place was really worth.

Five heirs signed. The sixth, the old lady who lived there, was now isolated and helpless. She finally moved out and relinquished her share for a pittance. But just before leaving, she got a voodoo priest to put a pierced rag doll in the dusty, deserted master bedroom. When Larry came in to inspect his new domain, he found the doll and ran out of the building. He was quite upset and told my father about the gris-gris he had found.

"What are you going to do?" my father asked.

"For one thing, not touch the doll. If I do, I'm cursed."

But Larry Borenstein was not a man to be deprived of his property rights, curse or no curse. For a fee of five dollars, he hired another voodoo priest to pour a reversing powder on the doll and carry it off in his anti-voodoo shroud.

Larry later told my father what he had done.

"You really do believe in this stuff?"

"No," Larry shrugged. "But for five *dollars*?"

Larry had a paranoid side. He was convinced that the *Times-Picayune* had a special editor whose job it was to see that his name was broken and hyphenated every time it appeared in print. But not all the slights were imagined. My father saw Larry stewing about something in the carriageway one night and asked him what was wrong. Larry said some newspaper photographer had just called him a "fat, dirty little Jew."

"That's terrible," my father commiserated. "What did you say to that?"

Larry shrugged and turned his palms skyward. "What *could* I say?"

I never got directly involved in their exchanges, of course, but I observed this intense relationship from a front-row seat. At a time when most of my contemporaries were at home doing their school-work or watching "Leave It to Beaver" on TV, I was getting an accelerated course in adult social relations. Not to mention game theory. Coming on top of the musical and cultural education I was getting from the mens, all of this was shaping my worldview far more decisively than anything I learned in high school.

I always liked Larry, who made me laugh with his lightning one-liners and took a kindly interest in my music. In fact, it was Larry who helped me solve the problem of my untunable horn by selling me a beautiful matched pair of Buffet Albert system clarinets. (I had by this time returned the clarinet I'd borrowed from George Lewis.)

After I had forked over one hundred dollars—a modest price even in those days—he told me an astonishing secret: "I didn't want to say this until you had already bought the horns, Tommy, but they belonged to Lorenzo Tio, Jr." Tio was a legendary early player and the teacher of some of the city's greatest clarinetists, including Johnny Dodds and Sidney Bechet. Thanks to Larry Borenstein, I now had Tio's horns. It seemed to me like a sort of apostolic succession.

With Allan Jaffe, my dad had a warm, easygoing rapport. He felt sort of like an older brother to Jaffe, and Jaffe reciprocated. Allan was not much of a verbalizer, but I would sometimes hear him repeating things my father had said, like the idea that the old musicians were like heroes of *The Iliad* and *The Odyssey*. And one night my dad did what any guy would do when he saw his kid brother in trouble.

I was sitting with my parents in our usual corner seats when we heard a commotion outside in the street. My father jumped up and got to the front gate just in time to see some drunk break a hurricane glass over Jaffe's head. There were two or three other men with him. My father lunged at the glass-wielder and they tumbled together into the street. A few punches and curses were exchanged, then the guy got up and staggered away with his friends.

I thought my father was a hero that night. But he said it was foolhardy, something he did on old schoolyard impulses without thinking. "I'm just glad it ended before somebody got stabbed or shot," he said, "and we all wound up in the *Times-Picayune*—or the morgue—tomorrow morning." But I think that, deep down, he was proud that he had leapt to Jaffe's defense. And so was I.

The relationship with Sandy Jaffe was more complex. She could be effusive at one moment and give you an icy stare with those big blue eyes five minutes later. My father appreciated attractive women and always tried to charm them. But charm never got very far with Sandy. She had other priorities. She was fiercely protective of the Hall, the musicians, and the kitty basket that fed them all. And once she bore two sons, Russell and Benjamin, they of course shot to the top of the priority list.

Unlike her calm and unflappable husband, Sandy had an impetuous side. When the George Lewis band was about to embark on his big tour of Japan in 1963, my father contacted an old colleague at *Life* magazine to suggest photo coverage of this "historic event." The editor went for the idea and sent a crack team lead by Larry Burrows, a star photojournalist who was later killed in Vietnam. My father was ecstatic: this would be a huge P.R. coup for George, the Hall, and the Jaffes, who accompanied the band.

Shortly after they got back from Japan, my father asked Sandy how things had gone with the *Life* photographers. Sandy sort of giggled and said, "It didn't work out. They were trying to take over everything, telling the band what to do and where to stand, so I finally kicked them off the bus."

"You kicked them off the bus? Where?"

"On the highway between Tokyo and Osaka. I just told them to get off, and they did."

My dad was incredulous. Not only had his hope for a publicity coup gone up in smoke; Sandy had unwittingly burned up his last chit with his old friends back at *Life*.

Noel Rockmore was too much of a narcissist to offer true friendship to anyone, but my father found him intriguing. Larry Borenstein had met this promising young artist in New York in the early 1960s and commissioned him to paint a series of portraits of the old musicians. Larry set Rockmore up with a garret and a studio in exchange for the exclusive rights to sell his paintings. The artist jumped at the chance to escape the pressures of the New York art scene and work in what he called the "creative obscurity" of the French Quarter.

Endowed with a boundless ego, Rockmore claimed to be one of the world's greatest living painters. "Picasso hates me," he said. "He hates me because he fears me." He was no Picasso, of course, but he had a unique style. His portraits captured the essence of a personality—the brooding, seething soul behind the face. There was something noble, tragic, and profoundly human about his Preservation Hall portraits. But they weren't to everyone's taste. Dr. Edmond Souchon, a local obstetrician and Dixieland guitar-strummer, found them too gloomy. "I always thought jazz was supposed to be full of life," he told Rockmore. "These people look like they're already dead." Rockmore glared at him stone-faced and snapped, "That's the way I see them."

My father, happily immersed in this bohemian phase of his life, took an interest in Rockmore and used to bring me down to his studio to watch him paint. Sometimes he would put down his brush and pick up his classical guitar, which he played very well. And he talked about all sorts of things, from Marx and Freud to Bauhaus architecture and zen Buddhism. During one of these sessions, Rockmore did a lugubrious pen-and-ink portrait of my father, emphasizing the dark circles under his eyes and the lines on his forehead. He signed it, "For Tom, with condolences."

I think Rockmore recognized a sort of fellow traveler in my dad—a writer and intellectual who had lived in New York and had some affinity with his world. And my father, who after all had written a novel about the egotism and eccentricity of a self-proclaimed artist—the zany, roller-skating Count Casimir—found a fascinating case study in this half-mad painter.

I didn't much like Rockmore myself. I was a little jealous of the attention my dad gave him, and hated the fact that Sally had found him "interesting."

Every night Rockmore would be at the Hall, silently scrutinizing the scene with his intense black eyes. He was a short man, built like a jockey, with raven-black hair, a marble-hard face, a deep voice, and an overload of testosterone. For if there was one thing

Noel Rockmore loved more than painting, it was women. And women loved him.

Borenstein was fascinated by his protégé's phenomenal success as a modern-day Casanova. "It's a kind of universal genius," he told my father. "I've seen him in New York just walk women off the street and into his bed." Rockmore himself once acknowledged his obsession to my dad: "I've got a gland problem."

Indeed, it sometimes seemed like there was no boundary between Rockmore's paintbrush and his penis. They were the twin focal points of his universe. He even painted a nude portrait of himself standing next to a canvas with a brush in his hand and all God gave him dangling proudly from his groin.

A woman walked into Larry's shop, where the painting was on display, and exclaimed, "My God! Who's the hung painter?" Larry told her it was Noel Rockmore. She immediately left the shop and went looking for him.

My blood ran cold one night when I saw him put the moves on Sally just before she left for San Francisco. He was standing in the carriageway, doing a quick oil sketch on a small canvas. Sally was standing next to him, watching the image take shape. Suddenly his brush touched her blouse and left a big splotch of paint right over her breast.

"Sorry," he said, with an impish grin. "Let me take you up to my studio. I'll get that off with White Spirit."

To my horror, she followed him up the rickety steps that led to his garret studio—and bedroom. I almost died thinking of what he might be doing to the object of my amorous fantasies.

When she came down twenty minutes later, the paint was gone from her breast. She was all red and flustered. I didn't dare ask what had happened. But when Rockmore reappeared in the carriageway, I overheard him telling Larry that Sally was the "coldest woman" he'd ever met. I was reassured.

Rockmore never became the great painter he always imagined he was. He acquired a certain local following, but no national success. Eventually, the obscurity got the better of the creativity. As he drank and womanized himself into decadent marginality, French Quarter wits started calling him "Rockbottom."

CHAPTER THIRTY

While I was exploring the jazz world, my cousin Claudia was moving in the city's upper social circles. She was a sorority girl at Newcomb College, a maid of honor in some of the top carnival balls, and the fiancée of a boy from a prominent New Orleans family—a match-up that Uncle Buck had eagerly encouraged. Like my uncle, Peter was a good-hearted guy who liked to party and drink hard. In fact, that seemed to be his main activity at Tulane University, where he was an active member of the Delta Kappa Epsilon fraternity, better known as the "animal house."

Partying to the music of black jazz bands was a time-honored tradition among the fraternity crowd Peter ran with, and he was often asked to organize the music for their boozy bashes. He got a kick out of the fact that Claudia's little cousin could play jazz alongside the old men—kind of like a young white hope—and would sometimes invite me to sit in with the bands he hired. That was how I found myself one night on a paddle-wheeler in the middle of the Mississippi River with six black musicians and a boatload of drunken Dekes.

The band, led by banjoist Papa French, was the successor to Celestin's famous Tuxedo Orchestra, one of the oldest groups in town. I pulled up a chair next to Joe "Cornbread" Thomas, the band's toothless clarinet player, and had a ball playing along on Celestin's old numbers, like "Marie Laveau," "Eh La Bas," and

"South." But as the night progressed, and the drinking got wilder, the South began to get the upper hand.

With a huge Confederate flag draped behind the bandstand, the partygoers started whooping rebel yells and shouting things like "Forget Hell!" and "The South's Gonna Rise Again!" Finally, they made the band play and *sing* "Dixie," which blacks consider the national anthem of slavery and segregation. The band members went along with all this. But I could see in their faces, and in the silent glances they shot one another, that this situation made them uncomfortable.

We docked just as the last set ended, and the musicians quickly packed up and left. I stayed around waiting for Claudia and Peter to give me a ride home.

As I sat alone on the bandstand packing up my horn, a tall guy with a clip-on black bow tie staggered over to me.

"Say, how come a white boy like you can play as good as the niggers?"

"Practice," I said curtly.

"You must practice a lot, my boy, 'cause you play pretty good."

"I know."

He looked at me silently for a moment, swaying unsteadily on his feet as he weighed my words. "But you know something?" he said finally. "Your talent is surpassed only by your arrogance."

"I'm not arrogant," I said. "I'm angry."

"Angry at what? You didn't get enough to drink? Hey, give this man a beer!"

"No, I'm angry that I had to sit here and watch you guys insult my friends."

"What friends?"

"The band members. You made them sing 'Dixie' in front of a rebel flag."

"And you think there's some kind of, uh, ramification in that?"

"It's no ramification. It's an insult to the humanity and dignity of those old men."

"Hell, boy, what side are you on anyway? They're just a bunch of niggers."

I never held that outrage against Claudia and Peter, neither of whom ever spoke that way in my presence. In fact, I later put together some of my own groups for Peter's parties, using foreign musicians and occasionally Punch Miller and the one-legged trombonist Eddie Summers. But the riverboat incident said a lot about the attitudes of white middle-class New Orleans—at least in those days—toward the music and the mens.

That lesson was reinforced the night I joined Valencia, the social club that Claudia and my sisters had lobbied to get me into. It was really a mini–country club for overprivileged teenagers, complete with swimming pool, billiard tables, and a big ballroom. Their dances usually featured local rock 'n' roll bands. But when I arrived for the new members' dance, I was amazed—and delighted—to see Sweet Emma's Bell Boys up on the bandstand.

The other club members were not so pleased to see a bunch of old blacks in place of their regular rock groups. As Emma and her boys—including the Humphrey brothers and Jim Robinson—did their best to entertain them, some of the snobbish youths began stomping their feet on the dance floor in an attempt to drown out the band. The club's organizers finally calmed the protesters, but not before they had humiliated the band—and reminded me once again of the gap between my two worlds.

After the dance ended, I approached the clarinetist, Willie Humphrey, as he was packing up.

"Hi, Willie," I said. "I sure was happy to see the band here tonight."

He looked surprised to see me there. "Hello, Tommy," he said. "You belong to this club?"

"I just joined. This was the new members' dance."

"Un-huh." Willie buttoned up his jacket and checked his watch. Then he lowered his voice and said: "You know, Tommy, I live just a few blocks from here, and I been playing at this place for many years. These society people always respected our music. But look like something got into the younger generation. I guess we too old-fashioned for 'em."

Maybe Willie was right. His remark made me feel very lonely. But there was at least one other new member who had dug their music that night: Quint Davis. The son of a prominent local architect, Quint briefly tried his hand at the drums, and even showed up for a couple of Punch Miller's jam sessions. But he soon abandoned the drums and started playing tambourine and dancing à la Mick Jagger with a local rock band. Some years later, he was taken under the wing of the famous music impresario George Wein and reemerged as the producer of the New Orleans Jazz and Heritage Festival. Together, they turned the event into one of the most successful jazz festivals in history.

CHAPTER THIRTY-ONE

I eventually got over the fright Sweet Emma had given me the first time I walked into Preservation Hall. But I could never think of her as "sweet." Whenever anyone asked how she got that name, she would say it's because she was always nice to people and "just went along with the program." In fact, Emma Barrett always made up the program herself and if you didn't like it, that was tough.

She absolutely refused to fly, so whenever her band went on tour, they had to put her on the train a day early. A lifelong insomniac, Emma never slept in her own hotel room on the road, but insisted on curling up in a chair in somebody else's room. She would call Allan Jaffe in the middle of the night and chat for hours about her aches and pains or some imagined slight. She hated doctors, and if ever Jaffe brought one around her house when she was ailing, she would snap, "What are you doing here, you old sawbones? I ain't gonna croak."

Emma was a strange-looking woman, bordering on the grotesque, with jutting, snaggly teeth, and sagging lips. But in her youth, as a svelte, light-skinned girl with bright black eyes and high cheekbones, they say she had passed for a great beauty. She married Ricard Alexis, an outstanding trumpet player-turned-bassist, but they were long since divorced. Alexis died in 1960.

One of the rare "womens" among the mens, Emma never re-married. But rumor had it that Sammy Penn, Kid Thomas's cigar-chomping drummer, had a longstanding relationship with her.

People said he used to put rags over his license plates whenever he visited her house so nobody could trace the car back to him.

Emma was proud of the fact that her father, Captain W. B. Barrett, was a black volunteer in the Union Army during the Civil War and later served in the state senate during Reconstruction. She kept his yellowed newspaper obituary in her purse. It was at Capt. Barrett's insistence that Emma started taking piano lessons in the early years of the twentieth century. She learned the instrument so quickly that she landed a job with Papa Celestin's Tuxedo Orchestra at age twelve.

Emma left Celestin three years later and played with a variety of different groups until she organized her own band in the 1950s. Sweet Emma's group soon became one of the top bands in the city, and was one of the few regularly working units in town at the time Preservation Hall opened.

Allan Jaffe immediately recognized the show-business potential of this lively ensemble and took the band on tour. One of their first trips was to Memphis, Tennessee, right after the Civil Rights Act was passed in 1964. Memphis was in the heart of Jim Crow country, and Jaffe was determined to sign in the band as the first black guests at the King Cotton hotel. They were all standing on a fancy red carpet in the middle of the lobby while Jaffe went to the reception desk to sign the register. Emma was clutching a brown paper bag. All of a sudden, the bottom of the bag fell out and a dozen eggs splashed all over the carpet.

There was a reason for the eggs. Just as she didn't trust banks and doctors, Emma didn't trust room service or restaurants to provide her food. She wouldn't even eat Buster Holmes's red beans and hot sausage, which she disdained as "pee warmers." Her main diet seemed to consist of Sarah Lee pound cakes and soda crackers. She would send Jaffe's assistant, Chris Botsford, out to buy them between sets and consumed them right in front of the piano. Jaffe once found a dead mouse inside the instrument, apparently clubbed to death by a piano hammer as it nibbled on Emma's crumbs. Bill Russell felt bad for the mouse.

Emma, for her part, had no love of animals. Years earlier, her husband had bought a monkey that caused no end of trouble. "Ricard paid fifty dollars for him," she said. "He even had him christened and threw a big party. But that monkey was very devilish. He used to go out in people's yard, take all their clothes off the line, and drop 'em on the ground. He'd go in the kitchen and dump coffee grounds all over my stove. Then he'd get into the liquor and get drunk. I finally made Ricard get rid of that damn thing."

The monkey was hardly the only object of Emma's ire. In fact, there was no one she wouldn't snap at. She would throw water on people who tried to take her picture. Whenever fans at the Hall asked her age, she would snarl, "None of your damn business." When the French movie actor Alain Delon was introduced to Emma after a concert, she told him, "Who the hell are you? I never even *heard* of you."

Yet when Emma sat at the piano and started to play, you had to forgive her cussedness. For all her eccentricity, she was a star and an artist to the tips of her small but powerful fingers. Her chords were always impeccable and she was one of the great timekeepers. And Emma really knew how to drive a band. "I've always been strong, from a youngster coming up," she said. "Stronger than some men. And I always had plenty of nerve. Me, I'm cheeky."

She was also a wonderful vocalist, with a smoky contralto voice that could bring tears to your eyes on ballads like "Whenever You're Lonesome, Just Telephone Me" or gospel tunes like "A Closer Walk with Thee." When Sweet Emma sang, the melancholy soulfulness of her voice seemed to justify the nickname that was so at odds with her cranky personality.

Emma was a shrewd judge of musicianship. She knew who could play and who was faking it and wasn't afraid to tell you. And once you got past the initial snarls and dirty looks, she had good advice for young musicians trying to master the old style. "When you love something, you'll learn it," she said. "You've got to have the *feeling* for music and rhythm born in you. It's something you have to put your whole heart and soul in if you want to make a success. If you love music, you'll learn that horn."

But the greatest lesson Sweet Emma had for the rest of us was her courage. After a near-fatal stroke paralyzed the left side of her body in 1967, she came back in a wheelchair and played with just her right hand. She went on like that for years, sometimes appearing two and three nights a week, because music was her life and she still had it in her.

CHAPTER THIRTY-TWO

Suddenly Sally was back. My heart jumped into my throat when I saw her sitting alone in the carriageway. She was as lovely as ever, but there was a kind of sadness in her eyes. She looked like she had been crying. Then she told me her story.

"Just before I went to San Francisco, I met this guy," she said. "He was a young doctor at the medical center where I worked. We dated a while, then things started getting serious, too serious for me. So I told him I wanted some time to think things over. That's one of the reasons I went out to San Francisco."

But the young doctor didn't give up easily, she explained. He kept writing and calling and begging her to come back and marry him. He even phoned Sally's mother and got her dress size so he could order her a wedding gown. She wasn't really in love with him, but finally relented. By the time she returned to New Orleans, she had become quite used to the idea of getting married and starting a family. But life is full of surprises.

"I called him when I got to town," Sally recounted with a slight quiver in her voice, "He said he had something important to tell me but couldn't do it on the phone. So I took a taxi to his apartment. He made me stretch out on the couch in what he called the 'shock position.' Then he told me he had fallen in love with somebody else and was going to marry her instead of me. He even had the gown refitted for the other girl—that bum!"

Sally began to cry softly. I wanted to hug her but didn't dare. Instead, I patted her on the back and consoled her as best I could. I was older and taller than when Sally had left town, and I sensed that she looked at me a little differently now. But whatever dreams I may have entertained of having an adult relationship with her soon ended. She met a young architect, married him on the rebound, and moved to Philadelphia. I thought I would never see her again.

CHAPTER THIRTY-THREE

Cathy, my high school girlfriend, used to say I had a condescending attitude toward the musicians. Whenever I told her stories about them, she said I made them sound like clowns and buffoons. She said my parents and I doted on them because it "flattered our sense of class superiority" and allowed us to "flout our white liberal magnanimity."

Well, this girl had a pretty cynical attitude in general, mixed with jealousy over all the time I spent with the musicians. But I wondered if there was any grain of truth to what she said. Were we really amused by the antics of these noble old men in the same way that Huck Finn was amused by the "nigger Jim"? The very idea seemed preposterous to me.

My father had based his early career in journalism on the crusade for racial equality. He'd even gone North to be able to express his views more freely. As for my mother, whatever prejudices she may have grown up with in Mississippi couldn't have survived long once she married Tom Sancton and moved to New York. When they lived up there, they socialized with black intellectuals, ate soul food in Harlem, and made friends with the blues singer Leadbelly—his wife, Baby, even showed my mother where to buy turnip greens in New York. And even after my parents had moved back South, visiting black intellectuals like Roi Ottley and Henry Lee Moon were welcomed into our home.

No, my mother was no racist. But she was basically going along for the ride. It was impossible to know what she felt deep down inside because she hid it under a veil of Southern belle charm and humorous patter. She was incapable of saying, "This is what I believe," or "This is what I want." Maybe that's how she dealt with her own pain and disappointments. I know her affection for the musicians was genuine, but in this, as in so many things, she was following Daddy's lead. And to some extent, at least in the beginning, I guess I was too.

My father had more than admiration for the mens. He felt a bond with them, a sense of shared destiny, even though he had grown up on the other side of the color line. He laughed out loud one night when Larry called him a Southern gentleman, and later told me the reason why: "Hell, I'm the last man in New Orleans who could be called a Southern gentleman. I grew up an orphan and essentially a pauper. Even today, I can never be sure a twenty-five-dollar check will clear the bank. I live in a big house that I bought for peanuts because it was a wreck and nobody wanted it. I've lived in jeopardy all my life. And that is the real basis of my brotherhood with the men."

I don't think his talk of brotherhood was just the knee-jerk rhetoric of a political liberal. He felt it deeply, not just out of a sense of shared poverty and precariousness, but because he found a healing solace in the company of these old men following the failure of his books. The literary establishment had rejected him, failed to acknowledge his genius, so he embraced the folk culture of this excluded slice of humanity. Most important, perhaps, the musicians knew nothing about his failed books or his abandoned career up North. They judged him by no standard other than friendship and human decency. As George

Lewis once told him, "Tom, people know what kind of man you are."

But what about me? What strange force drove a white middle-class teenager down that road with such passion and single-mindedness? Was it just the beauty of George Lewis's tone and the throb of Booker T's bass drum? Or was it a way to win the approval of a father who was so obviously enthralled with the musicians and their culture? Or did I see the mens themselves as father figures and role models? Maybe it was all of that.

Our motivations were varied and complex, but they did not include condescension. Sure, most of the musicians were uneducated; their spelling was approximate and their speech was different from ours. Sure, they were funny—humor was one of their most effective weapons for dealing with poverty, pain, and hard times. They were showmen, but there wasn't an Uncle Tom among them. Even the ones who clowned around the most always kept their human dignity. And we felt privileged to be around them.

It was one thing to know that and feel it in my heart. But it was another thing to try to explain it to Cathy or other school friends who could never really understand my attachment to this coterie of old jazzmen. Most of them, in fact, did not know about it. It was my secret garden, until WWL-TV, the local CBS affiliate, did a little documentary on me as part of a series they called "Terrific Teens."

Their camera crew got permission to film me in the halls and classrooms of Benjamin Franklin High. But they also filmed me at Preservation Hall, sitting in with Kid Sheik's band, and talking with Sheik and others about learning their music. The day after the show aired, I thought I would be greeted in school like a big star. Instead, people avoided me in the halls. The gym teacher, Coach O'Neal, took me aside and said, "I thought that show was going to feature Franklin. It was all about you and those people at Preservation Hall." He didn't need to be more explicit. I understood then that even in the relatively liberal environment of Ben Franklin, a public school for "gifted" students, a young man trying to live in two worlds was considered weird.

CHAPTER THIRTY-FOUR

Apart from his wife, Pearl, the only thing Jim Robinson loved as much as his trombone was his "groceries." That's what he called the bottle of whiskey that he brought to the Hall each night and joyfully sipped in the courtyard between sets. He ran out of liquor one night and leaned over to my father with his empty plastic glass in his hand. "Oh, Tom," he said, scratching the glass with his fingernail, "If I don't get this . . . then I be mad at *everybody!*"

My dad went to a package store on Bourbon Street and bought him a half-pint of his favorite whiskey, I. W. Harper. After that, he often found himself supplying Jim's groceries. Daddy's reward for this was an annual gift of Pearl's sweet potato pie at Christmas time.

Jim and my father were great buddies. They had first met in New York, where my parents used to hear him playing with Bunk Johnson and George Lewis in the 1940s. "Yeah, Tom," Jim said. "I used to see you at the Stuyvesant. You was in there with a different girl every night. Man, you was awful!"

"You must have me mixed up with somebody else, Jim," my father protested. "I was always with Seta."

But Jim kept laughing and mischievously wagging his finger. "You was terrible with them womens, Tom. Terrible."

This became a standing joke, and Jim would delight in bringing it up every time my parents sat by him in the Hall.

It was impossible not to feel good when you were around Jim Robinson. He took joy in his music and radiated it to everyone around him. I thought he was the best trombone player in New Orleans. But the genius of his personality was even grander than his musicianship. Jim loved people, and people loved him.

He was tall and powerfully built, with a broad face and high, Indian-like cheekbones. When he smiled, his gold-capped front teeth gleamed, his eyes narrowed to little slits, and his nose crinkled up.

Jim loved to share jokes with the other musicians, or friends in the audience, slapping his thigh and laughing lustily at his own quips. Sometimes, when other men were taking solos, he would get up and do a kind of pigeon-toed dance, with his skinny butt sticking out and his enormous hands clapping time. Whether he did this in Preservation Hall in front of ten people, or in Carnegie Hall with the touring band, he would soon have the whole audience clapping along. And when he played the trombone, with his big, brassy tone and his flawless timing, Jim left his listeners spellbound. His specialty number, "Ice Cream," was always a showstopper.

For all his onstage antics, there was nothing buffoonish about Jim Robinson. Nor was this some put-on act for the tourists. When you saw Jim at his home, he'd put on one of his records and do exactly the same thing—the dance, the thigh-slapping, the good-natured laughter. "Listen at what I do on this number," he'd say excitedly, waving a finger in the direction of his record player. "Ain't no other trombone players can make that." Sometimes, when he had no gig and no visitors, Jim would take his trombone down to the corner barroom and play along with the jukebox. All the music in him just overflowed.

Jim was born Christmas Day 1892 on Deer Range plantation, thirty-five miles downriver from New Orleans, and grew up in what must have been a slave cabin in the old days. His father was a teamster and a breaker of mules and horses; his mother, a plantation worker. Jim would accompany her down the muddy roads to the fields each day. He was just a young child when she died, but the memory of that loss never left him.

"Tom," he told my father during one of our visits to his house on Marais Street, "when my mother died, I was so sorry I could hardly make it. I was just little, about six or seven. People worried about me. They were sayin', 'Jim you got to stop cryin'.' Then one evening I saw my mama coming down the road to the house and she saw me in the front and she said, 'Go around to the back by the kitchen, son, I want to talk to you.' So I went to the back and she met me there. And she said, 'Jim, I be a spirit but I ain't gonna hurt you. I want you to try to feel better. I want you to know I love you and I'm gonna stay with you. And quit worryin'. It's all right.' Then she be gone. And Tom, I come out of it and I never worried about her being a spirit again. She straighten me out."

Jim might have spent his life walking those muddy country roads, if he hadn't been drafted into the army in 1917 and sent to France with a segregated road repair unit. The outfit had a band and Jim soon found himself playing trombone instead of digging ditches.

When he told us about this experience, my mother asked if he had learned to read sheet music with the army band. "What?" he exploded. "Me read music? Naw, Miz Sancton. All them little black dots make me dizzy!"

After he got out of the army in 1919, Jim spent a decade with the famous Sam Morgan Band. When Morgan died, he gigged around with obscure little groups until he was recruited for Bunk Johnson's first recording. From there, Jim's career had followed the rising fortunes of George Lewis, with whom he played and criss-crossed the world for the next two decades.

For the first couple of years at the Hall, I could hear essentially the same Lewis band two nights a week—Jim, George, Kid Howard,

Joe Watkins, and Slow Drag. But something happened in the mid 1960s, and Jim and Howard suddenly stopped playing with George. Howard even abandoned Jaffe's place altogether, and switched over to Dixieland Hall—a veritable apostasy.

I asked Jim about all this but he was evasive. His wife Pearl volunteered that George was "too sly" and had a "big head." I never knew what the real reason was—maybe Jim thought George hogged the spotlight or cheated him on the money—but I thought it was almost tragic that that great ensemble would never be heard again. To me, it was like the breakup of the Beatles.

Jim never seemed to miss the old band, though. By that time, he was a regular with the Preservation Hall touring group. He loved the big audiences, the good money he made on road trips, and the camaraderie of the band bus.

I once tagged along with a Preservation Hall band tour and sat next to Jim much of the way. He chatted about everything from the old Morgan band to baseball to Pearl's cooking—but not a word about George Lewis. And he told me something I never thought I'd hear from an old jazzman: "My tax man told me I can't do no more tours this year. He say I'm makin' too much money."

When we stopped at a motel in rural Pennsylvania, Jim discovered that his room had a kitchenette in it and decided to throw a party. Buster Holmes was accompanying the band, so Jim got him to cook up a huge pot of red beans and rice to eat after the concert.

There we were at midnight milling about on the balcony with paper plates full of Buster's beans, passing around a magnum bottle of Tabasco sauce and cans of beer. Bewildered motel guests stuck their heads out to see a bunch of old black guys—Jim, Willie Humphrey, Billie and DeDe Pierce, Cie Frazier and Buster—partying with Allan Jaffe, road manager Chris Botsford, and a skinny white teenager.

The next morning I went to see Jim and found him pouring gallons of leftover beans down the toilet. They had sat on the stove overnight and went sour. "You 'bout to cry, ain't you?" Jim laughed when he saw the look on my face. "I know you love them red beans."

As much as he liked to clown around, Jim had an ironclad sense of dignity that would tolerate no slight. Jim downed too many "groceries" one night and got to stumbling around on the bandstand to the point where Sandy Jaffe called him a taxi and told him to go home. He became indignant and refused to pack up his horn. "You can't talk to me like that, Miss Sandy," he said, wagging his finger at her. "I'm a man, you hear? I'm a *man*. I'm a man *amongst* men." And he was.

CHAPTER THIRTY-FIVE

When it came to asserting pride and dignity, nobody could outdo the Creoles: men like Guesnon, Louis Cottrell, and Albert Burbank all seemed to have a patrician sense of their special place in the world. Apart from Guesnon, none of them talked about it, but you could feel it in their quiet self-assurance.

Burbank had a head like a Roman senator. He was light-skinned, with a high forehead, wavy white hair, clear gray eyes, and a long, straight neck. He played the clarinet with a polished elegance—textbook posture, effortless breathing, rich tone, fingers that found their place so naturally on the instrument that they hardly seemed to move. The thing he was proudest of, though, was not his clarinet playing but his fishing camp on the north shore of Lake Pontchartrain.

One night, as he was packing up after playing at the Hall, I asked him if I could come around his house for some lessons. "Aw, man, I ain't got time for that," he said. "What you want to take lessons with me for?"

"I'm trying to learn the clarinet, Albert, and you're a clarinet master."

Burbank laughed and waved both hands in the air as if swatting flies. "Aw, man, listen at this shit!"

When I persisted, he came back with a counteroffer. "Look, I play all the clarinet I want to play down at the Hall. But I tell you what—I'll take you over to my camp and teach you how to fish. How that sound?"

That sounded great to me. Frank Naundorf, a German trombone player who had settled in New Orleans, was standing nearby and asked if he could come, too. "Yeah, man," said Burbank. "The more hooks we put out there, the more fish we gonna catch."

The next day, Burbank picked us up in front of Buster's at 7 a.m. and we headed out to the lake. From the top of the old Highway 11 bridge, Burbank pointed to a row of fishing camps over on the left. "See that yellow one there? That's mine. I call it my 'Yellow Heaven.'"

Burbank's camp was just a one-room wooden cabin built on a pier, with a few kitchen chairs and a folding card table for furniture. In one corner lay a heap of crab traps, fishing nets, and cane poles. A large ice chest with rusted hinges stood in the other corner, next to a galvanized tub. We filled the chest with ice then put in the cold cuts and beer we had bought at Schwegmann's supermarket on the way to the camp. "We don't have no toilets around here," Burbank explained. "You just got to go where you can."

It was a clear day, with sunlight shimmering on the water and a warm breeze coming in from the lake. Gulls circled and crowed overhead, sometimes diving to the surface of the water to scoop up a shrimp or a small fish. We tied some chicken necks into the round, double-hooped crab nets, attached their strings to the pier, and threw them over the side.

The fish weren't biting much, and the croakers we did catch were so small we threw them back. The real thrill was pulling up the crab nets and finding those big blue-claws—sometimes even two or three of them—gorging on the soggy chicken necks. We'd draw the nets in ever so slowly, then put a foot down on the crabs' backs and seize them by the rear flippers so they couldn't nip us with their claws. We caught more than a dozen good-sized crabs that way.

Toward the end of the afternoon, all beery and sunburned, we helped Albert build a driftwood fire on the beach. He brought out the galvanized tub, filled it with water, threw in some salt and a couple of packets of Zatarain's spicy crab-boil. Then he emptied the basket of crabs into the boiling mixture. They wiggled and snapped their claws for a second, then settled motionless on the bottom and their color began turning from dark green to a brownish pink and finally a deep red.

Frank Naundorf, a melancholy guy with a heavy dose of German *weltschmerz*, shook his head with a sardonic smile as he contemplated their agony. "Burned alive," he muttered to me. "Just like Dresden."

When the crabs were done, we emptied the tub and poured cold water from the ice chest onto their steaming shells to cool them off. Albert threw them into a big Schwegmann's grocery bag and packed them in the trunk of his car.

He didn't say much on the way back to New Orleans. When he dropped us off in front of Buster's, we hopped out and thanked him for the outing. He just nodded. We were originally going to split the crabs with Burbank, but he told us to take them all.

We brought the day's catch back to Frank's apartment, spread newspaper on the kitchen table, and feasted. Soon our fingers were smeared with yellow crab fat; our hands, forearms, and faces were covered with crumbs of meat and bits of shell.

The next time I saw Albert, I told him they were the best crabs I had ever tasted.

"Listen, what you done wit' them crabs?" he asked.

"We ate them, Albert. Why?"

"I thought you was gonna throw 'em out. I seen how that boy look at 'em, like he was disgusted or somethin'. I was really burned.

We live kinda rough over there, but we ain't no low-lifes. That tub was clean. Weren't nothin' wrong with them crabs, man."

I tried to explain that Frank was German and that seeing the crabs boiled alive made him think of all the people who burned up in the Dresden firestorm during the war.

Burbank thought this over for a moment, then replied, "Weren't nothin' wrong with them crabs, man."

He didn't want to know about Dresden. We had insulted him, scorned his hospitality, and hurt his Creole pride.

I can remember at least one other occasion when I unintentionally offended one of the musicians: Percy Humphrey, longtime leader of the Eureka Brass Band and the Preservation Hall touring band.

Percy used to be a powerhouse in the street parades. But he slowed down a lot in his later years. He was overweight and out of breath and had trouble with his dentures. His response to that was to take it easy and pace himself. "He done got to the point now where he's old and lazy," said George Guesnon, laughing at the lengths to which Percy would go to get his rest. "Boy he's a lazy ass. He'll start off a number, *toot-too-ta-loota-loot*, then he take down. He give the trombone six choruses, give the clarinet five, give the piano four, give the banjo two—one time I even caught him sleepin' up there."

But it was not just laziness with Percy—it was a survival tactic. And one night, without realizing it, I became part of his strategy. Just back from an exhausting overseas tour, he called me up and invited me to come down to the Hall and sit in with his band. I told him I would do my best to make it, but I had to go to a party and would be there for the last set. Well, I didn't get away from the party in time, and the band was just finishing up the last number when I walked into the carriageway. Percy glared at me over the top of his glasses and hardly spoke a word when he left the bandstand. I figured he was insulted, thinking that I had spurned his invitation. So I decided to go see him the next day and apologize.

Percy lived in a neat white cottage at 4519 South Robertson Street, not far from our house. He had a shiny new Oldsmobile parked in his carport and an air-conditioner humming in his front window. Percy was the only musician I knew with an air conditioner. He'd made a decent living selling life insurance, and the Preservation Hall band tours had nudged him into relative affluence for a jazzman.

I found him in his reclining chair watching a baseball game in his T-shirt and boxer shorts. He grunted a terse greeting when he saw me in the doorway. I could tell he was still sore.

"Percy," I said, "I'm sorry I didn't show up earlier last night. I didn't mean to hurt your feelings."

"Hurt my *feelings?*" he shot back. "Man, you hurt my *chops*. I just come back from a tour of England and my lip was busted. I was lookin' to you to play the last set."

"You were really counting on me?"

"Sure I was countin' on you," he said. "I told Sandy Jaffe, 'I'm a lay down sure 'nough on that last set, when I have two clarinet men with me.' I was depending on you coming and relieving me."

"If I'd known that, I would have played the whole night. I wouldn't have let you down."

"Ain't no use cryin' over spilled milk now," he said.

Percy got up and turned down the volume on the TV. Then he slumped back down in his chair and looked over at me.

"You know the number I wanted you to play?"

"'Burgundy Street'?"

"That's it."

Percy, who had worked with George Lewis for years, must have heard the master play it a thousand times. I was quite flattered that he wanted me to play George's famous solo for him. Maybe it reminded him of the old days. Then I thought about it for a while and realized the tune also had a nonmusical attraction for Percy: it takes about six minutes to play, plenty of time for a nice breather.

CHAPTER THIRTY-SIX

The bane of New Orleans, apart from the heat and the mosquitoes, is hurricanes. Every summer, and into the fall, they well up in the Atlantic, the Caribbean, the Gulf of Mexico, or the Bay of Campeche off the coast of Mexico. Then they suck up tons of water and pack swirling winds that strike land with devastating force.

Landfall can be anywhere along the arc from Mexico to the tip of Florida. But New Orleans, lying along the Mississippi River, and ten feet below sea level on average, is a particularly vulnerable target. People always said that if "the big one" ever came up the mouth of the river, the Mississippi and Lake Pontchartrain would sweep the levees away and a flood would destroy the whole city like some Biblical retribution for all the sin and frivolity that reigns there. But it was like the story of the boy who cried wolf: we had heard it so often that we didn't really believe it.

We had some near misses when I was growing up there. In June 1957, Hurricane Audrey headed our way with winds of one hundred and fifty miles per hour. As they usually do under a hurricane threat, everybody in New Orleans stocked up on flashlight batteries, canned food, and bottled water, parked their cars on the highest ground they could find, nailed plywood over their windows, and then turned on the TV and watched local weatherman Nash Roberts pronounce on their fate.

We were lucky that time—far luckier than the residents of Cameron Parish, in the Cajun country of southwest Louisiana:

Audrey destroyed everything in her path and literally wiped the town of Cameron off the map, leaving 435 dead.

New Orleans would also be spared in August 1969, when Hurricane Camille, the most powerful storm ever to hit the mainland U.S. up until that time, shifted eastward at the last minute. She smashed into the Mississippi Gulf Coast with winds of two hundred miles per hour and tidal surges of twenty-five feet, killing 143 and devastating the coastal towns.

In September 1965, though, we were not so lucky. A monster hurricane named Betsy, which had been heading up the Atlantic seaboard, suddenly turned west, crossed Florida, and made a bee-line for New Orleans, blowing gusts up to one hundred and fifty miles per hour. We anxiously tracked its course on our TV screens and prayed that it would hit somebody else. But Betsy kept boring in on us, picking up ever more wind and water as she made her way across the Gulf.

When it finally hit, our tall, wood-frame house, located on an exposed street corner, trembled with the periodic gusts. Trees were bent almost parallel to the street, their branches breaking off and crashing into cars and houses. The wind peeled the tin roofs off sheds and garages like a can opener, sending them flying in all directions, along with metal garbage cans, street signs, flower pots, cardboard boxes and other bits of debris. Telephone poles snapped and electric wires whipped the air like black snakes.

As we hunkered down around the dining room table, we listened to the ghostly shrieking of the wind and the muffled sounds of flying objects smashing into things down in the street. Suddenly we heard a mighty shattering of glass in the living room. "It's the bay window," my dad shouted. "Come on, Tommy, we have to board it up, or we'll have a foot of water in there."

We all dashed to the living room. I struggled to hold a large sheet of plywood up against the gaping hole while my dad began nailing it to the window frame.

Before he had planted the last nail, we heard what sounded like an explosion coming from the dining room. We rushed back there and recoiled in horror. One of the brick chimneys had blown down, crashed through the roof and the floor of the attic, and pulverized the dining room table. The chair my dad had been sitting in not five minutes earlier was now no more than a pile of splinters lying under a ton of bricks. "God Almighty," my father gasped, as torrential rains poured in through the open roof, "I'd be a dead man if that window hadn't blown out."

Indeed, it was only that random event that kept my father becoming one of Betsy's seventy-five victims. But some of our friends weren't so lucky, including the old clarinetist Israel Gorman, who caught pneumonia when his house flooded and died shortly afterward.

Our house was on relatively high ground, so we were spared the flooding that engulfed the low-lying neighborhoods. Even so, the rain waters that poured through the gaping hole in our roof did massive damage to the floors, ceilings, walls, rugs, and precious antique furniture inherited from my mother's side of the family.

It was at that point that my father made the shrewdest move of his life. Before we even began to clean up, he started snapping photos. He shot the house from every angle, inside and out, filling five rolls of film with dramatic evidence of the storm's devastation. Then he sat at the typewriter and wrote out a detailed report on the damage in the graphic, grainy style he had learned on the old *Item*.

The next day, long before our ruined rugs and furniture had dried out, he handed a fully documented claim to his insurance agent.

When the man came out to inspect the damage, he found every-thing the way it was the morning after the storm, including the pile of bricks and the crushed chair. As other claims began to drift in and accumulate into mind-boggling backlogs, my dad's early-bird file got a prompt—and generous—payout.

Suddenly my dad was rich. At least he felt rich for a while. Soon workers were hammering, sawing, and painting all over the house. They redid all the floors, walls, and ceilings, put in new closets, bookshelves, and partitions, and rewired the whole house. My parents bought new furniture and appliances—sofas, armchairs, dish-washer, clothes dryer. The crowning touch was a powerful central air-conditioning system. For the first time in my life, we lived in a house that was clean, comfortable, functional, and presentable.

That terrible, capricious storm was my dad's greatest triumph. But the golden age of the Sancton "mansion" did not last. Nine years later, long after I moved out, an idiot tenant downstairs left a ciga-rette burning on the edge of a table while she took a shower. It fell onto a pile of newspapers and started a fire that quickly swept through the wood-frame house. No one was hurt, but the damage was heavy. The losses included most of my parents' wedding presents and an oil portrait of my mother as an eighteen-year-old Jackson debutante, holding a camelia and looking forward to what life would bring her.

My father again got a handsome insurance settlement. This time, though, following a tortured logic that made sense to no one but himself, he decided not to get a professional contractor to fix up the house. "They're all crooks," he fumed. "As soon as they see it's an insurance job, they double the price." Beth, who by that time had gained considerable experience in buying and renovating old houses, offered to send her own contractor over to do the job. No way, said my father, indignant that one of his children would dare offer help and advice.

Daddy had a better idea. He would use part of the money to pay off the mortgage and use the rest to fix up the house himself. So he paid off the two percent loan, which was probably costing him all of one hundred dollars a month, bought some paint and plaster, and dabbled for a while at a massive repair job that was far beyond his ability to carry out alone. For years thereafter, my parents lived among charred timbers, with orange industrial extension cords strung through the transoms and bare plywood nailed over a hole in the floor where the flames had burned through. It looked like a Deep South version of Mrs. Havisham's ruined manse in *Great Expectations*. The upstairs, where my parents lived, finally received basic repairs. But the rental apartment downstairs, their only steady source of income, was boarded up the day after the fire and has stayed that way for the past three decades.

On August 29, 2005, the "big one" finally hit. Hurricane Katrina blasted Louisiana and Mississippi with winds of one hundred and fifty miles per hour and a tidal surge of up to thirty feet. The Mississippi Gulf coast was virtually wiped out from Bay St. Louis to Biloxi and beyond. And New Orleans, though it was spared the brunt of the storm winds, was innundated after the swollen waters of Lake Pontchartrain breached the levee at the 17th street canal and gushed into the bowl-shaped city. Though the French Quarter and the Garden District were largely untouched, eighty percent of the city was under water at one point, including many of the neighborhoods I had paraded through as a young man—never thinking or believing that the dire predictions of catastrophe would one day come true.

CHAPTER THIRTY-SEVEN

By the time I was seventeen, grown tall and lanky, I looked old enough to start playing in local clubs and bars. The prospect of gigging on and around Bourbon Street was exciting. But I soon realized with a shock that passing for an adult meant I'd be judged as an adult. All this stuff about being "good for my age" didn't mean a damn anymore. When you played in the French Quarter clubs, you had to be good, period.

There was no more demanding a bandleader on Bourbon Street than trumpeter Wallace Davenport. He had played for years in the Count Basie and Ray Charles orchestras before returning to his home town in the late 1960s. Wallace led a combo at the Maison Bourbon, a touristy jazz club on the corner of Bourbon and St. Peter. He had iron chops, fast fingers, and little patience for any musician who couldn't "cut it." He was a moody, dark-faced guy with penetrating eyes that bored right through you if you hit a wrong note.

Though he was playing old-style jazz for the tourists, Wallace was a sophisticated musician whose taste went to modernish licks bordering on bebop. He got bored with the traditional repertoire, so he tried to spice it up by calling swing tunes, pop tunes, and complicated ballads that no one in Preservation Hall ever played.

Wallace had heard me sitting in at the Hall and asked me to replace his ailing clarinet player for a couple of weeks. It was the middle of summer vacation and I had lots of time on my hands, so I jumped at the chance.

Jumped in over my head, in fact. The first number Wallace called was "I Never Knew"—and I didn't. He kicked it off at a racehorse tempo. By the time I'd figured out the key, the damn tune modulated to a minor key in the bridge, then back again. It was a musical roller-coaster ride.

When the song ended Wallace glared at me. "Shit man, don't you know that number?"

"No," I said. "I never even heard it."

"Well, can't you hear the changes?"

Hear the changes? Alas, playing with the likes of George Lewis, Kid Sheik, and the Olympia Brass Band had not tuned my ear to diminished sevenths, augmented fifths, flatted ninths, whole-tone scales, and all the harmonic sophistication that Wallace had picked up on the road with the big bands. I knew I had some serious woodshedding to do.

Wallace had another trick. He would call tunes in impossible keys—the "natural" ones full of sharps and flats. He said he liked to do that to keep everybody "on their toes" and make things more interesting. I think he did it to show off his technical prowess—and embarrass his sidemen. A lot of the older musicians, even some of the best, just couldn't get around those weird keys.

Fortunately, I had been warned about Wallace's penchant for key changes. And I had a secret weapon. My cherished pair of Lorenzo Tio clarinets included a horn in the key of A, which allowed me to play in all the natural keys with ease. I set both of my instruments up on the bandstand. Whenever Wallace modulated into some bizarre key, I'd grab the A and go effortlessly up and down the horn.

Wallace seemed impressed at first, then he got to watching what I was doing. "You just fakin' it, man," he said. "A real musician can play every key on the same horn."

His "real musician" remark stung me. And once his regular clarinet man returned to the job, Wallace never again asked me to play with him.

It wasn't long before I found another gig—this time with my piano-playing buddy David Paquette. His parents, Fred and Filly, were jazz addicts who had recently moved down from Connecticut to be near the music. David had taught himself the piano by listening to his parents' vast record collection. He was the first kid my age who shared my passion for jazz, and we hit it off from the start.

David and I were roaming through the quarter one summer night looking for some place to jam. We wandered into a bar on Dauphine Street that had an unoccupied piano. The place was half empty, so we asked the barman if we could play a few tunes. "Sure," he said, "anything that can bring some customers in here." Pretty soon the two of us had the place rocking with tunes like "Daisy," "Peg O' My Heart," and "I Wish I Could Shimmy Like My Sister Kate." By the time we took a break, my clarinet case was full of tips.

A tall heavyset man waved us over to his table in the back corner. "I'm Eddie Abadie," he said. "I own this joint. You boys sound pretty good together. Y'all want to play here regular?"

Sure, we said.

He promised us twenty dollars a night plus ten percent of the cash register receipts. "If I make a thousand, you get a hundred. If I make ten thousand, you get a thousand. How's that sound?"

We said it sounded great.

"Terrific," he said, giving each of us a bone-crunching handshake. "Now you see that guy behind the bar? That's Albie. He's my flunky. Everybody needs a flunky, right? Check with Albie at the end of the night. He'll show you the cash register receipts and give you your cut."

We came back the next night and had a great time. The place was jammed. But when we checked with Albie, we learned that the bar had only taken in two hundred dollars. "They all a bunch of shoo-shoos," Albie said. "They clap and whoop it up but they don't buy no liquor."

Next night the take was two hundred and fifty dollars; the night after one hundred and eighty dollars.

Eddie Abadie came in the third night and asked how it was going.

"Terrible," I said. "We're not making any money."

Abadie told us not to worry. He had big plans for buying ads in the papers, getting us matching tailor-made costumes, putting in a good sound system, big posters of us in front of the place, selling records.

"Wait a minute, wait a minute," said David. "Before you go off the deep end here, you should know we're still in school. We're not gonna be able to play every night once classes start."

"Shit, I thought you boys wanted to be professionals. Get the fuck out of here."

Not long after that, David landed a regular job in Pat O'Brien's piano bar and embarked on a career that would eventually take him around the world. I went back to school.

I had to cut back on the late-night gigs once the new semester started. About that time, though, three of my foreign buddies—Lars Edegran, Orange Kellin, and Trevor Richards—landed a trio job at the Caverns, on Bourbon and St. Ann. The Caverns was a big, open club with a dance floor that was packed every night. It soon became a hot jazz scene, especially when guys like Jim Robinson, Kid Sheik, and Capt. John Handy, the town's hottest alto sax player, started showing up to jam after their regular gigs.

I was dying to go over there and play with them. But there was a problem: the music didn't start until 11 and went on until 3 a.m. There was no way my father would allow me to stay out that late.

But Daddy went out of town for a few days and I seized my window of opportunity. My mother was partly deaf and slept like a log. So I figured I could snatch the car keys and sneak out the back door after she went to bed. She'd never know I was gone. And just in case she did notice my absence, I left a note on my bed that said, "Don't worry. I've just gone down to play at the Caverns. I'm a big boy now and can fend for myself. Be back soon."

Jim Robinson and Handy were playing with the trio when I arrived. Jim grinned and waved me over to the bandstand. I took out my clarinet and played a long set with them, mainly the funky, driving blues and boogies that Handy specialized in.

During the break, I stood at the bar chatting with Handy over a cold beer. He was telling me about a job he had played that afternoon at a Catholic church picnic. I thought that was hilarious, since Handy's sax playing was a pure distillation of sex and sin. "That's what I'm talking about," he said, "Man, I looked out at all them Jesus people and I just couldn't tunk."

I stayed at the Caverns until the last note was played. It was well after three. Suddenly I was gripped by remorse and panic. What if Mother had woken up and found my empty bed? She'd be worried sick. She'd call the cops. I'd get in big trouble. Or worse, what if someone had slipped in the unlocked backdoor and murdered her in her bed?

There was little traffic that time of night, so I sped back uptown as fast as I could. I also ran a stop sign one block from home. As soon as I did that, a pair of headlights hit my rear-view mirror. It was an unmarked police car that had apparently been following me with its lights off. I pulled up to the curb, right in front of my house.

"Let me see your license," said the cop.

I felt in my back pocket and my heart sank. In my haste to sneak off to the Quarter, I had left my wallet on the top of my dresser. "It's right upstairs, officer. I'll just run up and get it."

"No you won't, son. The State of Louisiana requires drivers to have a valid license on their person at all times. You're under arrest."

Just then I heard my mother's voice calling from the screened porch upstairs. She had been waiting up there for me to return. "Is there something wrong, officer?" she said. "That's my son."

The cop looked up at her and said, with a perverse satisfaction, "Your son's going to jail, ma'am."

Next thing I knew, I was in the back of a police car, with no inside door handles and a heavy wire-mesh screen separating me from the driver.

"Where are you taking me, officer?" I said.

"Central Lockup."

Central Lockup was the place where all the local criminals— rapists, murderers, drug dealers, and car thieves—passed on their way to prison. How could that wonderful jam session have led to this? Didn't they know I was just a kid, just Tommy Sancton out playing his clarinet with the mens? This was all terribly wrong.

When the car pulled up in front of police headquarters on Tulane Avenue, site of the main city jail, I could hear the prisoners shouting through their barred upper-story windows. "Hey, you fat-assed cop down there," one shouted. "You think you bust me, motherfucker? You ain't bust *nobody!*"

The arresting officer took me through a series of heavy steel doors and told the desk sergeant to book me for "speeding, running a stop sign, and driving without a license." It's a good thing they didn't test my breath, too or I might have faced a DWI charge.

The sergeant made me fill in some forms, then took my belt, shoes, and pocket change. Another cop gripped my arm firmly and led me down a corridor to a heavily barred holding pen.

It was about ten feet square, with a concrete floor and steel benches bolted to the walls. There were blood smears on the floor, along with stinking puddles of urine, vomit, and what looked like a fresh discharge of sperm.

I wanted to throw up, but I didn't dare because a man was sitting on the other side of the pen and staring intently at the new arrival. He was a white man, about thirty, with a rumpled sports jacket and his shirt unbuttoned to the waist. He was very drunk.

"What are you in for?" I said, trying to make conversation.

"Molesting a female, unless they change it to rape."

Thank God it was a female! I had heard horror stories about what happened to guys in prison.

"What'd they get you for?" my cellmate asked sullenly.

"Traffic violations," I said.

He shot me a contemptuous look.

After an hour or so, I was taken to an individual cell. It was smaller than the holding pen and didn't stink as much. They told me I could make one call—to a lawyer, bail bondsman, or an elected official, who could have me released on his cognizance if he saw fit. I woke up Maurice "Moon" Landrieu, a state representative who was later to become the last white mayor of New Orleans (and whose daughter Mary is currently a U.S. Senator). Landrieu knew my father from his newspaper days and promptly took care of the matter. By 5 a.m., I was back out on the street.

"Where you goin', motherfucker?" someone shouted from a prison window. "They let all you little white boys out, but the brothers gotta stay here."

"Get on home, boy," said another voice. "Get on home to yo' mama!"

I flagged a cab and headed back uptown. As I suspected, Mother was still waiting on the upstairs porch. "Darling," she said. "What on earth?"

I told her everything that had happened that night—the Caverns, the jam session, the arrest, central lockup. She didn't yell at me. She knew she didn't have to: nothing she could have said would have made me feel worse than my own sense of guilt and shame. We agreed to keep the matter to ourselves, so my father never learned of his son's brief sojourn in Central Lockup.

Not that I didn't find other ways to run into trouble. On one warm September night, I took a high-school classmate to hear the band at Luthjen's, a white dance hall in a rough downtown neighborhood behind the Quarter known as Faubourg Marigny. My friend, Bruce King, got some funny looks with his shoulder-length hair, but nobody really hassled him. New Orleans was full of hippies in those days.

We shared a table with some of the Luthjen's regulars, including Fred and Filly Paquette. I sat in with the band on a few numbers, then we hung around listening, talking, and drinking beer until almost midnight.

Bruce and I were feeling no pain when we left. We were walking down Charters Street toward the Quarter when we heard the whine of an engine. A car screeched to a stop next to us and somebody shouted out, "Hey, you fuckin' hippies! Get outta the goddam road!"

Without thinking, I shot them the finger. We instantly heard car doors slamming and feet hitting pavement. One of the guys punched Bruce in the face and busted his lip open. Another one smashed a whiskey bottle on my head. If the bottom of the bottle had hit my skull, it would surely have crushed it. But it struck me at just the right angle—and my head was just hard enough—that the glass shattered into a million shards instead of killing me.

I fell to the ground and they began to kick me all over—in the head, in the ribs, in the groin. Somebody grabbed my clarinet case and tried to rip it out of my hand. But that was the legendary Tio horn, and I clutched the handle for dear life.

"Let go, asshole," someone shouted, "or I'll fuckin' kill you!" He kicked the case, splitting the wood and knocking a chunk off the end. But I held on with all my force. They finally gave up and sped off in a squeal of burning rubber.

We stumbled back to Luthjen's in a daze. Bruce's face and shirt were scarlet and I had trickles of blood oozing from superficial wounds in my scalp. "Holy shit!" said Fred. "What happened to you guys?"

He took us into the men's room and put my head under the tap to wash the glass fragments out of my hair. Bruce splashed cold water on his face and dabbed his split, puffy lip with Fred's handkerchief.

I explained to Fred what had happened and he said, "Jesus Christ! Don't you know enough not to shoot the bird at a car full of New Orleans drunks?"

I guess we didn't. We were also too dumb to call it a night, so we left Luthjen's and wandered back into the Quarter. We went to one of my favorite soul-food restaurants, Smitty's, and decided to have some more beer.

We must have been a sight—Bruce with his split lip, bruised cheek, and bloodied clothes, me with my matted hair and cuts on my forehead.

A brawny black guy kept staring at us from the bar, and finally staggered over to our table. He bent down low and squinted at Bruce's face. Then he pulled a .22 pistol out of his jacket pocket and waved it in front of us. He was drunk and slurred his speech.

"I'm a shoot you, man!" I heard him say. "I'm a shoot you!"

I thought that was it—first we get out heads busted by some white drunks, and now this black drunk is going to plug us.

But he kept talking and I finally realized what he was actually saying: "Who misused you, man? Who misused you?" He was commiserating with us and offering to lend us his gun so we could avenge ourselves. We declined—politely—and bought him another drink.

CHAPTER THIRTY-EIGHT

Next to his tuba and his record collection, Allan Jaffe's most cherished possession was a film. It was made by a German TV crew that had come to town to do a documentary on the local music scene. The director cast his pretty red-haired daughter as a curious German fraulein wandering around New Orleans and poking into various jazz venues. One segment shows her visiting Preservation Hall. Jaffe welcomes the girl at the gate and steers her inside, where the Louis Cottrell band is playing. (This was filmed before Cottrell moved over to rival Dixieland Hall.)

The band plays a great rendition of "Bugle Call Rag"—an exciting up-tempo number that features four-bar breaks for all the instruments, followed by solos all around. The camera moves in on each musician: Cottrell, with his balloon belly and fast but imperturbable fingering; trumpeter Kid Howard, rolling his eyes up like Armstrong and punching out his fiery, wide-vibrato phrases like the world depended on them; drummer Paul Barbarin, grinning and staring out through his enormous glasses as he flails at his woodblocks, cowbells, and cymbals. The soundtrack was as good as the images.

We never saw the film on German TV, of course, but the producer sent Jaffe a copy. My father had a Bell & Howell projector that he used in his P.R. business and offered to show the film at the Hall one afternoon so Allan, Sandy, and Larry could judge the results. They all agreed that it was an outstanding document.

One day, my father saw a way to score points with one of his most important P.R. clients, a famous New Orleans architect with a booming international business. The architect had a big meeting coming up in Frankfurt and my dad thought he could make a hit by showing that great German TV film about the New Orleans jazz culture. But he knew Jaffe would never part with that precious reel. So, in what he later called "one of the jerk passages in my life," he asked Jaffe to lend it to him so he could watch it alone at home and "stimulate his thoughts" about some jazz writing he planned to do. Jaffe let him borrow the film.

What can go wrong will go wrong. The client took the film to Frankfurt and showed it at his meeting. Then he shipped it back to New Orleans—that much is proven by a bill of lading—but it never turned up. My dad put a trace on the shipment, had the client search his New Orleans office, even tried to buy another copy from the Germans. But the production company had gone out of business and the TV station had no copies. Where the film went remains a mystery to this day.

Now my father had to explain to Jaffe what he had done. Allan and Sandy were furious. So was Borenstein, who still owned an interest in the Hall and knew all too well the dollars and cents value of such a document in promoting his increasingly lucrative business venture. The Jaffes, while not indifferent to all that, grieved mainly over losing a personal memoir of this ephemeral moment in the Hall's history.

Allan might have been willing to let the matter drop to save a friendship that he valued. But Sandy could not digest the offense and called my father late one night to say she was going to sue him over the loss of the film. (She never did, of course.) Larry fumed about it for years, referring to it as "your dad's faux-pas."

My father, stung by deep regrets and his own enormous wounded pride, never set foot in the Hall again. In fact, he never even went into the French Quarter again. For him, that was the end of an era. He still visited the musicians and showed up for their funerals, which followed one another in all-too-rapid succession from the late 1960s on. But for him, the Hall was history.

The film fiasco marked a big turning point in my life. From that moment on, my parents stopped going to the Hall—Mother didn't drive and would never have gone there without my dad. So I would go by myself on the streetcar. The Hall and the music suddenly became my thing, not our thing. And what had previously united me with my parents began to divide us.

They still loved the music, but they didn't like my lifestyle once I started hanging out in the Quarter alone. I'd stay out late, go over to Johnny White's bar and drink beer after the Hall closed. Sometimes some of the old guys would be there, drinking and talking and telling stories—people like Sing Miller and Sheik and Kid Thomas. But mostly it was my foreign buddies—Lars Edegran, Orange Kellin, Clive Wilson, and the steady stream of fans and musicians from overseas who came to visit New Orleans for long or short periods. Whoever they were, my father didn't approve of me hanging out with them.

Neither did George Lewis. He told my dad, "Keep an eye on Tommy, he runnin' with a bad crowd." I really resented George for spying on me and reporting to my father behind my back. Was he jealous that all the attention I used to focus on him had now spread out to include a lot of other people? Or maybe he didn't like to see the cute little kid he used to teach getting older, more "mannish" as the musicians put it. Or perhaps he was just suspicious of foreigners.

It's not like I was hanging out with dope dealers. They were just a bunch of young Brits, Swedes, and Germans who loved the music, and also loved their beer. But my dad, who had so eagerly welcomed Sammy and others into his home in the early years, now thought they were a bad influence. In fact, he turned against the whole scene the way a reformed alcoholic turns against liquor. Speaking of which, it didn't help matters when I would come home smelling of beer, which the old teetotaler loathed and forbade me to drink.

I guess my adolescent rebellion consisted of trekking down the road he had put me on, after he'd decided to abandon it. He changed the rules on me. That's when my jazz odyssey moved into uncharted territory.

Things got to the point where my going down there at night became a source of constant conflict. Sometimes, when I came home really late, he would lock me out of the house. "Nothing good happens in the French Quarter at three o'clock in the morning," he'd tell me. "There's a bear on that road." It was the beginning of a tension between us that would become even more strained after I went off to college.

My father always wanted to feel in control, despite all the things in his life that had escaped his control and gone terribly wrong. "I know you kids have always resented me because I was the cop of the family," he would say. "I had to be the cop—your mother was too sweet-natured to administer discipline." Now that he saw me, a headstrong eighteen-year-old, starting to escape his control, he tried to turn the screws even tighter.

I know he was concerned about my safety—and he had a right to be in that violent town. But it was more than that. I think he feared that I was heading toward a career as a marginal jazz musician rather than getting a good education and doing something respectable. He did everything to make sure that didn't happen. "Son, don't let jazz steal you away from your schoolwork," he wrote me as I began my last year of high school. "Don't forget that I am the George Lewis of words, of thought, of ideas, of reading, metaphor. I do not want you to desert my side of the street of life. If you have any practical judgment, and survival skills, you will absolutely put jazz aside through the weeks and months ahead."

Not that I had my heart set on a musical career at that point. I never even thought about it in those terms. Music was my passion and I wanted to play as much as I could. But I also did my schoolwork and managed to stay near the top of my class, in spite of all the parades and jam sessions. My father was intent on me going to a good Ivy League college and I didn't want to let him down. And in my own ambivalent feelings, I also wanted the respectability and security that would come with that, even as I dreamed of becoming a great jazz musician.

CHAPTER THIRTY-NINE

My senior year at Benjamin Franklin High School set the stage for some big transitions in my life. In contrast to my former assistant principal, who couldn't figure out why I was hanging out at Preservation Hall, I finally found an educator who not only understood my passion for jazz but shared it. He was my English teacher Charles Suhor, a pure product of the working-class Ninth Ward, who played drums and moonlighted as the New Orleans correspondent for *Downbeat* magazine.

Suhor was intrigued by my interest in the music and encouraged me to write about it. I did a profile of Punch Miller for a school assignment, and Suhor liked it so much he submitted it for a national essay competition. To my amazement, it won a citation. He also sent it off to his editor, Don De Michael. Several weeks later, I got a letter from *Downbeat* saying they planned to publish it in their next issue—complete with a photo of me and Punch playing together at the Hall. I was euphoric.

The essay honors and *Downbeat* article played a key role in the other piece of good news that I got that year: my acceptance by Harvard University in April 1967. I was a pretty good student, but everyone knew that you had to have something extra to get into the Ivies. In my case, it was my music and my writing. Charlie Suhor—he was always Mr. Suhor to me in those days—had enabled me to document both in a way that would jump out at an admissions committee awash in superachiever applications.

My parents were overjoyed by my acceptance letter. My mother made me a breakfast of grillades and grits the next morning as a special treat. When I emerged from my bedroom at noon after a long night of celebrating with my friends, she remarked that "Harvard men sure sleep late." My father, who had spent several months at Harvard as a Nieman Fellow in 1942, now considered the famous college a "family tradition," ever referring to himself on occasion as a "Harvard graduate." He also had a way of taking biological credit for my achievements, saying it was all due to his "genes." That logic never seemed to apply to the dumb things that I did.

My dad's more tangible contribution was to help me put together my application. For all the strains that had crept into our relationship over my late nights in the Quarter, getting me into Harvard was an overriding goal that we both embraced. My father always told me you had to find a way to get ahead of Otho B. Gatewood—his mythical version of the dutiful but conventional striver. Otho was going to hit the Harvard admissions committee with stratospheric SAT scores and Rotary Club awards up the wazoo, he said. But nobody was going in there with such a rich, original lode of personal experience. So he made sure I included lots of photos of me playing with the mens at parades, funerals, and at the Hall. To top it all off, he advised me to package it all in an eye-catching red binder so it would stand out. He always regarded my acceptance as his greatest P.R. coup—and maybe he was right.

I know he was very proud that I got into Harvard. But he would not act proud on my graduation day, four years later: he pretended not to have any film for his camera and didn't take a single picture that day. When I later asked why, he muttered, "Because I didn't want any pictures of the pathetic people who would have to be in them." The "pathetic people" were my roommates, whom he apparently took for a band of homosexuals because they had long hair—like ninety percent of all American college students in those days. It was the beginning of a long estrangement between us. But that's another story.

During the summer before my freshman year, I totally immersed myself in the music. I think I sensed that it was the twilight of my jazz apprenticeship, perhaps my last chance to live and play alongside the men who had taught me their craft and would be gone from the scene all too soon. I played a lot of parades and funerals with the Olympia, did Tulane fraternity gigs with Punch Miller and some of the foreign musicians, and sat in with bands at the Hall and local white dance joints like Luthjen's downtown and Munster's uptown. And there were lots of backyard parties, with washtubs full of ice and beer, pots full of red beans and gumbo, and nonstop music.

I also got a part-time summer job with a local television station. It consisted of booking guests to appear on a popular kiddie show, "Johnny's Follies," and supplying them with fruit juice and doughnuts on the set. Only problem was, Johnny got canned in the middle of the summer. Enraged mothers called me to bitch about the show's cancellation, so I told them to send letters to the station management. Deluged with hate mail, the bosses fired me for organizing a "protest movement."

I didn't really care. I had spent most of my office hours following the world's biggest news event of 1967—the Six Day War and its aftermath—on the station's ubiquitous TV screens. Like most Americans at that time, I looked on Israel as the Athens of the Middle East, a besieged oasis of democracy threatened with annihilation by its Arab neighbors. I didn't have to be a political junkie to be gripped by the drama of this embattled little nation rising up to defeat its aggressors. What was Johnny's silly tap-dancing compared to Abba Eban's dazzling United Nations speeches and the prospect of a world-shaking Middle East conflict?

Toward the end of the summer, I said my farewells to all my old friends at the Hall—George Lewis, Punch Miller, Kid Sheik, Jim Robinson, Harold Dejan. Some of them wondered if leaving town might mess up my style. Others seemed to think I was heading off to a "music school" up North. It never occurred to any of them that I might be destined for a career other than jazz.

There was one special teacher I didn't see at the Hall: Creole George Guesnon. So I went to say good-bye to him in his little "bird cage" on North Roman Street.

I hadn't been there in quite a while and he let me know it. "Well hello, stranger," he said. "I ain't seen you since March the nineteenth. What you think of that? March the nineteenth! Look like you 'shamed to come around the old spook's house anymore. You done joined the White Citizen's Council on me or somethin'?"

"You know better than that, George," I said. "I've been real busy packing up to go to college. I'm leaving in a few days."

"Goin' off to college?" George repeated. "God Almighty! Seem just like yesterday you was a little boy comin' in here with your clarinet case in your hand and your tennis shoes all untied. Now look at you—a big, fine man fixin' to go to college. Where you goin'?"

"Harvard."

"Well, that's a fine school. That's a fine school. But, like I say, don't go forgettin' all the things I told you. I taught you stuff them Harvard people don't know nothin' about. Ain't that right?"

"That's for sure," I said, taking a seat on my old stool while George settled slowly into a straight-backed chair. I noticed he was breathing heavily.

"Well, it's a good thing you come, Tommy," he said, "'Cause I ain't gonna be around much longer."

"What do you mean?"

"Oh, you know, my blood pressure been worryin' me. Doctor say I got to lose weight. I get tired just walkin' around the block. But that's all right, my man. I done what I had to do. I have done it to perfection. God gave me my talent in 1927, and I'm fixin' to give it back to him."

"Don't talk like that George," I said. "You're only sixty. You still have a lot of good music to play for people."

George shook his head. "Shit, man, I don't play for the people. Everything I've done, I never done it for nobody but me. That's why I play so well, 'cause I am my own harshest critic."

Bitterness had always been part of the mix with George—along with humor, ambition, and an unshakable belief in the big break that was waiting just around the corner. Now the bitterness seemed to be getting the upper hand.

I looked around the room. The familiar photos and clippings were still on the yellowing wallpaper. But the place seemed strangely empty. "George," I said, "where are all those stacks of sheet music and manuscripts you used to keep on the floor?"

"Aw, man, I took most of that stuff out in my backyard and burned it, sheet by sheet. I hardly got a cent from my compositions all my life, so ain't nobody gettin' rich off it when I'm gone. I'm just sorry I didn't burn it all. The thing I loved most, I sold to the man I hate most in this world."

"Who's that?"

"Larry Borenstein. He come around here askin' me to sell him a short story I wrote. I had wanted to get it published, but, what the hell, I was hungry and he give me a hundred bucks for it. But he ain't gettin' the rest of it. It's *gone*."

I was relieved to see that George still had his banjo propped up in the corner. I hadn't seen him at the Hall for a long time and I'd even heard that he quit playing. "Looks like you're still making that pretty stuff on your banjo."

George turned his head and looked at the instrument. "Oh yeah. I mean, you know, I play a little bit for myself, just to pass the time. But I don't go down to the Preservation Hall no more, cause they got too many phonies down there. That boy want to tell me how to run my band—play like this, don't play like that, make the tourists happy, keep that almighty dollar fallin' in the basket. Shit, nobody tells Creole George Guesnon how to run his band."

"Jaffe won't hire you anymore?"

"Oh, man, I could go work down there tonight if I want. They gonna *make* room for me soon as I hit the door. But I don't want to abuse my talent. So you ain't gonna see me down there no more. The only place you gonna see me is at my wake. I want you to come back down here when I die and look at me, you hear? Come look at the old man."

"I'll come look at you all right, but I'll do it right here in your bird cage when I come home next summer. We'll play some pretty tunes together. Now you take care of yourself."

"Same to you, young man. Like the song say, 'Good-Bye, Good Luck to You.'"

He stood in his doorway as I walked through the gathering dusk toward the bright avenue a few blocks away. When I got to the corner, I turned and waved. All I saw was the outline of that massive head and shoulders silhouetted against the light from his front room.

That was the last time I saw Creole George Guesnon. He died eight months later, on May 5, 1968.

I didn't make it back for the wake, and I'm glad I didn't. People who were there told me that his body was almost unrecognizable:

for some reason, the undertaker had decided to shave off the thick eyebrows he'd always been so proud of. At least they'd gotten the music right. As George had requested, Emanuel Sayles had stayed by his casket the whole time and played the banjo.

When I came home on my first summer vacation, I made it a point to go see George's common-law wife, Corinne Monroe, who lived in a housing project a couple of blocks from the bird cage. Corinne was a heavyset, light-skinned woman from the sugar cane country near Thibodeaux, Louisiana. She worked as a cook for a white family uptown. She and George had been together for twenty-seven years, but never married because George still had an estranged wife out in California. So they kept separate apartments rather than "live in sin in the eyes of the church," as George put it.

Married or not, she was now a grieving widow struggling to cope with the huge vacuum that George had left in her life.

"Oh, I just miss George so much," she told me. "It happened so fast."

"Were you with him when he died?" I asked.

"Yes, thank God, I was. I had just gone over there after work with some fried chicken. He was so happy. He said he hadn't had anything to eat all day. And, boy, he grab him a big old drumstick and start to chew. Then all of a sudden, he drop the drumstick and clutch at his chest. He say, 'It's my heart, baby, it's my heart.' Then he fall down dead, right there on his kitchen floor."

Corinne said that George often talked about me, and that he had left me a special "legacy." She went into a back room and returned with a package that had been carefully wrapped in brown paper and secured with twine. On the top of it, George had written: "For a fine young man and a fine clarinet player, Tommy Sancton, with my prayers and best wishes. Creole George Guesnon." I untied the twine slowly, taking care not to rip the paper bearing his precious inscription.

The package contained two items. The first was a prayer book he had received the day of his first Communion, bookmarked to a prayer on eternal life. The other was George's personally annotated copy of the book *New Orleans Jazz, A Family Album*.

The book, which I knew well, contained photos and brief biographies of hundreds of New Orleans jazz musicians. But George had transformed it into his personal album, pasting dozens of photos and clippings onto its pages and writing marginal comments on everything from music and art to politics and race relations. On the future of the "Negro race," he wrote, "I predict here and now that there can be only two answers: either mass annihilation or back to slavery."

The last pages of the index were plastered over with raunchy black and white pictures of nude women in provocative poses. Next to them, George had penned the caption: "Memories of Storyville, showing in detail the frank, and candid, atmosphere of the old Basin St. whorehouses in N.O. where jazz was born." Even from the grave, George was gleefully mixing the divine with the profane, the sublime with the vulgar—after all, he would have said, that's what jazz is all about.

But the thing that really caught my attention was a typewritten letter from my father, dated August 29, 1967, that George had pasted onto the flyleaf. It confirmed what I had long suspected about my father's sense of personal identification with George Guesnon.

"Dear George," he wrote, "I appreciate the privilege of being able to call on you as a friend. . . . You are a great man in my book. Every theme you handle is done with the drive of a born artist—the lucky kind, the kind who can work with total belief in what he's doing. I worked that way as a writer for many years—with total belief in the worth of my writing. I do not have it now. I believe it is going to return to me some day. The example of your life—its bravery, its drive, its pride, its artistic purity—has probably been one of the reasons which has kept alive my own hope as a writer."

The letter said a lot about both men. George had simply labeled it "A fan letter." Probably the only thing that counted for him was the effusive praise of his own genius; I don't think he took any notice of my father's torment. But for Daddy, it seemed to me that the admiring words about George were really aimed at himself. It was the kind of adulation he wanted desperately to bask in, but never got.

George's posthumous gift had left me a key to understanding my father's paralyzing self-doubt during those years. I had never fully realized before how much the failure of his novels had shattered his confidence, leaving him unable to hold down a steady job or follow any project through to completion. Yet this remarkable confession also made clear the bedrock of strength and solace that he drew from his friendship with the mens.

CHAPTER FORTY

I hadn't been home long when I headed over to Buster's for a plate of his down-home red beans—something I didn't get in the Harvard Freshman Union.

I found Kid Sheik standing at the bar in front of a cold Dixie. He was chewing on a cigar stump and chatting with Miss Fannie, Buster's assistant chef and bottle washer.

"'Bout time you got back here, Tommy. When you got in?"

"Couple of days ago. I was just over at Corinne Monroe's place. She told me about Creole George."

"Yeah, man. Died eatin' chicken, right in front of his old lady. What a shame. And you heard George Lewis been in and out the hospital again? Had pneumonia or something, but he's back playin' now. That cat got nine lives."

I rapped my knuckles on the wooden bar. "Hope so."

"And here the *big* news—Joe Watkins is gettin' back on his feet. They say he's even startin' to play the drums again."

"You're kidding! Last I heard, they'd sent Joe to a rest home"

"I'm tellin' you, man, Joe's back home now. Go see for yourself."

Joe lived at the top of a dark, narrow staircase at 832 North Galvez Street. The door was open when I got there, so I walked right in. I found him sitting at his kitchen table, drinking coffee and calmly perusing the *Times-Picayune*. When he looked up and saw me, he smiled just like the old Joe Watkins I used to know. He had gained weight; his face was fuller, his eyes brighter.

"When you got in town, pops?" he said. "Sit down and I'll fix you some coffee."

I was astounded to see him stand up and step over to the stove. Before he went to the rest home, he was using a walker. His movements were still slow and his step hesitant, but he was so much better than the last time I had seen him that his recovery seemed to border on the miraculous.

"What happened, Joe?" I asked. "How did you get back on your feet?"

"Well, you know I was at that convalescent home," he said, setting a cup of coffee down in front of me. "And they took pretty good care of me. They was nice folks. But I would just lie there and look at the ceiling and tell myself, 'Joe, you gonna die right here in this bed if you don't pull yourself back together.' So one day I just told them I was goin' home."

"Just like that?"

"Yeah, Tommy, that's just what I told 'em. They didn't believe me at first, but they called my landlady—you know Louise, lives downstairs? Well, Louise said she'd look after me. Next thing I knew they brought me back home in an ambulance. I was so happy to be back in the old place, I just kinda pepped up, you know? And look like God give me the strength to try to make it back."

"Did you get any therapy?"

"Well, Pickles come over once in awhile to help me walk, and I just tried to do a little more every day. When my legs got stronger, I got my sticks out and started practicin' my snare drum. It's comin' back, Tommy, it's comin' back."

There was no better therapy for Joe than to get him on a bandstand again. He was still too weak to play a whole evening at the Hall, but some of the young musicians had been rehearsing with him in the afternoons.

During the time I spent at home that summer, I played several jam sessions with Joe. His foot was still a little weak on the bass drum, but his hands were working fine, his tempo was steady and his voice was strong on the vocals. One of his favorites was Jelly Roll Morton's "Doctor Jazz": "Hello central, give me Doctor Jazz, he's got just what I want, I'll say he has . . ." That was probably the real medicine behind Joe's recovery.

I got the idea of making a comeback album with Joe, and George Buck offered to issue it on his G.H.B. label. Joe was thrilled. He had cut more than fifty records with George Lewis—including some on big labels like Atlantic, Blue Note, and Verve—but probably none had made him as excited as this one. "Ooh, man, we gonna make us a nice record, Tommy," he said. "And I want to sing, too—some of my old favorite vocals."

As for the other musicians, we got Yoshio "Kid Claiborne" Toyama on trumpet, his wife Keiko on banjo, Lars Edegran on piano, and Sylvester Handy (Capt. John's brother) on bass. The trombonist was Frank Demond, a Californian who had recently moved to New Orleans and later replaced Jim Robinson in the Preservation Hall touring band. Peter Ecklund, a visiting trumpeter from Connecticut, also joined the band on several tunes. The recording engineer was old Bill Russell, the man who had rediscovered Bunk.

The session took place in our attic on Gen. Pershing Street. But the music had to be put on hold for a couple of hours while we ate. My mother, with her Mississippi sense of hospitality, could not conceive of having a house full of people without offering them "a little something to eat," so she had made a huge turkey dinner with all the fixings.

As we all sat around our big dining room table, chewing and drinking and talking excitedly, I thought what a strange and varied assemblage this was: a Swede, two Japanese, a Connecticut Yankee, a Californian, a former Mississippi debutante, a Southern writer, a college student, a historian, and two old black men born in the first decade of the century. Jazz had an amazing capacity to pull people together.

The really strange thing, though, was the fact that we had company at all. It had been years since my parents had invited anyone over to dinner. For that matter, apart from special occasions like Thanksgiving or Christmas, I hardly recalled having sit-down meals together as a family. It wasn't our style. Nor could my father have been comfortable at the table with some of the young musicians he didn't like me hanging around with at night. But he put up with it for Joe's sake. In fact, once he got into it, I think my dad really enjoyed the evening.

Getting Joe up into the attic after dinner was a challenge: his weak legs couldn't make it up the narrow wooden steps. But my father had an idea. He had rigged up a pulley and a rope with a big metal hook on one end so he could ratchet his heavy file boxes up and down. According to some logic I never understood, his files had to be in the attic at some times, downstairs at other times, and in the basement at still other times. But the pulley was just what we needed to hoist Joe into the attic.

We tied him into a kitchen chair and hooked the rope onto the back of it. From down below, my dad pulled on the other end of the rope while I climbed slowly up the stairs, holding onto Joe's legs to keep him from swaying back and forth and banging into the walls. Joe was scared to death. "Name of God, Tom," he cried out. "Don't let go that rope. Oh, sweet Jesus!"

Joe was pretty shaky when he reached the top and got untied, so we gave him a shot of my mother's bourbon. By the time we had finished ratcheting up his drum kit and setting it up for him, he seemed fine. A few practice rolls, and he was ready to go.

The session went well. Joe wanted every number played back again and grinned ear to ear at what he heard, especially his favorite vocal numbers like "Tishomingo" and "Just a Little While to Stay Here."

We were all exhausted by the end of the evening, but we knew we had a nice record in the can. Joe even seemed a little more relaxed when we tied him back in his chair and lowered him down from the attic. I guess you can get used to anything.

The day after the session, I saw my father brooding on the front steps. He had a melancholy streak, and I was used to his frequent bouts of depression. But this time, I sensed that something specific was bothering him and I asked him what it was.

"It's something Joe said when he was leaving here last night," my dad explained, his bushy eyebrows knotted in anguish. "He stood at the gate here, shook my hand, held it, and said, 'Tom, I want you to know something. I really appreciate you having me into your house like this.'"

"That was a nice thing to say, Daddy," I said. "Why does it make you feel bad?"

"Because this great man did honor to us by coming up our stairwell. I should have thanked *him*. But in Joe's eyes, Seta and I must have the silhouettes of big, rich white people—if he only knew the truth. It was a big deal for him to come into our house and eat at our table."

"He enjoyed it, he appreciated it," I said. "That's what counts."

"That's just the point, son. Instead of one night, Joe might have enjoyed ten nights at my table—fifty nights. The same for George Lewis, the same for Guesnon, Jim Robinson. That would have been the perfect way to honor these men, show my respect and love for them. Why didn't I think of this before?"

My dad never got the chance to invite Joe back to dinner. Not long after our recording session he got a phone call from Louise. She said Joe fell down in his kitchen while he was eating dinner and started talking "all out of his head." She had called an ambulance and they rushed him to Charity Hospital.

"It's Joe Watkins," my father told me. "Sounds like a stroke."

We jumped in the car and sped to the hospital. My dad was always at his best when he could leap into action and deal with a crisis.

The emergency room was a bedlam of shooting victims on bloody gurneys, pregnant women rushing in to have their babies delivered, old ladies in wheelchairs, kids with crushed fingers and broken arms and split lips. But no Joe Watkins.

We went to the main admitting desk and inquired about Joe. The young man on duty told us he had been released.

"Released?" said my father. "The man's had a stroke."

"Sir, according to my records, there is nothing wrong with this patient. He's checked out and waiting for an ambulance to take him home."

We roamed through the labyrinth of grim neon-lit corridors and finally found Joe lying on a gurney alone and unattended. His eyes were half-closed and there were tears on his cheeks. He opened his mouth and groaned but couldn't speak.

"What's this?" my father said, and fingered something out of Joe's mouth. It was a piece of half-chewed bread from his dinner.

"Sons of bitches didn't even clear the food out of his mouth," he said. "Indigent old black man, looks like he's about to die, so they send him home and free up a bed. They call it triage. I call it racism. There's gonna be hell to pay for this! But first, we have to take care of Joe."

My father went to a pay phone and called his old Heart Fund contact Alton Ochsner, a prominent gerontologist. Ochsner told my dad to rush Joe over to the hospital that bore his family name.

My dad collared an ambulance driver and told him to take Joe to "Ochsner Hospital over in Jefferson Parish."

We rode in the back of the ambulance. Joe was batting his eyelids and making gurgling noises, but couldn't speak. I held his limp hand in mine.

Twenty minutes later the ambulance pulled up in front of an emergency room and the driver jumped out to open the rear door.

"Where are we?" my dad asked.

"East Jefferson hospital," replied the driver. "You said Jefferson, right?"

"I said Ochsner, goddammit," my father shouted. "They're waiting for him at Ochsner. Get us the hell over there fast."

The driver turned on his siren and sped off.

We arrived at the hospital ten minutes later, and Joe was wheeled into the emergency room. Dr. Ochsner was there, as promised, and took him under his care. We hoped that the lost time would not prove fatal.

As we rode home in a cab, my father was still fuming over the ambulance driver's incompetence and, especially, over Charity's refusal to treat Joe. "That hospital was built for the poor people of New Orleans—most of whom are black," he said. "But they treat blacks like cattle. Worse than cattle."

"Maybe they're just understaffed," I said.

"No," my father shook his head. "I think it's racism. Jaffe once told me an outrageous story about Billie Pierce. She had gone to Charity for some routine treatment and suddenly found them wheeling her into the operating room for a hysterectomy. Jaffe was convinced it was to demonstrate the operation for medical students. They just grabbed the first old black woman they could find. Wouldn't surprise me—all the medical students in this city used to learn their trade by cutting up the cadavers of black paupers from Charity."

Dr. Ochsner called the next day to say that Joe had come out of his coma, but he couldn't determine the full extent of the damage for several days.

We drove over to visit Joe in the hospital's geriatric ward. He was conscious and glad to see us, but he seemed confused.

"So how was your trip overseas?" he asked me.

"It was great, Joe," I replied, though I had never been out of the country in my life. "I had a wonderful time over there."

He nodded and closed his eyes. "That's good," he said. "That's good."

There were a few more mumbled exchanges, then his eyes suddenly welled up with tears.

"I was sleepin' before you come, Tom," he said to my father. "Jesus come to me and we talked and he was dressed like the Mardi Gras Indians except all in white—no colored beads or nothing, all in white like a chief with a big white headpiece. And he said, 'Joe I'm disgusted with people, how mean they can be. And I'm gonna walk right out of this world!' That's what he said, Tom, 'I'm gonna walk right out of this world!'"

I wasn't sure if I would ever see Joe again. But I knew he had played his last note of music. Not even Dr. Jazz could reverse the effects of a massive stroke.

When our record finally came out, several years later, it bore the grim title, "Joe Watkins: Last Will and Testament." And if Precious Joe ever heard it, it was not from this world.

CHAPTER FORTY-ONE

The call came on December 31, 1968. It was Dorothy Tait, George Lewis's long-time manager and former mistress. "Well, Tom," she told my father, "George slipped away from us last night."

I was stunned. I knew George was in the hospital again—this time with pneumonia—but I assumed he would pull through as he always did. After all, he was only sixty-eight. He had played at the Hall two weeks earlier, just before I returned for my Christmas vacation. His treatments had gone well at first, and it looked like he would be back home in a few days. But Dorothy told us he had picked up the potent Hong Kong flu virus in the hospital and it sapped his strength until his frail body just couldn't fight any more. "The end came peacefully," she said.

It was inconceivable that he was gone forever, that the world would never again hear the sound of his clarinet. When I looked at my shelf full of George Lewis records, and saw the smiling photos of him on my bedroom walls, I felt sure that, somehow, somewhere, George was still present. He had to be. All that force, all that power, all the beauty of that celestial tone could not end with a heartbeat.

I shut myself up in my closet, turned the light off, and put on one of his records. And George was there with me. I heard his voice, his horn, the applause after each number. But once the record ended and the dark chamber fell silent, I knew he was gone. As much as my youthful idealism had been shaken by the assassinations of

Martin Luther King Jr. and Robert Kennedy just a few months earlier, nothing matched the grief I felt over George's passing.

When I arrived at Blandin's Funeral Home for the wake, I saw the trombone player Louis Nelson standing on the front porch. It was a cold, humid January night and he was bundled up in a heavy overcoat. Nelson was always a quiet, solitary figure, better at charming women with his rugged good looks and breathy melodies than at verbal communication. But at this moment, he looked especially somber and very much alone. He had been George's best friend and, after Jim Robinson quit the band, his regular trombone man.

"Hello, Nelson," I said. "I never thought we'd see this day."

"He knew it was coming," Nelson grunted. "He told me in the hospital he'd never see the end of the year."

There was a large crowd inside, maybe two hundred people. Some were sitting on folding chairs, some milling about in the aisles, others standing up in the back. Two adjoining rooms were also packed with mourners, whispering, murmuring, a few of them softly weeping. There were cameras, floodlights, and newspaper and magazine reporters. NBC had sent a crew. So had a Japanese TV network and a French radio station. This was an international event.

Almost every jazz musician in New Orleans was there: the old men who played with George, the young ones like me who idolized him, and those who hardly knew George but respected him as a fallen brother.

George's family was sitting in front—Shirley, George's other grown children, and many of his thirteen grandchildren. Near them, like members of a grieving harem, sat George's women: two ex-wives and two former mistresses.

At the back of the room there was a cloth-covered casket flanked by large floral wreathes. One was in the shape of a clarinet, another formed the insignia of George's Masonic lodge. A black man in a mason's uniform sat next to the catafalque holding a book and a symbolic trowel in his white-gloved hands. On the wall above the casket was a stained-glass portrait of Jesus, lit from behind like a neon sign.

I walked up to the coffin and looked down. It was hard to comprehend that the small black figure inside was George Lewis. The face was stony and the hands, with those beautifully tapered fingers, now looked like dried sticks.

George's last instructions had called for "a lot of music" at his funeral. So the family asked some of the young musicians who admired him to play at the wake. In an adjoining room, I took out my clarinet and played some soft hymns along with Claiborne and Keiko Toyama.

I had always tried to sound like George. This time I didn't try, the music just came out by itself. I heard the clarinet but was hardly conscious of playing it. I felt like his spirit was blowing through me.

Some of the old musicians were standing around us and nodding their heads. Percy Humphrey whispered to my father, "George Lewis will never die as long as that boy is alive."

Punch Miller appeared with his trumpet and sat in with us. He called "Just a Closer Walk with Thee," and instinctively put a bluesy little growl into his horn that lightened the mood. Punch was reminding us that, in New Orleans, even death has room for humor and sassiness.

When we finished playing, Willie Humphrey came up and said, "George would have been proud of you tonight, Tommy."

His wife, Alma, also shook my hand and offered condolences. "I know this is a sad day for you, young man," she said.

I thanked her, then suddenly wondered if Willie felt hurt or offended by the fact that I had always preferred George's playing to his. But Willie Humphrey had never been the kind of guy to worry about things like that. He was having too much fun playing his clarinet. Besides, he knew, and I knew, that I never had the chops or fingers to do what he could do. I had always gone for the tone.

The next day, we buried George across the river under gray, rainy skies. There were three marching bands, the Eureka, the Olympia, and a group made up of George's young fans who had come from all over the world. I started with this pickup band, playing a high-pitched E♭ clarinet, the same kind that George had used in his old brass-band days with the Eureka.

With thousands of mourners, tourists, and curiosity-seekers trailing behind, the musicians played hymns and dirges as they followed the hearse from the funeral home to the Olive Branch Baptist Church, just across the street from George's house. George was a devout Roman Catholic, but he was denied a Catholic funeral because he was a mason. This black Protestant Church, with its full-throated choir and its fiery preacher, was in fact much better suited to the spirit of his music.

They placed the casket in the front of the altar and the pastor mounted the steps to his pulpit.

"Let all mortal voices keep silent," he began, "for a mighty prince has fallen this day in Israel."

Amen! . . . Yes, sir! . . . That's right!

Shouting out the words in measured cadences, banging his fist on the lectern, and punctuating his phrases with explosive grunts, the Rev. S. J. Ellison told the congregation that "God has just received brother Lewis—huh!—And he told him, 'I been expectin' you, George.'"

Oh yeah! . . . Uh-huh!

"And George say unto the Lord, 'I worked hard all my life—huh!—I loved my wife, and I loved my children. But I also loved my music—huh!—Yes, I loved it as much as my wife and children.' And God say, 'That's what I know—huh!—You a honest man, brother George, and the gates of heaven are open unto you!'"

Yes, sir! . . . Amen!

"And the Lord said, 'All power is in my hands'—huh!—I can strike down the sinner—huh!—and I can make the lion lie down with the lamb—"

That's right! . . . Amen!

"It was *early* that George Lewis heard the voice. It was *early* that he learned his lesson—huh!—and start playin' his music, oh yes, and tellin' the world in song that Jesus is king!"

Yeah, you right, brother! . . . Tell 'em about it!

"Brother George and *all* the musicianers makin' everybody call His name—huh!—So if you walkin' with the King, continue to walk with him! . . . If he holdin' your hand, let him hold your hand."

Oh yeah! . . . That's how it is!

"Cause you got to *work* until the day is done—huh!—You got to *work* until the settin' of the sun—huh!—You got to *work* until you hear His voice sayin' unto you, 'SILENCE! . . . Silence! The battle is fought and the victory is won. Come and enter my Kingdom!'"

Amen! . . . Praise the Lord!

Church bells tolled mournfully as they brought George out under a cold drizzle. Harold Dejan grabbed me by the arm. "Tommy," he whispered, "I want you to play the rest of this with my mens. You belongs with us." So I fell in with the ranks, alongside Louis Nelson, Manuel Paul, Milton Batiste, Booker T, Papa, and all my old Olympia buddies.

The muffled drums rolled and we launched into the one hymn that George had specifically requested for his funeral, "The Old Rugged Cross," the same tune he had played on the porch of his father's shack in Mandeville. That moment flickered in my memory like an old film as I marched along to the band's swaying cadence and played high, sweet notes for my fallen idol.

Our feet sloshed through muddy puddles as we made our way slowly, slowly toward McDonogh cemetery, a mile or so away from the church. Manuel Paul's fat, rich tenor sax moaned to my right; the biting brass of Nelson's trombone sounded on my left. From behind, I heard Book's throbbing bass drum and Batiste's loud, shrill trumpet.

Up ahead of us, detached from the Eureka and walking alone in front of the hearse, Percy Humphrey sounded his high, pure clarion call, like Gabriel at the gates. It made me think of a verse by Walt Whitman:

With music strong I come, with my cornets and my drums,
I play not marches for accepted victors only,
I play marches for conquer'd and slain persons . . .
I beat and pound for the dead,
I blow through my embouchures my loudest and gayest for them.

The bands and crowds trampled the sodden ground of the cemetery as they followed the pallbearers to a simple plot with a whitewashed concrete border. "G. Lewis" was painted on it in plain black letters. George's mother lay in an adjoining grave. She could rest easy now. His train had finally arrived.

We played one last hymn at graveside as they lowered the casket into the ground. Then the pastor threw a handful of dirt into the hole and recited these words: "One generation passeth, another generation cometh, but the earth endureth forever."

Yes, a mighty prince had fallen, and the world would never see the likes of him again. For me, this cold, damp day marked the final act of a great play. It had its prologue in the strains of Civil War marches and work songs, rags, and blues; the first act came when Buddy Bolden's cornet found a powerful new voice and called his children home; the second unfolded with the young century, when the whorehouse professors, marching groups, and dance hall bands created a strutting, pulsing, foot-tapping music that some of them took upriver and gave to the world. The third act was played by the men who stayed behind or returned to their roots—Bunk, George, Jim, Guesnon, Punch, Joe, and all the rest—who stoked the dying coals and briefly, too briefly, revived the old fires.

The remains of those dwindling ranks, those who could still walk and play, were on stage that afternoon. It was my chance and privilege to have a front row seat before the curtain fell. Yes, there would be other bands, other songs, more good times and bad times. And some would say all this had just been a prologue to some new thing still to come. But for me, the play was over. Whatever else might happen in my life, I knew it had been changed forever, ennobled and enriched, by my brotherhood with the mens.

So when the bands reached the cemetery gates and Booker T pounded his drum to signal the exuberant finale, I played my loudest and gayest for George.

EPILOGUE: THREE DECADES LATER

I never became a professional musician, as my old friends had always assumed I would. In fact, I quit playing music entirely for a dozen years. Instead, I landed a job with *Time* magazine, fulfilling, perhaps unconsciously, the career that my father had abandoned to write his novels. I married a beautiful French woman named Sylvaine, raised her daughter, Sandrine, and our son, Julian. We finally settled down in Paris after two long stints in New York. But I always stayed in touch with New Orleans, and made regular trips home.

Much has changed over the years. My grandmothers died long ago, both of them pushing one hundred. So did my Uncle Buck, and my Mississippi uncles, Julian and Clay. My dear Aunt Pat wound up in a nursing home after breaking her hip at age ninety. Wendy and Claudia are both divorced and happily remarried. Beth, widowed, twice divorced, and beautiful as ever, finally achieved her Scarlett O'Hara dream of owning an antebellum mansion in Pass Christian, complete with horse stables and an alley of oak trees (until Katrina blew it all away). My mother, long since retired from her library job, published a charming volume of childhood memories, *The World from Gillespie Place*, and continues her church work after surviving a quadruple heart bypass and major abdominal surgery. And my father . . . well, my father may yet surprise us all. We long since healed the breach that separated us during and after my university years. In fact, my dad offered some helpful advice as I cast about for my first job, at age thirty, just after getting my history doctorate at Oxford. Recalling the red binder on my Harvard application, he suggested that I blanket the New York media outlets with carefully crafted job-hunting kits so I could leapfrog over poor Otho B. Gatewood again. It worked.

My father was proud to see my byline in a prestigious magazine. He even bought dozens of copies each time I wrote a cover story. He mailed some of them to his friends and stacked the remainder in the basement as "insurance" in case I ever had to go job-hunting again. I thought he was being a tad overexuberant, but deep down I was gratified by all this fuss over my articles. What man doesn't seek his father's approbation?

But as my father watched and cheered my journalistic career—with lots of coaching from the sidelines—what was left of his own career just seemed to wither away. Since he lost his last client three decades ago, he hadn't done anything but letter-writing and file-moving and collecting rent at the rooming house that he inherited from his mother.

But then a strange thing happened. My dad started writing again in his late eighties—not just letters or notes, but a real book. He finally decided to forget about the mythical third novel and write an autobiography. "If I can just find the golden voice," he told me, "I'm going to write a book from my guts that people will love to read. Not a novel, but my story. If it was handled by anybody else, it would bore me, because I'd come off looking like a fool. But, handled the right way, with the right voice, people would understand that I couldn't have lived any other life."

He firmly believes, and I desperately want to believe, that this book will be his final, game-winning Hail Mary pass. For most people the clock would be running out, but my teetotaling, non-smoking father apparently intends to live forever, aided by the

Sancton arteries and years of jogging. If and when his book is ever published, I'm sure he will tell his story very differently from the way I have done it. Then maybe I will understand the things I never understood about him—and cherish all the more the things I admired. For I now know that I would not be who I am if my father had been any other way; that the very things that distressed and disappointed me over the years—his impracticality, his eccentricities, his obsessions—gave him the drive to push me ahead; and that his early passion for civil rights and black folk culture made him lead me to the mens. What other father would have taken his teenage son to Preservation Hall every night and cheered him on as he began that improbable, enchanted apprenticeship? What more precious gift could a father offer the boy he loved?

As for the music scene, almost everything has changed. Allan Jaffe died of cancer in 1989, at the age of fifty-two. Bill Russell went three years later, at eighty-seven, just after completing a seven-hundred-page masterpiece on Jelly Roll Morton—stunning proof that games can be won in the fourth quarter. Larry Borenstein died of a heart attack, and Noel Rockmore finally drank himself to death. But the Hall stayed open with Sandy, her sister Resa Lambert, and her son Ben at the helm.

For many years, I would still see the dwindling band of jazzmen during my annual treks home. I remember running into Kid Sheik on his way to a French Quarter gig one spring day in 1989. He was all duded up in a cowboy hat, a loud Hawaiian shirt, and a gold medallion dangling around his neck. "I just made the big eighty, man," he said with his guttural laugh, as if his longevity was a big joke on the fates. "Still tryin' to make it. Like the song say, we got to ramble till the butcher cut us down."

I went to see Harold Dejan at his house on Mexico Street on one visit. His hair was snow white and he could no longer march in the street parades. But he was still "the grand old man of the Olympia Brass Band," and proud of it.

Harold seemed very glad to see me and reminisced about the days when I cut my teeth playing with his band. "I'm tellin' you, Tommy," he said. "when you was *young* you could play that horn. I admired you so much, so ambitious and everything. No jive—you *played* that damn horn!" I didn't dare tell him I had given it up.

Harold went in his back room and came out with something I will always cherish: a photo of me at sixteen or seventeen, blowing my heart out in the middle of the Olympia and surrounded by a crowd of strutting second-liners. It gave me a momentary heart pang: I'd never be there again, never do that again, never have Harold at my side and a sea of black bodies heaving all around me.

Into the early 1990s, I could still catch Percy and Willie Humphrey at the Hall or the Palm Court on Decatur Street. Percy's trumpet playing was much weaker than in the old days, and he shuffled when he walked, but he still had that beautiful clear tone and knew how to lead a band. His older brother Willie seemed indestructible, taking interminable clarinet solos, his sound fatter than ever and his agile fingers only slightly slowed by time. Willie was so full of music that he would get up and play *O Sole Mio*, a cappella, after the rest of the band had packed up and left the stage at the end of the last set.

And then one day I saw Sally Fellon at the Hall. She was standing in the carriageway and holding a little girl by the hand. It was her granddaughter.

I hadn't laid eyes on Sally in nearly thirty years, but she was still beautiful. We talked briefly, but I sensed an awkwardness. To really say something meaningful to Sally would have required a long, quiet moment, and we didn't have that luxury. It was better to keep our memories sweet, innocent, and untouched by time.

Time, unfortunately, did not stop for the mens. Today almost all the old players are gone, felled one by one like giant oaks in the primeval forest—Punch, Jim, Willie, Percy, Sheik, Emma, Sing, Booker T, Chester, Nelson, Thomas, Harold, Papa, Batiste.

I rarely go into Preservation Hall these days. The place is little changed since the night my parents first took me there. It still has the same brooding Rockmore portraits, the same moldy pinkish-green patina on the walls, the same dusty, sweaty, humid smell—with less cigar smoke and more after-shave. But the space is inhabited by the ghosts of too many old friends.

The people who sit in their chairs today are mostly younger black musicians. Some are fine players, but most of them never really knew the mens, and, apart from a few dedicated scholars like Dr. Michael White, probably haven't even spent a lot of time listening to their records. They are doing their own thing, playing a mixture of traditional jazz, Dixieland, and rhythm 'n' blues with an occasional dash of bebop. Trumpeter Wynton Marsalis, probably the most talented and articulate of the contemporary jazzmen, has done a great service to the New Orleans tradition by stressing the importance of "checking out the roots." But he's fighting an uphill battle. For most young jazz artists, especially those outside New Orleans, the roots begin with Charlie Parker.

Out on the street, vibrant young groups like the Dirty Dozen and the Rebirth Brass Band have transformed the old marching band tradition, with its proud uniforms and harmonized voicings and regimental grace, into a brasher, funkier sound. They bear little resemblance to their predecessors—apart from their exuberance and the unmistakable New Orleans beat that underpins their music and delights new generations of second-liners. And that's okay. As much as I may regret the passing of the old guard, I know that a living culture must be in tune with its times. Only a fool could expect a musical tradition rooted in the late nineteenth century, tempered by the Jim Crow era and the hardscrabble Depression years, to survive intact into the twenty-first century.

Yet something still survives.

Many years after putting my clarinet under the bed, I was invited in 1987 to a reunion of the New Black Eagle Jazz Band, a Boston-based group I used to play with in college. I did a few tunes with them and suddenly realized how much I had missed playing the horn, how much of my inner voice was the pure tone of a vibrating reed. As Sing Miller used to say, "Once you got that music under your skin, even the doctor can't cure you." So I decided to play again, but only as a sideline, lest the old jazz addiction interfere with my sacrosanct day job. Even within those limits, it probably didn't help my career: how can people who run big magazines understand an editor who moonlights as a jazzman? Too bad. Being who I am was more important than being who I was supposed to be.

In the first year of the new century, I returned to New Orleans to play at the Jazz and Heritage Festival. I was invited to take part in a special tribute to George Lewis to mark the hundredth anniversary of his birth. The two other featured clarinetists were Michael White, one of the rare young locals to play the old style, and my former benefactor and hero, Sammy Rimington.

Sammy, though pushing sixty, was still the slender, hyperactive Brit I had met in the carriageway in the summer of 1962. We had crossed paths a few times since then, but this was the first time I found myself on a concert stage with him. I was a little nervous. Had I honored his gift? Had I learned the clarinetist's trade? Was I really worthy to be on a bandstand with the great Sammy Rimington?

All those trepidations melted away as soon as Sammy kicked off the first number. We played all the George Lewis standards, trading solos and licks the same way I had heard George and Sammy do it in the Hall nearly forty years earlier. We ended with a trio version of "Burgundy Street Blues," which brought down the house. Sammy and I hugged each other and walked offstage arm in arm. The circle was closed.

"If only George could have heard us," I said.

"Maybe he did," Sammy replied, as if he had summoned up George's spirit with his purported supernatural powers.

I saw Sandy Jaffe standing in the wings, smiling excitedly the way she did the night I first sat in with George. She had salt-and-pepper hair now and her black eyebrows—like my beard—were going gray. But she had the same effervescence in her eyes.

"I caught your set, Tommy," she said. "It was wonderful to hear you again. You've gotta come down and play at the Hall tonight."

I mumbled something about having family plans, taking my wife and son out to dinner or some such. "No, you've gotta come play. I'm hiring you. It's a paying gig."

I didn't need the money, but I didn't want to disappoint Sandy. So I said I would do it for old time's sake.

I showed up early with my eighteen-year-old son Julian and my mother, then eighty-five. They sat in our old corner seats, next to the drummer. My father stayed home, ever reclusive and probably still brooding over the old film fiasco.

I took my place on the bandstand, in George Lewis's old high-backed chair. As I warmed up my horn, I looked at my son sitting in my old place, and my mother, who had been younger than my present age when we first walked into this room so many years ago. I thought about time and fate and the cycles of human experience.

The band members were mostly young black musicians, including a fine trumpeter named Wendell Brunious. I did not recognize any of the other players. Suddenly I did a double-take: could that be Narvin Kimball in the corner tuning his banjo? Narvin had been there the very first night I ever walked into the Hall. He was gray-haired even then. He couldn't possibly be alive and playing in the year 2000.

"Narvin," I exclaimed, "it's so great to see you again."

He shook my hand and said politely, "Thank you. It's nice to meet you."

When the music started, I could hear Narvin next to me, churning out that unshakable rhythm, soloing on his trademark trilled chords, singing in his rich, smooth tenor.

After the last set was over, I leaned over to Narvin and told him how much I enjoyed hearing him and playing with him again. "Thank you, young man," he said. "You raisin' some hell on that clarinet, too."

I sensed that he didn't really know who I was. I wanted to explain, to remind him of the boy who used to come in with his parents, the one who took lessons with George Lewis and followed all the parades. But I decided against it. No point stirring up my memories, or confusing Narvin with some old story that might or might not mean anything to him. Instead, I took my clarinet apart and put it back in its case. Narvin packed up his banjo and disappeared into the carriageway.

I thought that was the last I would ever see of him. But he returned to the bandstand a moment later.

"I want to apologize to you," he said. "My wife just reminded me that we know you. But I just couldn't place you at first. I'm sorry."

"Don't apologize, Narvin," I said. "I was a little boy when you first knew me. I don't look the same."

He shook his head and tapped his right temple with a stubby finger. "It's not you," he said. "I'm ninety years old. I just can't remember everything anymore."

He narrowed his eyes and gazed at me for a moment, as if he was trying to recognize in my bearded face the boy he first met in the summer of 1962. I don't know if he really did make the connection. But he nodded slowly and gave me a faint smile.

"I want you to do something for me, young man," he said. "I want you to tell the people that you played with me when I was ninety years old, and I still had that beat. Tell them, please."

Yes, Narvin, old friend, noble banjo master, singer of hymns and ballads, keeper of the rhythm, joy-giver of ten thousand nights, yes you still had that beat. You were the last of the mens. I knew you all. I loved you. I laughed and cried with you. I learned your songs. And I will tell your story.

ACKNOWLEDGMENTS

As noted in the Introduction, this book was written before Hurricane Katrina battered New Orleans and added a tragic new chapter
to its history. Though the saga of my family and my city continues
to unfold, I chose to retain the original ending of this self-contained
account rather than try to update it in Katrina's aftermath.

Much of this book is the story of a boy's encounter with some
remarkable old jazzmen and his attempt to learn their lessons on
music and life. If scholars and experts should find errors of fact or
date, I would remind them that this is in no way intended as a work
of jazz history, biography, musicology, or discography. It is an
account of a human, and intensely personal, experience as seen
through my eyes.

I have reconstructed the story mainly from memory, aided by
my own notes, conversations, and interviews, a good number of
which were captured on tape over the years. My father, Thomas
Sancton, himself a central character in my story, helped me fill in
the gaps with his own extensive notes, clippings, and recollections.
I am not sure what he will make of what I intended as an honest,
loving portrait, "warts and all." But this book could never have been
written—indeed, my jazz apprenticeship would never have taken
place at all—without his enormous contribution.

In seeking to complete the story and gather vital facts and dates,
I have occasionally relied on other books and articles. In particular,

I should mention Frederick Turner's beautifully written and evocative *Remembering Song: Encounters with the New Orleans Jazz Tradition* (Viking, 1982); William Carter's comprehensive and well-researched *Preservation Hall: Music From the Heart* (W.W. Norton, 1991); Tom Bethell's scholarly and detailed biography, *George Lewis: A Jazzman from New Orleans* (University of California Press, 1977); Barry Martyn's interview compilation, *The End of the Beginning* (Jazzology Press, 1998), Al Rose and Edmond Souchon's *New Orleans Jazz: A Family Album* (Louisiana State University Press, 1967), as well as various articles and interviews appearing in such publications as *Downbeat*, *Jazz Beat*, *New Orleans Music*, *Footnote*, *The Second Line*, and *The Times-Picayune*. While my debt to such sources is willingly, and gratefully, acknowledged, I have refrained from including extensive citations or a formal bibliography because this is not a work of erudite research but of memory.

I owe a great debt of gratitude to those who helped me track down photos or authorized their use. Among them: Chris and Janie Botsford, William Carter, John Chiasson, André Clergeat, Ralph and Pat Cowan, John Daigle, Frank Demond, Kathy Edegran, John Edser, Lee Friedlander, Ben Jaffe, Resa Lambert, John McCusker, Edward G. Marks, Bruce Raeburn, Martha Ramsey, John and Dodie Simmons, Leo Touchet, and Clive Wilson. Thanks also to Rolf Wahl for sharing his memories and tapes of George Guesnon; to Dwight DeVane for his thoughtful comments on the manuscripts; and especially to my editor, Judith Gurewich, for believing in this book and helping me make it better.

To those who may feel that this or that musician was left out or given short shrift, I would simply say that I have concentrated on those I was closest to and knew best. There were dozens, perhaps hundreds, of musicians playing traditional jazz in New Orleans in those days. Most of those I was fortunate enough to hear and befriend are present on these pages, but others contributed no less to the extraordinary cultural, artistic, and human achievement that this book attempts to celebrate. To all of these noble souls, wherever they may be, I want to say thanks for these precious memories.